MICROECONOMICS

Ninth Edition

Panos Mourdoukoutas

ISBN 13: 978-1-781149-429-6

Acknowledgments:

p. 113: From *American Economic Review*, Vol. 70, No. 3 (1980): 320. Copyright © 1980 by the American Economic Association. Used with permission of the publisher via Copyright Clearance Center.

p. 116: From *American Economic Review*, Vol. 70, No. 3 (1980): 320. Copyright © 1980 by the American Economic Association. Used with permission of the publisher via Copyright Clearance Center.

p. 189: From the *Washington Post*, May 7, 1989. Copyright © 1989 by The Washington Post. Reprinted with permission of the publisher via Copyright Clearance Center.

p. 190: From the *New York Times*, October 29, 1989. Copyright © 1989 by The New York Times Company. Reprinted by permission of the publisher via Copyright Clearance Center.

4750 Venture Drive, Suite 400
Ann Arbor, MI 48108
800-562-2147
www.xanedu.com

CONTENTS

Chapter One

INTRODUCTION TO ECONOMICS

Preview

1.1   **Introduction**

1.2   **Definition and Scope**

     Economics in Ancient Times

1.3   **Economics as a Science**

     The Need for Abstraction

     How to Construct a Model

     Economic Models and Theories

     Economics, Theory, Experiments, and Statistics

1.4   **Economic Concepts**

     Human Needs

     Goods and Services

     Economic Resources or Factors of Production

          Labor

          Entrepreneurship

          Management

          Non-human Resources

          Land/Natural Resources

          Capital

          Technology

          Information/Logistics

     Economic Systems

     Firms

          Entrepreneurship: The Ultimate Advantage

     Markets

     Economics and Psychology

Preview

Not everyone reads newspapers and magazines and loses sleep trying to find solutions to economic problems and questions. Even students in economics classes often wonder, why should they spend several semesters studying economics? Yet some economic problems cannot be assumed away. Individuals, businesses, and government are all faced with economic problems that they must understand and deal with. Economics is the discipline that provides the concepts, the tools, and the theories that enable one to understand economic problems and evaluate alternative solutions. An introduction to economics, this chapter explains the reasons for studying economics, the method and the basic concepts that economists apply when analyzing economic problems.

1.1 Introduction

The world of economics is a complicated place. A place full of questions to be answered: What are the sources of inflation and unemployment? Does the government have remedies for these problems? How does a society make choices as to what commodities to produce? Why do some companies succeed and others fail? What determines commodity prices? Should the government be in control? Should the government restrict foreign investment? What are the costs and the benefits of economic associations like NAFTA and the European Economic Community (EEC) for the member economies? What are the problems of transition from one economic system to another? Why are prices of certain items so expensive in some countries?

The study of the world of economics is a rather difficult task. Being commingled with other social problems, economic problems are hard to isolate and study from one perspective only. Economics is, perhaps, a much harder discipline than other disciplines like physics and chemistry where problems can be more accurately defined and theories can be better tested in elegant laboratories. But how do economists do it? How do they choose which questions to study? How do they develop and test theories? How can students learn and apply economic theories? Addressing these questions, this book is an introduction to problems, concepts, theories and applications of economics.

The book is divided into two volumes. The first volume is a discussion of macroeconomic issues and theories, issues pertaining to the economy taken as a single unit. The second volume is a discussion of issues and theories of microeconomics, issues pertaining to the economy taken as a set of separate units. To make the book student-friendly and reflective of the trends of our times, our approach is based on four elements: (1) concepts and theories are applied to real world issues, (2) examples are up to date and reflective of the intercultural mix of the U.S. and world economies, (3) an analysis of the economies of other countries that have drawn considerable attention in recent years like Japan and Eastern Europe, and (4) an inquiry into modern fields of economics like Health Economics and Industrial Policy.

An introduction to the discipline of economics, this chapter explains the reasons for studying economics, the methods that economists apply in studying economic problems and the basic concepts they use to develop economic theories and to communicate with each other. This chapter is in six sections: The second section explains the definition and scope of economics. The third section reviews the method of economics. The fourth section looks at the basic concepts of economics. The fifth section analyzes the concepts of scarcity and choice and the sixth section concludes the discussion with a review.

1.2 Definition and Scope

An integral part of our lives, economics is not easier to study than other disciplines. By contrast, because so many people think of themselves as economists, it is getting harder and harder to draw attention to economics in the classroom.

When asked why they study economics, students give a variety of answers. Some typical responses are: "I do not know; I already know enough economics and I should not be here;" "I am here to learn how to make money;" "I am studying economics because I was told to by my advisor;" "It is a prerequisite if I want to pursue my studies in Marketing, Finance, Management, etc." We are sorry to disappoint those students who have signed up for an economics course because they expect to get recipes for making money; there aren't any. After all, if there were, economists would be millionaires, and it would be very hard to get them in a classroom to teach! Let us now turn to the "dictatorial" view, that students study economics because they have no choice. It is a requirement, and they must comply if they want to pursue a degree in business. But the requirement is not arbitrary. Economics is a prerequisite to studying applied business fields for a good reason: It provides the analytical skills and tools, the foundations, required in the study of business.

An analogy is to be made here, that of physics and engineering. Engineering school students cannot become engineers before understanding certain principles of nature which can be learned in physics. By the same token, students in business schools cannot become financial analysts or managers before they understand certain economic principles which can be learned in economics. **Economics is the science which investigates the allocation of scarce resources to alternative uses. Economics is the study of the production and exchange of commodities, the alternative mechanisms that can accommodate production and exchange, and the evaluation of government policies that may interfere with such mechanisms. Economics also studies the determination of the GDP and its components, the sources of economic growth, the problems of business fluctuations, and the alternative policies to pursue economic growth and to deal with business fluctuations.** Moreover, as the laws of motion of an economy reflect decisions taken by households, business organizations, and government institutions in pursuing their objectives, economics is a **behavioral science**. It deals with patterns of acquisitive behavior.

Rationalizing household decision making in allocating economic resources was the subject of the first book written in economics by Xenophon in Greek antiquity, when the term "economics" meant primarily the management of household affairs. If managing a household in the simple economy of ancient times was worth writing a book about, this subject may be worth several volumes in the complicated economy of our times.

Running a household in the U.S. is a serious business. It involves getting income, paying monthly bills, obtaining consumer credit, planning for taxes, choosing a career, choosing among investment alternatives, deciding whether and when to get married or divorced, shopping around for a mortgage, choosing between buying or leasing a car; planning for children's education, and planning for retirement.

Things become even more complicated in running business and government organizations. Business decisions involve issues of production, product pricing, hiring the appropriate labor force, borrowing capital, choosing among alternative technologies, investment in plant and equipment, developing new products, and expanding to new markets. Government decisions involve the evaluation of alternative social programs, building bridges, hospitals, schools, maintaining and expanding highway systems, preserving the natural environment, reducing income inequalities, and the pursuit of economic stability and growth.

In a democratic society, some other reasons for studying economics include the understanding and evaluating of the economic platforms of the various political parties that will enable citizens to cast their votes intelligently. For instance, the study of economics helps citizens understand the impact of government and trade deficits and the cutting of the capital gains tax on their lives.

Economics in Ancient Times

Xenophon
- The study of economics can be traced back to ancient Greek historians and philosophers.
- Like Xenophon (430BC), a historian who wrote *Oeconomicus*.
- A Socratic dialogue, which outlines the principles of managing household resources in Classical Athens.

Aristotle
- Aristotle (384BC) wrote a book called *Oikovouka—Economics*
- He takes a broader view of Economics than Xenophon.
- It outlines the principles of allocating resources at the household level and at the society level—the polis (city).
- And how economics can promote eudaimoneia—the good (or virtuous) life.

Confucius (551 to c. 479BCE)
- Confucius taught about the role of ethics in economics.
- "Joy can still be found in eating sparingly, drinking plain water, and using the upper arm for a pillow. Wealth and status attained immorally are like floating clouds to me."

To sum up, the study of economics provides for the understanding of the overall mechanics of an economy, it includes the foundations for rational decision making in business, in government, in society, in the better management of our households' economic affairs, and in the better management of a country's overall economic affairs.

1.3 Economics as a Science

Like any other science, economics seeks to explore, explain, and improve the understanding of a subject. Medicine, for example, seeks to explore and explain the functioning of a human organism and recommends cures for malfunctions (illness). Similarly, economics seeks to explore and explain the functioning of economic organizations, recommending cures for many problems. Many similarities and differences between economics and medicine can be found. They both make abstractions in the process of explaining phenomena. However, medicine deals with a certain human system which does not change over time and space. By contrast, economics deals with a system which does change over time and space. The U.S. economy is much different today than it was a hundred years ago. The U.S. economic system today is much different than those of the U.K., Germany, Sweden, the Soviet Union, etc. Moreover, medicine has the luxury of laboratories, where medical theories can be tested. Economics does not, at least not with such elegance. Testing of economic theories is primarily left to statistics.

The Need for Abstraction

Real world economies are complicated. They involve thousands of variables which are difficult to capture and explain all together at one time. In other words, it is too difficult to talk about all aspects of the U.S. economy, at once. The only way to get around it is to abstract all the complexities of the real world and create a fictional, simplified world where we can focus on critical variables in isolation. All variables should be analyzed one by one, in turn. This method is what scientists call abstraction. However, abstraction moves the discussion away from the real world to fiction, an ideal situation constructed for the sake of argument, a model. In other words, a **model** is an abstract construct, a simplification of a real world situation. It is an analytical tool economists make up in order to understand and explain the complexities of real world economies. Unlike models in sciences, which are concrete (a model of a BMW, a bridge, a jet plane), economic models exist only on paper in the form of tables, graphs, mathematical equations, or plain verbal descriptions (see box 1.1). This is the reason why social phenomena are more difficult to explain than natural phenomena.

Aristotle and other early scientists, perhaps, preferred the study of natural phenomena because it was easier. Actually a dichotomy between theory and the examination of evidence exists. Aristotle was the first scientist to examine physical evidence systematically but he also wrote two books on economics. Nevertheless one should be careful before concluding that the study of economics may seem to be unreal, when by virtue any theory is unreal; but no subject in science can be approached otherwise. However, although models are unreal they can nevertheless be used as a guide to real world phenomena.

How to Construct a Model

To construct a model one must, first, specify the phenomenon in question, then define the variables and the economic agents involved, and the relationship to be studied. Any model consists of four parts: **postulates**, **assumptions**, **decision rules**, and **refutable hypotheses**.

Postulates are behavioral statements which define the motives of the agents in pursuing certain objectives. Such objectives include love and affection for others, pettiness, revenge, and the acquisition of wealth, to mention but a few. Albeit economists recognize the existence of various human motives, in order to focus just on economic behavior, they postulate that economic agents are guided by *rationality*; i.e., the acquisition of wealth. To this end individuals prefer more of a good to less. They try to do the most with the least effort. For example, if the problem in question is what determines consumers' demand for automobiles, the consumer's motives must be specified: driving to work, driving to the stores, driving for pleasure, etc. In any case we postulate that individuals would try to get the most for their money. They will buy the car they like and can afford at the lowest price; otherwise they are not rational.

Assumptions are simplifying statements made for the sake of argument and serving as a means of abstraction. For example, it can be assumed that "price is the only variable which influences consumers' decisions to purchase cars." This is not always true, but it allows one to focus attention on a few variables each time. Arguments made on these grounds are "other things being equal" or *ceteris paribus* arguments. But how do consumers, workers, managers, and economic agents in general make decisions? What rules do they follow?

Decision Rules are rules which govern decision making; i.e., a set of instructions that direct economic agents to certain objectives. Decisions are made at the *margin*. Additional units of production generate costs and benefits and so are additional units of consumption. To determine whether they are better off, individuals must make comparisons. As long as the additional (marginal) benefit of an activity exceeds the additional costs, a larger production of consumption makes an agent better off. When marginal costs and marginal benefits are equalized, the overall benefit from that activity is maximized. To maximize profits, for instance, a company must produce up to the point where the revenue from the last produced unit is equal or larger than the cost of that unit. Likewise to maximize revenues, a company must produce up to the point where the revenue of an extra unit of output is equal to zero (more on this in the chapters on microeconomics). Decision rules lead to refutable hypotheses.

Refutable Hypotheses are relations between observable variables that can be tested with reference to empirical evidence. In other words, hypotheses are statements which are true under a set of postulates, assumptions, and decision rules and can be tested with reference to empirical evidence. For example, the statement, "Other things being equal, as the price of a commodity decreases the quantity demanded increases" is a refutable hypothesis. The variables involved are "price of cars" and "quantity of cars demanded." Both variables are measurable and the relationship can be either approved or disapproved with reference to empirical evidence. That evidence, in turn, can be obtained by looking at past records of car prices and consumer purchases to find out whether the hypothesis is consistent with the real world data.

Box 1.1
A Model: The Demand for Cars

Postulate: Consumers maximize satisfaction from income

Assumptions: (i) All cars are the same in quality, style, performance, etc.; (ii) consumers have a fixed income; (iii) price is the only factor that affects consumers' decision to buy a car.

Refutable Hypothesis: Other things being equal, as the price of cars decreases more people are willing to buy cars (see exhibit below).

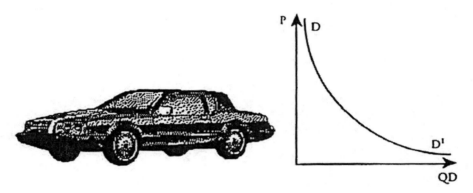

The relationship between price and quantity demanded is a hypothesis that can be tested against empirical evidence.

To sum up, the real world is too complicated to study in one session. To simplify matters, economists build models, analytical devices that keep the discussion simple and consistent. Models lead to hypotheses that can be tested against empirical evidence and become theories.

Economic Models and Theories

Models are logical systems. They cannot be proved true or false empirically. However, they can be proven logically valid or not valid. They lead to refutable hypotheses which can be tested against the empirical evidence. After a hypothesis is tested and found, in general, consistent with empirical evidence, it constitutes theory. Thus economic theory includes, in addition to economic models, empirical testing of hypotheses. Economic theories may diverge from the empirical evidence, because they are refuted by a set of specific facts, or because of logical flaws in the underlying models, or in both. Thus, **economic theory** is a set of generalizations (hypotheses), derived through both modeling and empirical testing, serving as a study guide of the complexities of real world economic systems.

We can compare economics with physics. For instance, if in physics falling bodies is the phenomenon to be explained, the theory that is being used is the "law of gravity." In economics, if the determination of prices is the phenomenon to be studied, the theory that is being used is the "law of supply and demand." The more general an economic law is, i.e., the more real world cases are explained by this law, the more powerful the law is. To quote Alfred Marshall:

> A science progresses by increasing the number and exactness of its laws; by submitting them to tests of ever increasing severity, and by enlarging their scope till a single broad law contains and supersedes a number of narrower laws, which have been shown to be special instances of it.

But how can economic laws be submitted to testing? Can economists subject economic behavior to the stringent requirements of a laboratory like physicists and chemists do with their own models?

Economic Theory, Experiments and Statistics

A distinctive characteristic of all social sciences when compared with those of physics and chemistry is the relative difficulty to perform experiments in them. For example, in a physics laboratory, we can isolate, with high precision, the effect of gravity on a certain object. We cannot be as handy in an economics laboratory. We cannot isolate with the same precision the effect of an increase in the price of automobiles on consumers from other effects, such as income, taxes, price of gasoline, etc. Nevertheless several economists have conducted experiments in various economic disciplines. For example, Chamberlin in 1948 experimented with various market structures and showed that monopolistic competition was a more appropriate model in explaining real world market performance. Hoggatt in 1959 experimented with the results of a market of three competitors. In 1982, Vernon Smith constructed experiments on the performance of markets where commodities have no intrinsic value; i.e., value is induced by the market participants. In the late 1980s the government spent $20 million on an experiment that tested the efficiency of the Job Training Partnership Act program.

These considerations point to significant differences between experimentation in positive science vis-à-vis economics. It is those differences that have led many economists to argue that economics is an "inexact science." In science, experiments deal with the testing of causality relationships (hypotheses) under a well-controlled natural environment. In economics, experiments test hypotheses under different real world markets that are hard to control. As a result of such difficulty, economists rely more on empirical observation, i.e., statistics rather than on experiments. **Statistics** provides the tools required to test hypotheses derived through economic modeling. For example, statistical techniques can be used to test the hypothesis, "as the price of beef increases, the quantity of beef demanded decreases." One can look at previous records on beef prices, and the quantity demanded, and find out whether the relationship between the two is consistent with the hypothesis.

To sum up, abstraction and statistical testing are the primary methods of mainstream economics. They do lead to refutable hypotheses and theories. But let us look at some of the concepts frequently used by economists.

1.4 Economic Concepts

As in any other discipline, economists have developed their own concepts and terms, scarcity, human needs, commodities, economic resources, economic system, market, and rationality—to mention but a few.

Scarcity—a situation where individuals, businesses, and society in general do not have enough resources to make the things they would like to have.

Ever since he appeared on earth, man is constrained by **scarcity**: limited means (material or immaterial) to attain alternative ends. To satisfy hunger primitive man had to allocate time and use tools in search of food, hunting, fishing and later on, in farming; to escape from cold, rain, and other adverse natural conditions man had to allocate resources to building shelters; the more time he allocated to one end, the less was available for the other. Albeit more complicated, modern life is still constrained by scarcity: limited supply of a certain thing as compared to the desire for it. Both limited supply and desire are necessary conditions to characterize a certain thing as scarce. However, in economic theory, it is not enough that something be rare in order to be scarce. Poison ivy is rare but not desired; it is not scarce. Automobiles are limited in supply and are desired by many; therefore they are scarce. The oxygen in our atmosphere, on the other hand, is needed by everyone but is unlimited in supply and therefore is not scarce. However, as air pollution increases in major world cities, even oxygen in the atmosphere may become scarce. One day, breathing may require masks that we have to pay for.

Coping with scarcity, i.e., providing commodities that satisfy human needs and elevating the standard of living are the most important goals of every economy. But what are human needs? What are commodities? How are they produced?

Human Needs—the feeling of missing something

Human needs may be classified in two categories, biological and social. **Biological** needs are feelings associated with the biological existence of human organisms, born with biological needs that carry until they die. Examples of such needs are feelings of hunger, thirst, shelter, etc. **Social** needs are feelings associated with the communal existence of human organisms, i.e., needs which arise because of membership in a specific society. Examples of such needs are friendship, traveling, and entertainment. Abraham Maslow classifies human needs into five categories, in the form of a pyramid.

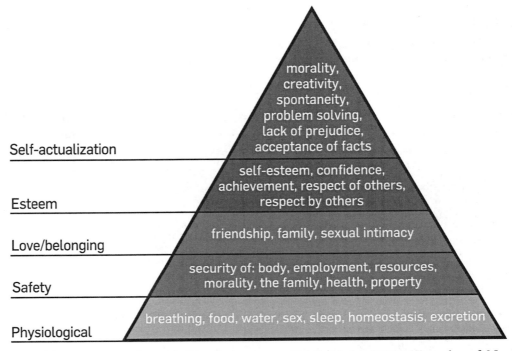

Source: http://upload.wikimedia.org/wikipedia/commons/6/60/Maslow%27s_Hierarchy_of_Needs.svg

There is no fine line between biological and social needs. For some people participating in a society and satisfying their communal needs is a precondition for the biological existence. To quote Aristotle's philosophical thinking, "Only Gods and crazy people can part themselves from the rest of the society."

Biological needs do not change very much from person to person and from society to society. The need to breathe existing in any person in any society today also existed in primitive societies. Unlike biological needs, social needs do change from society to society. The social needs of an individual who lives in a primitive society are very different than those of an individual who lives in an industrialized society. The dreams of a child living with famine in Africa are about bread and rice, while the dreams of a child living in the United States are about computer games, trips to Disneyland, trips to the Grand Canyon, trips to the moon, etc. But even within industrial societies the number and the type of social needs vary substantially. Actually, in advanced industrialized societies, it makes more sense to talk about **wants** and **desires** rather than needs.

Needs and desires progress over time along with progress in human logic and imagination. If people know that a trip to the moon is possible they may want to take such a trip, but only a few will have the money for it. As a result, economic resources are insufficient to keep up with growing needs. Getting richer does not necessarily mean being happier, a fact confirmed by the U.S. experience. Economist Tibor Scitovsky citing the results of several surveys about American happiness concludes that Americans get richer in income but no happier. Specifically, surveys show that for the period of 1946 to 1970, income adjusted for inflation increased by 62% but Americans were not happier in 1970. Thus no matter how fast economic resources have grown, they are still insufficient to satisfy all human needs and desires. But how are human needs and desires satisfied? With the consumption of commodities.

Goods and Services—the means of satisfying human needs.

Goods and services are the means of satisfying human needs. For example, a steak satisfies the need for food. A doctor's service satisfies the need for health care. An airline provides transportation services and satisfies the need for traveling, etc. Goods can be classified in various categories. One classification is that of durables versus nondurables. Durables are goods that can last for a long time, i.e., consumers can use them overtime. Television sets, microwave ovens, and refrigerators fall into this category. Nondurables are goods of a short life. Milk, fruits, meat, and most food items are all nondurable goods. Contrary to human needs and wants, commodities are limited because they are produced with the use of scarce economic resources.

Economic Resources or Factors of Production—the means of producing goods and services

Traditionally economists distinguished between three economic resources, labor, land, and capital. But as production of commodities has grown in complexity, another distinction between **human** and **non-human** resources is, perhaps, more appropriate. Human resources involve the use of human, manual, and mental capabilities in the production of commodities. To capture the complexities of production in advanced industrialized countries, we can further distinguish between three types of human resources, **labor, entrepreneurship**, and **management**.

Labor is the use of mental and physical human power in the production of goods and services. Labor power is the human ability to transform primary resources into commodities. It consists of human muscle, brain, etc. To the extent that different workers have developed their physical and mental capacities in different degrees we can talk about various types of labor. The labor of a coal miner is very much different than that of a medical doctor, which in turn is different from that of a lawyer. In this way, we can make various distinctions among types of labor, such as manual versus mental labor, skilled versus unskilled labor. But what differentiates one type of labor from another the most is investment in human capital. Through education and experience workers become more productive and adjust better to technological developments.

Entrepreneurship is the discovery and exploitation of new business opportunities. Entrepreneurship is normally spontaneous and innovative and can be very rewarding. Yankee entrepreneurial ingenuity, for instance, played an important role in the economic success of the U.S. in the second half of the 19th century. Modern entrepreneurs like Bill Gates, the chairman of Microsoft; Akio Morita, the chairman of Sony Corporation; and Chung Ju-Yung, the chairman of the Hyundai Group, have also played an important role in the economic success of major world corporations. But unlike the early times, when the money needed for new ventures came from a few wealthy individuals and families, in modern times money comes from millions of individuals. Today's large corporations are owned by thousands or even millions of stockholders who do not actively participate in day-to-day operations. Those activities are delegated to management.

Management is the use of human capabilities in the implementation and supervision of the production and distribution of commodities, a task that becomes more difficult as business organizations have grown in size and complexity. While in proprietorships and partnerships, management lies with the entrepreneur(s), in corporations, management is a separate entity. Managers act as agents of stockholders. They run the business and report back to stockholders.

Non-human Resources involve the use of auxiliary instruments at the disposal of human resources in the production of goods and services. In advanced industrialized countries we distinguish among four kinds of non-human resources: **land/natural resources, capital, technology**, and **information/logistics.**

Land/Natural Resources are resources found in nature. Acres of land used in the production of wheat, corn, grain, and other agricultural products. Energy materials such as crude oil, coal, and natural gas used in the production of electricity. Raw materials are used in the production of steel, plastics, detergents, etc.

Capital may be defined in many ways, depending on the discipline it is used in. In finance, for example, it is used in a very broad sense. It includes all assets individuals can hold in their portfolio—cash, stocks, bonds, etc. In economics the term is used in a very narrow sense. It applies only to **physical assets** used in the production of commodities. It includes things such as manufacturing equipment, office equipment, office buildings, shopping centers, transportation facilities, etc. In contrast to labor and land which exist as gifts of nature, capital is man-made, i.e., made up with the use of natural resources and labor.

Technology refers to the application of scientific knowledge and technical experience in the production of commodities. Technology may be classified in two categories, *process* and *product*. Process technology allows companies to change the way commodities are produced and raise the productivity of other resources. Product technology allows companies to improve the quality of existing products and to introduce new ones. In many cases, technology can be both process and product. Flexible manufacturing, for instance, has changed both the way commodities are produced and the types of products produced. Machines can be programmed to produce different models of the same product without any human interference.

Information/Logistics refer to a set of scientific techniques (mathematical and statistical models) used in gathering, processing, and application of statistical data. When applied to the production of commodities, such techniques contribute to the cost-efficient allocation of resources. Linear programming models, for instance, help airlines allocate airplanes over thousands of routes. Inventory models help firms tune their production to the market demand. And assignment models help firms allocate their labor to various tasks.

Information models applied for the first time by the American military in World War II played a major role in the coordination of the war military machine. The "just in time" inventory system developed by Toyota in the 1950s played a major role in reducing inventory costs and improved the company's competitiveness, and assignment models have helped corporations utilize resources efficiently.

Note that progress in microelectronics and biochemistry technologies are revolutionizing the workplace, dictating a reconsideration of the concept of economic resources. Robots and computers substitute for human muscle and human brain, and many commodities are produced with minimum human interference. New seeds increase the production of agriculture products per acre of land to the point where the contribution of land to the final product is limited. As such progress continues, the only scarce resource of the future may be knowledge. But how are economic resources allocated in the production of various commodities? Through economic systems.

Economic Systems—resource allocation mechanism

In a multi-person society, coping with scarcity is a social matter: production of commodities is the result of concentration and cooperation of resources in specific places at specific times. How is that possible? Through an economic system, a system that provides for a coordination of economic resources, maximizing the outcome of human cooperation. An economic system is a resource allocating mechanism, i.e., a way of allocating economic resources in the production of commodities and a way of allocating those commodities among consumers. Since there are various methods of allocating resources and commodities, there are various economic systems, market systems, central command systems, self-management systems, and mixed systems which we will discuss in Chapter Two.

Firms—institutions engaged in the production and distribution of goods and services

The firm is the central unit of modern economic systems. Firms are institutions in charge of economic resources allocating them in production and distribution of commodities. In other words, firms bring together the economic resources required to handle production and distribution of certain commodities. Motorola, for instance, brings together the engineers, the technology, the capital and the raw materials needed to make cellular phones. Boeing brings together the resources needed to make airplanes and Microsoft brings together the resources to develop computer software. There are various types of firms including proprietorships, partnerships, and corporations we discuss in Chapter Two. But how do firms acquire resources and sell their commodities? Through markets.

Entrepreneurship: The Ultimate Advantage

Entrepreneurship has become the slogan of a globalizing economy, and for a good reason. It is the only resource that cannot be easily transferred across corporate boundaries, and therefore, the ultimate source of competitive advantage in global industries where imitation, market saturation, and easier entry quickly erode business profits. Entrepreneurship must be nurtured within business institutions that release the imagination, ingenuity, and creativity of the individual and the group and transform them to new products, processes, and business models.

In its many different forms, entrepreneurship is the part of human nature that spins the world around on its axis, shifting it into a new orbit. When freed from religion, monarchy, and oppression, people sailed the vast seas, traveled to far away lands, discovered new ways to improve their living. In the pre-capitalist world, entrepreneurship in the form of land expeditions and sea explorations became a major source of economic progress and prosperity.

In the late Song dynasty China (960–1274), land expeditions reached to Africa and the Near East for ivory, rhinoceros horn, precious stones, and pearls. In the late Middle-Age Europe, expeditions reached to the Middle-East for China dishware, perfume, Persian carpets, and Indian cloth. In the European *Renaissance*, Western European explorers and merchant adventurers sailed the seas to discover new routes and acquire exotic products, technology, and new ideas. The Portuguese with Vasco da Gamma sailed around Africa, searching for an east sea-route to Asia. The Spanish with Christopher Columbus sailed the Central and Atlantic Ocean, searching for a Southwest sea route to Asia. The British, the French, and the Dutch sailed the North Atlantic, searching for a northwest passage to Asia.

In the capitalist world, entrepreneurship in the form of land and sea explorations and industrial innovations has been at the center of economic activity. In the individual capitalism of the pre-industrial and the early industrial eras, entrepreneurship in the form of land expeditions and sea ventures opened up new markets creating industries. At the eve of the American Revolution, for instance, New England and Delaware sea ventures opened up new market frontiers to the West Indies and Africa, giving rise to the fishing and shipping industries of the colonial Northeast American economy. In the post-revolutionary period, new merchant ventures expanded the market frontier of the new Republic across the Atlantic and the Far East, while land expeditions expanded the domestic market frontier to mid and western United States.

In the individual capitalism of the early industrial era, entrepreneurship in the form of industrial innovations spurred new industries. Eli Whitney's cotton-cleaning engine (gin) and Singer's sewing machine gave a new impetus to the textile industry, while Colt's revolver and the interchangeable manufacturing process spurred the gun-manufacturing industry. Alexander Graham Bell's discovery of the phone that replaced the old Morse telegraph sparked-off the telephone industry, while Edison's light bulb and commercialization of electric current marked the beginning of the electric utilities industry.

In the corporate capitalism of the first three-quarters of the 20th century, entrepreneurship in the form of research and development delivered new products and processes fueling the growth of yet new businesses and industries. Ford's development and mass-manufacturing of the T-model at the turn of the century, for instance, turned the corner for the automobile and the steel industries. The development of a number of breakthrough products by the "Big Three" U.S. chemical companies provided the foundation of the metal alloys, nylon, plastics, and optics industries, allowing large corporations to diversify and overcome saturation in mature product markets. The invention of transistors, semiconductors, computers, and lasers provided the foundation of yet another host of industries that eventually led to the information revolution.

In the network capitalism that began in the last quarter of the 20th century and continuing to the present day, entrepreneurship in the form of software and hardware development, strategic innovations, and new business models continued to be at the center of economic activity. Software from Microsoft, for instance, made computers user friendly, sparking a host of applications that accelerated the growth of the industry. New distribution channels by Dell Computer and Amazon.com turned market niches into mass markets, as did retail outlets like Walmart, discount investment service providers like Charles Schwab, and low-fare airliners like Continental Airlines.

Markets—mechanisms that allocate goods, services and resources, and set prices

A market is a mechanism that facilitates the exchange of commodities and resources, i.e., it brings buyers and sellers of a resource or a commodity together and determines the price and the traded volume. Firms can buy raw materials, hire labor, rent land and acquire technology in resource markets. Those resources are supplied by households. Bargaining between the two sides determines the price for each resource. In turn, firms can sell commodities in commodity markets, where households are the buyers (more on this in Chapter Two). What behavioral principles, what objectives guide the behavior of firms and households? Rationality.

Economics and Psychology—the rational and the emotional side of humans

Humans are both intelligent and emotional beings. As intelligent beings, humans decide by reason, by carefully examining the parameters of the environment they live in, setting goals and priorities and crafting alternative strategies and tactics to reach them. Intelligent consumers, for instance, carefully examine their economic situation, taking stock of their human and non-human resources, ranking and prioritizing their needs and desires, the need to be satisfied first, second, and so on, in order to derive the maximum return from their human and non-human resources, as it is taught in standard economic books.

As emotional beings, humans decide by impulse rather than reason, fueled by anxiety, anger, fear, greed, complacency, etc., ignoring the environment they live in, failing to set goals and priorities, and craft strategies and tactics to reach them. Emotional consumers, for instance, fail to take stock of their human and non-human resources, and to prioritize their needs and desires. Instead, they act out of impulse, rushing and racing to buy products filling the needs and desires of ruthless marketers, rather than those of their own.

To sum up, coping with scarcity is the ultimate purpose of every economy. Human needs are satisfied with the use of commodities which are produced with the aid of human and non-human resources. Such resources are brought together by an economic mechanism, a set of institutions that allocate resources in the production of various commodities. Firms and markets are the two most important economic institutions of most western economies. Rationality is the most important behavioral principle of the members of an economic system. But let us look at one of the models economists have developed to analyze scarcity and choice.

1.5 Scarcity and Choice: The Model of Production Possibilities

Individual, corporate, and government resources are scarce. Individuals have an open list of objectives, things they would like to consume but limited resources to pursue those objectives. Corporations have an open list of objectives, products they would like to produce, but limited resources to pursue those objectives. Governments have an open list of social programs they would like to pursue, but they, too, are on a limited resource budget.

Faced with scarcity, economic agents must make choices. They must choose what to produce and what not to produce. Choosing to go to school, for instance, means the giving up of many nice things a student could have done with his/her resources. Choosing to make more mainframe computers, for instance, a computer company must cut down on another product line, PCs; and in choosing to spend more on health programs a government must spend less on other programs.

To demonstrate the problem of scarcity and choice, economists have developed the model of production possibilities. The model postulates that economic resources are limited and assumes: (i) only two commodities are produced, chairs and tables; (ii) chairs and tables come only in one style; and (iii) economic resources used in the production of the two commodities are perfect substitutes with each other, i.e., they can be switched back and forth between the production of chairs and the production of tables.

With limited resources, a trade-off between the production of chairs and tables exists, to produce more chairs the economy must forgo some tables, and vice versa. This is true for the simple reason that the production of more chairs requires the transfer of resources from the production of tables to the production of chairs. Exhibit 1.1 depicts this trade-off between the production of chairs and the production of tables as a straight line—called the **production possibilities line**. It shows the maximum number of chairs and tables the economy can produce with the available economic resources. Note that the straight line, one-to-one trade-off between the production of the two commodities, reflects the assumption of perfect substitution of economic resources: Resources can be transferred back and forth between the two production processes without a problem. What about the case where economic resources are not perfect substitutes? The trade-off between the production of the two commodities is not one-to-one any longer and the graph of the production possibilities is a curve rather than a straight line.

Exhibit 1.1

The Production Possibilities Line for Chairs and Tables

The trade-off between the production of chairs and tables is a straight line. It reflects the similarities in the production processes of the two commodities, which make economic resources perfect substitutes. The Economy must give up the production of exactly one table in order to produce one extra chair.

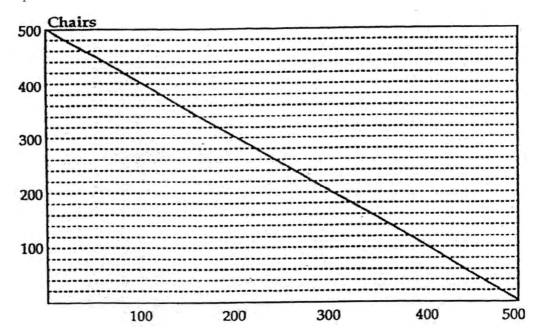

Postulate: Resources are limited
Assumption: 1. Society produces only two commodities.
               2. Economic resources are perfect substitutes.

The Production Possibilities Schedule for Chairs and Tables

Chairs	Tables
500	0
450	50
400	100
350	150
300	200
250	250
200	300
150	350
100	400
50	450
0	500

To understand this case, let us assume that an economy produces hamburgers and jet fighters. Unlike the case of chairs and tables where the same machines and workers could be interchangeably used in the production of chairs and tables, this is no longer the case. As workers are transferred from Big Macs to jets, the production of the jet fighters increases but not sufficiently enough to compensate for the production losses of hamburgers. Reflecting this disproportional trade-off, the production possibilities become a curve (see Exhibit 1.2).

Exhibit 1.2
A. Production Possibilities Schedule for Hamburgers and Jet Fighters

Hamburgers	Jet Fighters	Opportunity Cost
1,000	0	–
900	200	2.00
800	350	1.50
700	450	1.00
600	520	.70
0	550	.05

This table provides a set of attainable alternatives. One choice of the society is to produce 1,000 hamburgers and no jet fighters. Another choice is 900 hamburgers and 200 jet fighters and so on, until the combination is no hamburgers and 550 jet fighters.

B. The Production Possibilities Curve for Hamburgers and Jet Fighters

The Production Possibilities Curve for Hamburgers and Jet Fighters

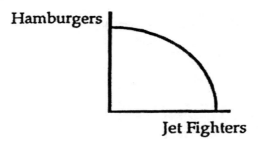

This exhibit is an image of the possible production alternatives of hamburgers and jet fighters. The society can attain any combination of the two commodities on or within the curve—but nothing beyond.

The **production possibilities curve** is the set of all combinations of the maximum production of the two commodities may be produced with a given volume of resources. It expresses the productive limits of the society. The economy can produce any combination of the two goods on or within that frontier but none beyond it.

To sum up, the production possibilities model is an illustration of the feasible production alternatives with limited resources. The model emphasizes the trade-off between the production of one good versus the production of another good. To elaborate more on this trade-off, let us discuss two important concepts, efficiency and opportunity cost.

Real World Snapshots

Jobs, Jobs, Jobs! Can the Government Raise Employment?

The idea of the government creating jobs is very popular, especially in recessions when more people are unemployed. The first budget of the Clinton Administration, for instance, earmarked $1.3 billion for summer youth jobs. But can the government do it? Can politicians create more jobs in the government sector, without affecting the number of jobs generated in the private sector? Economists are divided on this issue. Some economists say yes: if those workers are already unemployed and are put back to work, there is a gain in efficiency and production, and employment can increase in the government sector without a decrease in production and employment in the private sector. (Can you draw the production possibilities curve in this case?) Other economists say no. Governments have no resources of their own. To pay wages, governments must raise taxes, cut spending elsewhere, print money, or issue debt that takes resources away from the private sector. For every thousand new jobs the government generates, another thousand are lost in the private sector. Put differently, government programs to stimulate the economy and create jobs just expand the government sector and employment at the expense of the private sector. (Can you draw the production possibilities curve in this case?)

Efficiency

With scarcity taken for granted, efficiency is the buzz-word in economics. With a given amount of resources, the welfare of an individual, the performance of a corporation and the welfare of a society all depend on the way economic resources are utilized. When economic resources are used without care and are wasted, welfare declines. When consumers pay more for commodities they need or buy commodities they do not need, economic resources are wasted and consumer welfare declines. When corporations use more resources than necessary to produce a commodity or they produce commodities they fail to sell, they waste economic resources and sooner or later will fall behind the competition. Likewise when societies use too many resources for the commodities they produce or they produce commodities that are wasted, they are doomed to fall behind other societies that use resources wisely.

Bearing these considerations in mind, economists have developed two concepts of efficiency, technical efficiency and economic efficiency:

Technical efficiency means producing the most of commodities with the available resources: producing the maximum number of chairs and tables, jet fighters and hamburgers, etc., with the available resources. By definition, any production combination on the production possibilities line is technically efficient; likewise, any point on the production possibilities curve is efficient: it represents the maximum the society can produce in hamburgers and jet fighters given the available resources (see Exhibit 1.3).

Technical waste is the opposite concept of technical efficiency. When resources are not well coordinated or fully utilized, production of one or both commodities is less than the maximum. By definition, any production combination inside the production possibilities line or curve is not efficient; resources are wasted (see Exhibit 1.3).

Technical efficiency is the necessary but not the sufficient condition for maximizing welfare. Producing the maximum quantities of the two commodities may be still wasteful if there is no need for them. Making the largest pie with a fixed amount of resources is still a waste if no one is willing to eat it. Likewise, making computer mainframes where the market demands PCs is also a waste and so is the making of submarines when there is no need for them. To address these points, economists have developed a more broad concept of efficiency, economic efficiency.

Economic efficiency means getting the maximum satisfaction out of certain resources: getting the most out of commodities that are useful to someone. Thus, the concept of economic efficiency is stronger than that of technical efficiency. To get maximum satisfaction from a given level of income, for instance, consumers must purchase only commodities they need and shop around until they pay the lowest prices for them. To maximize the return on certain resources, companies must produce commodities that consumers are willing to buy and produce them with the least amount of resources; the same principles apply when it comes to social resources and production.

Assuming that economic resources are allocated efficiently, there is a trade-off between the things we can do. When choosing to produce more of one commodity, less of another commodity must be produced. This idea is explained with the concept of opportunity cost.

How Efficiency Affects Business Performance

Technical Efficiency ↑→ Productivity ↑→ Cost ↓→
Performance (Profit) ↑
Example: Wal-Mart

Economic Efficiency ↑→ Sales ↑→ Performance ↑
Example: Microsoft

Exhibit 1.3
Technically Efficient versus Inefficient Production

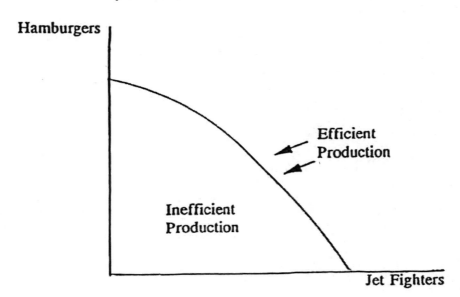

Opportunity Cost

As discussed earlier, scarcity implies trade-off among choices. When resources are committed to a certain objective, alternative objectives are not satisfied. **Opportunity cost is the value of the next best alternative when scarce economic resources are committed to a certain objective.** When an individual chooses to allocate resources to schooling another alternative is sacrificed (see end of the chapter for more details). When a corporation chooses to allocate resources to one product line, another product line is sacrificed. And when a government decides to build an extra jet plane, another social program is sacrificed. But how can opportunity cost be measured? How can alternative resource uses be valued?

Opportunity cost is a subjective concept, i.e., it is relevant only to the agent who makes the choice. Sacrificing an hour to go to school means different things to different people. For someone, it means the money that he could make for an hour's work in a fast food store. For another the time taken away from child care, drinking beer and watching his favorite TV show or lying on the beach (Exhibit 1.4). These considerations further suggest that opportunity cost does not always translate to money but to the next alternative someone would enjoy with scarce resources. Opportunity cost may also change each time the agent is faced with new decisions. The opportunity cost of attending school may be different for each student a few years later (see the real world link, at the end of the chapter).

To demonstrate the concept of opportunity cost we return to the table used to draw the production possibilities curve (Exhibit 1.2). Moving from one production combination to another or from one point on the production possibilities curve to another, the production of hamburgers increases while the production of jet fighters drops. For example, moving from the first combination to the second, the society must sacrifice, give up 100 hamburgers for 200 jet fighters. Moving from the second combination to the third, the society must sacrifice an extra 100 hamburgers for an extra 150 jet fighters (see third column of Exhibit 1.2). In other words, at some point, a given sacrifice of hamburgers "buys" fewer and fewer jet fighters.

The concept of opportunity cost is general and applies in the evaluation of individual corporate and social resources. For instance, the time a student spends preparing for an exam in economics may compete with time needed preparing for a chemistry exam, when the number of hours available for the two courses is fixed. Assuming that the student is equally able in chemistry and economics, a ten point higher grade in an economics exam translates to a ten points lower grade in a chemistry exam (Exhibit 1.5). In another example, time workers spend to commute to work has an opportunity cost that can be measured in terms of hours lost from work (see special reading).

Exhibit 1.4
The Opportunity Cost of Four Students Attending a Lecture in Introductory Economics

Student	Mr. Smith	Mrs. Collins	Mr. Brown	Mr. Mors
Opportunity Cost	Working in a fast food restaurant	Looking after children	Watching favorite TV show	Lying on the beach

This exhibit is a hypothetical example of the opportunity cost of four students attending an economics class. It demonstrates the idea that opportunity cost may differ from individual to individual. For Mr. Smith staying in the class means a sacrifice of the earnings he could earn working in a fast-food restaurant. This could translate into $6, $8 or whatever the going wage is in that line of work. For Mrs. Collins, coming to the class means using child care which could, again, be translated into dollars, whatever Mrs. Collins must pay for a babysitter. For Mr. Brown and Mr. Mors, coming to class means giving up leisure, whatever dollars they translate it to.

Opportunity cost is not confined just to the value of forgone opportunities over material things but to immaterial things as well. By the way, have you thought of the opportunity cost of marriage? The value of things one could enjoy as being single instead of married. Have you thought of the opportunity cost of breaking the law and going to jail? The opportunity cost of getting addicted to drugs. Here are two examples to practice your knowledge of opportunity cost!

Exhibit 1.5
Student's Production Possibilities in Economics and Chemistry

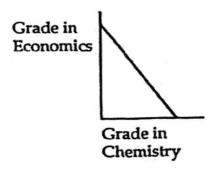

Exhibit 1.5 is a demonstration of a student's production possibilities model. On the horizontal axis we measure the student's performance in chemistry, while on the vertical axis we measure the student's performance in economics. Both performances are measured in terms of the grades the student can attain. Given a certain amount of time the student has available for studying economics and chemistry, he cannot improve his performance in chemistry without deteriorating this performance in economics.

The Law of Increasing Opportunity Cost

You might have already observed that, as we move from the left of the production possibilities curve to the right, at some point, opportunity cost is increasing, i.e., the society must forgo a larger and larger number of hamburgers for additional jet fighters (see relevant column in Exhibit 1.2). Why is it so? Because of the assumption that economic resources are not perfect substitutes.

Economic resources employed in various industries are seldom perfect substitutes for each other. If things were so, the sacrifice and the gain would correspond one-to-one as in the case of chairs and tables (see Exhibit 1.1). In that exhibit, the production possibilities for chairs and tables is drawn as a straight line because of the similarities in the production processes of the two commodities, which make economic resources perfect substitutes, i.e., as productive in both industries. However, in most cases production processes are not similar, and economic resources may not be substitutable. Highly specialized workers, for instance, in one industry may not have the skills required in other industries. As additional workers switch from the production of one commodity to the other, the last workers are less productive in the latter industry than the former. Therefore, the production lost in one industry will not be balanced by an equal increase in the output of the other industry. This implies that the transformation of an economy from one set of industries to another can only be slow and painful. America's difficulty in switching from defense-oriented industries to civilian industries since 1985 is a case in point. Highly specialized aerospace and computer engineers cannot be switched to hospitals and schools without proper training that will slow down the transformation from one industry to another.

Opportunity Cost, Specialization, and the Division of Labor

As human skills are allocated unevenly in society, the opportunity cost of an activity differs from individual to individual. The opportunity cost is highest for the activity an individual can perform best. The opportunity cost of doing something else instead of singing is high for singers. Likewise, the opportunity cost of doing something else other than teaching is high for teachers and so are activities other than plumbing to plumbers.

Exhibit 1.6
Over Time, the Production Possibilities Frontier Expands

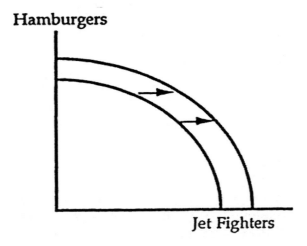

Over time, due to an expansion of both human and non-human resources, the production possibilities curve shifts to the right (the shift may not be symmetrical). This means that the economy can produce more hamburgers and more jet fighters.

Relative differences in opportunity cost is the foundation of specialization and division of labor. It makes sense for singers to specialize in singing and buy from others goods and services that they cannot do as well. Likewise it makes sense for teachers to specialize in teaching and plumbers to specialize in plumbing and buy other goods and services from other specialists.

The same reasoning can be applied to the international division of labor. Countries should specialize in the production of commodities they can produce the best and buy the rest of commodities from other countries (more on this in the discussion of the theory of pure trade in another chapter).

Opportunity Cost, Specialization, and the Division of Labor

- As human skills are allocated unevenly in society, the opportunity cost of an activity differs from individual to individual
- The opportunity cost is highest for the activity an individual can perform best
- Relative differences in opportunity cost is the foundation of specialization and division of labor
- The same reasoning can be applied to the international division of labor, countries should specialize in the production of commodities they can produce the best and buy the rest of commodities from other countries.

Three things have become clear from the discussion of scarcity: (1) maximization of individual, corporate, and social welfare requires that economic resources are allocated efficiently in production and consumption; (2) economic resources have an opportunity cost, the value of the next best forgone alternative; and (3) opportunity cost is the basis for specialization and the division of labor. How does the discussion change if resources become less scarce?

Economic Growth, Technology, and the Production Possibilities Curve

Allocating resources efficiently and attaining the maximum production and consumption is not enough in a dynamic society. Somalia and the Sudan may attain the maximum production and yet people starve. Economic growth, the rising of the economy's potential is essential not only for poor countries but for rich countries as well. As long as the economic pie grows larger, everyone's piece become larger and the struggle over the distribution of income and wealth becomes less intense and problems over government deficits and welfare become smaller. But how is the economy's potential expanded? With the expansion, enrichment, and enhancement of economic resources, especially technology.

So far in drawing the production possibilities curve, we have assumed fixed economic resources. Such assumptions that may be valid in the short term, are not so in the long term when economic resources may expand and along with them the production possibilities curve. Human resources may expand with the natural increase in population. A larger number of workers, entrepreneurs, and managers become available with a population of 300 million instead of a population of 250 million. Non-human resources expand with savings, improvement in technology, information, etc. With positive savings more money is available for machines, shopping centers, highways, etc., and therefore, workers have more means at their disposal to produce commodities. Over time, scientific knowledge and experience in producing commodities advances, and along with it, the production possibilities frontier. All these factors move the production possibilities out (see Exhibit 1.6). You should notice, however, that technology may not advance equally in both industries, and therefore, the production possibilities curve need not shift equally at both ends.

1.6 Review

1. Economics issues and problems dominate every man's life—from presidents and corporate executives to consumers and workers. The study of economics enables people to become (i) better students of business disciplines, (ii) better managers of their own resources, (iii) better-educated citizens, casting their votes more intelligently.

2. Economics is the science which investigates the laws that govern economic systems. It deals with issues such as the allocation of limited resources over unlimited human needs. Issues of production and exchange, the determination of the GDP and its components, economic growth, business fluctuations and the policies to deal with them.

3. Studying economics is not any easier than studying sciences. Economists investigate economic phenomena with the use of models, abstractions of real world situations. A model includes four parts—postulates, assumptions, decision rules, and refutable hypotheses.

4. Economic theories are derived out of models and empirical evidence, serving as a guide to investigating real world phenomena. As in any other discipline, economists have their own concepts and terms to communicate with each other, scarcity, commodities, economic resources, economic systems, markets, and rationality.

5. Scarcity is the major issue in economics. It refers to a limited supply of resources in relation to the demand for them in the production of various commodities.

6. The Production Possibilities Curve is a model, a tool describing production choices with the available resources; every point on the curve shows the maximum that can be produced with those resources. Among other things, the production possibilities curve is used to discuss two important concepts, economic efficiency and opportunity cost.

7. Efficiency in economics means that an agent produces a maximum of commodities from certain resources. Economists distinguish between two concepts of efficiency, technical and economic efficiency. Technical efficiency means the maximization of production of a commodity with the available resources. Economic efficiency means the maximization of both production and consumption of commodities.

8. Opportunity Cost is the value of the next best forgone alternative of a given resource. Any time an individual firm or society makes a commitment to a particular choice it results in the sacrifice of the benefits from the next available alternative not chosen. For example, the choice to produce missiles is associated with a sacrifice of other alternatives—the benefits from more hospitals, more schools, better highways, etc. And as resources are often non-homogeneous, such a transition may be painful.

9. Due to growth in the supply of economic resources, such as labor and capital, as well as advances in scientific knowledge, technology, and management systems, the production possibilities of the society expands; the production possibilities curve shifts to the right.

Real World Link 1: Why Does It Cost Less to Attend College at an Earlier Rather Than a Later Age?

Key Concept:

Opportunity Cost: The sacrifice of the best alternative associated with the commitment of economic resources to a particular activity.

Given the benefits you anticipate from a college education, is yours the right age to attend college? Or should you wait a few years? When is it least costly to attend college?

People attend college for various reasons. In addition to self-enrichment and the quest for understanding and exploring the natural and social environment, they attend school for economic reasons. College prepares them for better and higher-paying careers. In this sense, going to college is an investment in yourself. You commit your resources of time and money—time to go to college and study for the course assignments, money spent on tuition, books, etc., in anticipation of higher earnings (compared to the earnings you could make without a degree).

Assuming that tuition and other school costs, as well as individual learning ability, remains the same irrespective of age, when is it cheaper to start college, at the age of 17, or at the age of 35? One of the resources you are committing is your own time, and this time is not without cost. It must be taken away from other alternative uses. For example, instead of the twelve hours you go to school every week, you could work in a restaurant and earn five dollars an hour, and this is the opportunity cost of each hour you spend in college. Does the opportunity cost increase or decrease as one grows from the age of 17 to that of 35? Yes, the opportunity cost of time increases with age, because of the higher earning capacity that comes with experience. Thus, on purely economic grounds, going to college at an early age costs less than at a later age. In addition, the time stream over which benefits are gained is longer.

Real World Link 2: The Three Rules of Intelligent Shopper

Key Concepts:
- Technical Efficiency
- Economic Efficiency
- Opportunity Cost

Last night my wife came home from the shopping mall really upset. I wondered what had happened. As it turned out she couldn't stay long enough on line to buy a pair of shoes for an upcoming holiday party. But does she really need another pair of shoes? That's an open question. What isn't an open question is that the shoes were selling at a deep discount!

If you are heading for the shopping mall to buy merchandise at deep discount this holiday season, you better think twice. You may end up buying things you don't need, wasting your time and money, especially if you are an emotional shopper.

Humans are both intelligent and emotional beings. As intelligent beings, humans make decisions by reason. They carefully examine the environment they live in, setting goals and priorities. They craft alternative strategies and tactics to reach them. Emotional beings decide by impulse, fueled by anxiety, anger, fear, greed, and other emotions.

The intelligent and the emotional sides of human beings come out in shopping. Intelligent shoppers begin with the "Big Picture," the things that are important in their lives, setting needs ahead of desires. Before they grab a piece of a merchandise and head for the cash register, they always ask three simple questions:

Do I need the product?
Is the price right?
Is this merchandise the best use of my money?

Emotional shoppers, by contrast, act by impulse, passion and hype. They rush and race to buy products filling the dreams and aspirations of ruthless marketers, rather than their own. They see the "Big Picture," upside down, often placing desires ahead of needs. They rush to buy merchandise just because it happened to be on sale without asking whether they really have a need for it in the first place; whether the price is right; and whether it is the best choice for their money. They end up subscribing to magazines they never read; joining health clubs they rarely visit; buying clothing they never wear; purchasing tools and accessories they never use; and bringing home toys their children hardly touch.

Obviously, intelligent consumers allocate their resources efficiently and effectively, while emotional shoppers waste their resources. But why consumers do that? Why they shop with emotions rather than intelligence?

Because emotional shoppers allow themselves to be manipulated by marketers who hype their emotions by sales events like the Black Friday, Cyber Monday, and Black Saturday. They are too concerned with the prospect of missing out on sale opportunities on Sony's flat panel TVs, Apple's iPhones and the iPads, Decker's and Nike's (NYSE: NKE) shoes, and Ralph Lauren's and Coach's Apparel; they are buying merchandise indiscriminately, irrespective of the need for it, and its priority.

The bottom line: Before you head out for the stores on this holiday season, ask yourself the three simple questions of intelligent shopping, so you can be a victor rather than a victim of this holiday's shopping season.

Source: *Forbes Magazine*

Real World Link 3: The Six Rules of Success

Key Concepts:
- Economic Efficiency
- Technical Efficiency
- Opportunity Cost

Of all human abilities, one stands out, the ability to see the Big Picture, the things that are important in life, and not to be distracted by small, trivial, and irrelevant things; the intelligence to separate the message from the background noise.

'The Big Picture' is about the grand goals; the big dreams and aspirations people treasure in every stage and aspect of life. But how can you grasp and hold on to the Big Picture? What does it take?

Six rules that have been successfully tested in business and everyday life:

1. Get your Priorities Right

Setting priorities right is about making intelligent choices, deciding what goals to pursue in which order, which takes vision and foresight. Intelligent people rise over the hills and valleys of the present to gaze over the hills and the valleys of the future and see the invisible and the challenges it holds. Renowned entrepreneurs like Microsoft's founder Bill Gates, Apple's founder Steve Jobs, and Facebook's founder Mark Zuckerberg had such vision and foresight; they could see how technology could change the lives of everyday people; and came up with products and services that will turn their vision into reality.

Getting your priorities right is about choosing whether to go to school, start your own business or working for somebody else; whether to get married or stay singled; whether to have children or not; whether to stay married or get divorced; whether to remarry if widowed or divorced; and you have to choose how to spend your money.

2. Use Resources Wisely

Using resources wisely is also about making intelligent choices. It is about deriving the most value out of limited resources; shopping around for the right merchandise by asking three simple questions: Do I need this piece of merchandise? Is the price right? Is this merchandise the best use of my money?

In some cases, using resources wisely means more than shopping around for bargains for the right merchandise. It also means paying the least interest and finance charges for the things you buy on credit. Shop around for the lowest interest rates on a home mortgage; refinance when interest rates fall sufficiently; and stay away from consumer debt and finance charges that add to the price of the merchandise you buy.

3. Stay Focused

Staying focused means sticking with your priorities and goals; focusing on the message, not on the background noise; and executing. Take the right steps to reach your goals. That's all that matters in the end.

It takes patience, persistence, and discipline to stay focused. Patience to overcome the hurdles that stand between you and your goal; persistence to overcome the failures, setbacks, and temptations that may take you off course; and discipline to play the game right, to comply with all the rules: know what you are doing, be punctual, and work out all the details.

4. Develop the Right Relations

Reaching a certain goal requires moral and psychological stamina. It takes skills and resources no single individual possesses. This means that in pursuing personal success, people need friends and partners to overcome the many obstacles that stand between them and their personal goals. At school, friends can provide the moral and psychological support to endure and overcome the pressure that comes with class lectures, homework, exams, and term paper deadlines. Partners provide the information and expertise to go over complex concepts and to complete coursework projects, sharing of class notes, participating in discussion groups.

At work, friends provide the moral and psychological support to endure and overcome workplace-related stress, meeting project deadlines, handling customer complains, and dealing with internal politics. Partners provide skills and expertise to complete complex projects that require cooperation among several parties.

Friendships and partnerships is a trait shared by many successful company founders, including HP founders Bill Hewlett and Dave Packard, Google founders Sergey Brin and Larry Page, and Microsoft founders Bill Gates and Paul Allen.

5. Don't be Greedy

Greed is the idolization and relentless pursuit of something that lets people distinguish and set themselves apart from others—money, power, status, and so on; the feeling that they never have enough of it, and nothing can stop them from amassing and accumulating it.

Greed is an obsession that—like alcohol—numbs people's senses, blurs their vision, and makes them lose sight of the Big Picture. Greed leads people to live a life of imbalance and disproportion, a life of reckless and dangerous behavior. People who want everything in life fail to negotiate with others and compromise, and end up losing everything. People, who want everything from personal friendships and partnerships and become selfish and arrogant, end up destroying them.

6. Don't be Complacent

Complacency is the opposite of greed. It's the idolization of things people have accomplished, the feeling that they have reached the telos (ultimate destination).

This may sound contradictory to what was argued earlier about staying focused, but success isn't an entitlement. It cannot be taken for granted. Successful people cannot afford to be complacent because good times do not last forever, especially in a rapidly changing world. That's why complacency is dangerous. People who are complacent with their accomplishments fail to catch up with the rest of the world and are left behind. At school, students who are complacent about their performance at the beginning the semester eventually lag behind their peers and end up failing the course. At work, workers who become complacent and take their jobs for granted fail to keep up with the demands of the marketplace by upgrading their skills and are the first in line to be laid off in an economic downturn. In marriage, people who become complacent about what they have accomplished and take each other for granted, end with apathy and indifference for each other.

Source: *Forbes Magazine*

Discussion Questions and Problems

1. What are the five most important problems of the 1990s?
2. Why study economics?
3. What are the four steps in constructing a model?

4. What is the difference between models and theories?

5. Can economists test their theories with experiments?

6. What is the difference between the production possibilities line and curve?

7. How would you draw the trade-off between the production of donuts and croissants?

8. Can the government create jobs in one sector without destroying jobs in another?

9. What is the difference between economic and technical efficiency?

10. Is opportunity cost of an activity the same for each individual?

11. Why may the opportunity cost of shifting resources from one activity to another be increasing?

12. Does school cost only out-of-pocket expenses? Does the opportunity cost of education increase with age?

13. Who should look after children, the husband or the wife? When does it pay to hire a babysitter?

14. Mrs. Smith is a careful shopper. She uses coupons to save money. But she ends up getting items that she never uses. Mrs. Brown is a careful shopper too. She only buys items that she needs but she never bothers to use coupons and save money? Do Mrs. Smith and Mrs. Brown allocate their income efficiently? What is the difference?

15. For years IBM focused on mainframe computers while the market was moving in favor of personal computers. Did IBM allocate its resources efficiently? How did such strategy affect IBM's performance?

Homework 1

1. Define the following terms:

   Economic Models

   Economic Theories

   Human Needs

   Economic Resources

   Scarcity

   Opportunity Cost

   Economic Efficiency

   Technical Efficiency

2. John is a medical doctor. Why does it pay to have someone cut his lawn?

3. Why is the opportunity cost of going to school higher for older students?

4. What is the opportunity cost of signing up for my class?

5. It is often said that governments cannot create jobs because they don't have resources of their own. Do you agree? Explain.

6. In some countries the government bails out declining industries. How do such policies affect the allocation of resources?

Chapter Two

ECONOMIC PROBLEMS, ECONOMIC SYSTEMS, AND THE U.S. ECONOMY

Preview

What are the fundamental economic problems facing any society at any time? What are the economic mechanisms providing solutions to these problems? How are economic mechanisms different from economies? What are the characteristics of the U.S. economy? These are some of the questions we discuss in this chapter.

Introduction

The collapse of the Soviet Union and the Socialist economies of Central and Eastern Europe marked the end of a social experiment which placed economic resources and decision making for allocating these resources to government. It further revived the controversy surrounding the ways different economic mechanisms and institutions can satisfy individual and social needs. What are the advantages and the disadvantages of an economic system? What is the difference between economic systems and economies? What are the characteristics of the U.S. economy? Addressing these questions, this chapter is in four sections. The first section is a discussion of the fundamental economic problems. The second section is a discussion of the different types of economic systems, the third section is a discussion of the difference between economic systems and economies, and the fourth section is a brief discussion of the U.S. economy.

2.1 The Economic Problems

Ever since he appeared on earth, man has been faced with scarcity: limited resources to cope with unlimited needs and desires. Scarcity gives rise to four fundamental economic problems:

- What commodities should be produced?
- How much of each commodity should be produced?
- How should commodities be produced?
- For whom should commodities be produced?

Because economic resources are scattered among the members of society, the efficient solution of these problems requires a mechanism, an economic system, that will coordinate efforts. Economic systems may vary from society to society. For instance, in Greek antiquity, allocation of economic resources varied significantly across city-states. While the Athenian economic system relied more on individual ownership and trade of economic resources, the Spartan system relied on social ownership of economic resources that were allocated through governmental channels. Significant differences can be observed in the economic systems of contemporary societies. In the U.S. economic resources are, primarily, owned and allocated by individuals (under certain governmental rules), while in China and Cuba economic resources are, primarily, owned and allocated by government authorities. And while the U.S. and the British economic systems are similar, government rules that set the stage for individual ownership and allocation of resources are stricter in Britain than in the U.S. Which system is better?

Given the diversity and the changing nature of economic systems, providing an answer to this question is not simple. To make things simple, economists have attempted to classify economic systems into a smaller number of categories and apply a narrow range of criteria, such as efficiency, fairness, and flexibility for judging the performance of each system.

2.2 Types of Economic Systems

At the turn of the 20th century economists and social scientists classified economic systems into three major categories: Capitalism, Socialism, and Communism. By the middle of the century, this distinction became more and more ideological, therefore becoming blurred, confusing, and less operational. To avoid this confusion, economists adopted a more operational classification which included four economic systems: the Planned or Command System, the Self Managed System, the Market System, and the Mixed System.

The Planned or Command System

The Soviet model command system is a resource allocation mechanism that relies on central planning and control. Economic resources are socially (government) owned, and in the command of a central authority which provides solutions to the four fundamental economic problems. The central authority makes up the list of social hierarchies regarding the types and the quantities of the commodities that must be produced, and which economic resources will be allocated accordingly. If the central authority regards jet planes to be of high priority and soap of low priority, a relatively large number of jet planes will be produced. The central authority also decides how and for whom commodities should be produced. The main instrument through which these decisions are made and implemented is the Central Plan.

The Central Plan, which is normally made for a period of five years, includes four stages. In the first stage, the **central committee** of the Communist Party sets up national priorities, i.e., lists the types and the quantities of the commodities that must be produced.

In the second stage, the list is turned to the **Gosplan**, an agency responsible for coordinating the various sectors (ministries) of the economy. The Gosplan, which in the meantime has been collecting information about the availability of resources in the various sectors of the economy, attempts to match what is desired by the central committee to what is feasible with the available resources. After a tentative matching is reached, the Gosplan sets up production targets that are sent out to the ministers and the enterprises of each sector of the economy.

In the third stage, the enterprises of each sector review the targets set by the Gosplan and through the departmental minister convey their responses back to Gosplan. In the fourth stage, the Gosplan revises the original targets in view of the responses received by each ministry, ironing out any inconsistencies in the production targets across the economy.

It is important to notice that central planning is a system of vertical communication among the various economic units. Information flows from the central unit to peripheral units, and then back to the central unit; horizontal communication, i.e., the exchange of information among peripheral units, is not permissible. Such communication channels have three major drawbacks. First, the system is inflexible to any change in the economic conditions. Faced with any unexpected circumstances, managers of various enterprises must communicate with their superiors, who must communicate with departmental ministers, all the way to the central authority. As a result, when a decision is made, it may accomplish too little too late. Second, as information travels through long channels, it may be intentionally or unintentionally distorted, leading to wrong decisions. Third, as neither workers or management have a direct stake either in the resources or the output, they may lack the incentives to pursue the objectives set by the central planning authority.

It is very difficult to find any system which strictly complies with the characteristics of the command system. Perhaps the only good example one could think of is the system of War Communism in the Soviet Union between the years 1918–1921. During that period, trade in commodities was abolished, money as a medium of exchange and as capital was eliminated, workers were assigned to various tasks in a militaristic fashion, and equal wages were paid for equal work, and farm output passed into the hands of state authorities.

Today's remains of the Communist system in China and Cuba replicate several of the principles of this central planning, but they very much diverge from those set by the early revolutionary regimes. But even the late Soviet Union system of the Gorbachev era very much diverges from the system of war communism established in the early years of the Bolshevik revolution. In what was known as *Perestroika* (reform), several aspects existing in market economies, such as profits and incentives, emerged side by side with central planning.

The Self-Managed System

The self-managed system is a resource allocation mechanism that also relies on social ownership and control of the means of production. However, unlike in the command system where "social" practically means governmental, in a self-managed system it means labor ownership and control. Workers decide about what, how much, how, and for whom to produce. This system is decentralized in the sense that firms make decisions without the binding consent of a central planning authority. Some of these decisions are left totally to union leaders, while others are made through workers' conventions. Central planning does exist, in a weak sense, to insure a balance between demand and supply across the economy and consistency among individual labor interests and national interests. The market mechanism also exists side by side with planning and labor control; it facilitates the exchange of commodities and resources between enterprises (horizontal communication). Thus, the product mix of the economy is the result of interplay between the labor councils, the plan, and the market.

Examples of Command Economies

- North Korea
- Cuba
- Turkmenistan
- Myanmar
- Belarus
- Laos
- Libya
- Iran

Advocates of this system, between central planning and the market system, claim that it combines the best of both. Is there any real world system close to this ideal? No. Before collapsing into a bloody civil war, the Yugoslav system came close to it, or at least complied with some of the principles of self-management. In the former Yugoslavia, the labor force is divided into 30,000 workers' co-ops covering most spectrums of economic activity. Workers participate in all levels of decision making, including those of employment compensation benefits, and investment decisions.

Despite some success in the sixties and the early seventies, the Yugoslavian economy slid into mounting foreign debt and high inflation, joining many of the third world countries with similar problems. In 1988 alone, inflation was running at a rate of 175%, similar to that of many Latin America debtor nations, a factor that has contributed to social unrest, and the ultimate collapse of both the system of self management and the country.

The Market System

The market system is a resource allocation mechanism that includes the following: private ownership of the means of production, individual decision making, voluntary exchange of goods and services, the power of the market mechanism to coordinate individual decisions, and a limited role of government.

Exhibit 2.1 gives a sketch of a market system. On the left side of the chart are households which own economic resources selling them to firms (on the other side of the chart), in exchange for economic rewards (wages, interest, rents, profits). Firms, in turn, assume command over these resources allocating them in the production of goods and services which are sold to households at a price. Thus, the inner cycle of the chart represents the flow of commodities and resources: resources from households to firms (lower part), and commodities from firms to households (upper part). The outer cycle represents flow of money: expenditures of firms which ultimately become income to households (lower part) and expenditures of households which ultimately become revenues to firms (upper part). Thus, in this system a regular voluntary exchange takes place between firms and households. That exchange is carried out through markets, i.e., demand and supply. Since the object of exchange in the upper part are commodities, we call those markets commodity markets, while we call the markets in the lower part resource markets.

How does the market system provide solutions to the problems raised in the four fundamental questions?

The Problem of What and How Much to Produce: Consumer Sovereignty

What kinds of commodities and in what quantities should a market economy produce? Should there be more private jet planes produced, or more bread, more video players, or more cars? Who should make these decisions?

As was explained earlier, in the market system, production of goods and services is privately organized by various types of firms in anticipation of profit (the difference between revenues and costs). To pursue this objective, i.e., to make profits, firms must first produce and supply those goods and services which consumers desire and are prepared to pay for. Second, they must provide those commodities and services at the same or lower prices than their competitors. Firms that provide commodities at competitive prices are rewarded with profits while noncompetitive firms are ultimately driven out of the market. In other words, in a market economy what is to be produced is determined by consumers' preferences. Firms in the pursuit of profit will produce those commodities which consumers value the most. This is the well known principle of **consumer sovereignty**, i.e., the economy allocates resources to the production of goods and services consumers prefer most. If consumers prefer donuts, resources will be allocated in the production and distribution of donuts. If consumers prefer illegal drugs, resources will be allocated in the production and distribution of drugs, police enforcement, and medical treatment for drug addiction.

To put it differently, firms choose to produce those commodities which consumers value the most, i.e., commodities for which there exists a great demand. The greater the demand for a commodity the stronger the incentive is to produce more of that commodity. Conversely, the lower the demand for a commodity, the weaker the incentive is to produce that commodity. However, production is restricted by the availability of economic resources which will determine the supply of the commodity. In other words, the consumers' demand on the one side and the producers' supply on the other jointly determine what and how much are to be produced, with the former having the leading edge. Moreover, competition among firms will ensure that commodities are sold at the lowest price.

The Problem of for Whom to Produce: Income and Wealth Distribution

For whom are hamburgers, cars, video players, produced? These commodities will be produced for those who prefer them and are prepared to pay for them. However, although there is no limit to what consumers prefer, there is a limit on what they are prepared to pay. Consumers with higher incomes are prepared to pay for larger baskets of commodities than consumers with lower incomes. Thus, the allocation of commodities among consumers is determined by the allocation of income and wealth. Unequal income distribution means that there are a few people on the one side who can afford a large basket of commodities including luxury items such as Rolls Royces, private jets, servants, etc. Conversely, equal income distribution means that everyone can afford an average basket of commodities, and few luxuries will be produced.

The Problem of How to Produce: Competition

Depending on the nature of the commodity, there may be many different ways to produce it. Although firms can often choose among several ways in combining human and non-human factors of production, competition does not leave them much room for choice. To survive in a competitive market firms must use the most efficient production methods. Thus, in a market system of unrestricted competition, resources are allocated efficiently in the production of goods and services, meaning that the society gets the most value out of scarce resources.

The Mixed System

Are economic systems moving closer to a mixed system, i.e., a system of combined characteristics of all other systems? The answer is yes. In an era of ever-growing international interdependence, it becomes harder and harder to draw fine lines among systems. In most societies, individual ownership of the means of production coexists with social ownership, individual decision making coexists with collective decision making, and the market mechanism coexists with central planing. Government agencies own a large proportion of resources and allocate them according to hierarchies which often contradict those of individuals. Large corporations and powerful labor unions have more to say about economic matters than individuals. Although firms interact with each other through the market mechanism, business operations inside a firm follow a centralized process. Many decisions are the result of detailed strategic planning by expertise at the top of the firm's hierarchy, carried out by the various operating divisions, and labor unions constrain management decisions.

What and How Much to Produce

In a mixed system organizations such as corporations, unions, and government have replaced the individual as the primary decision making unit. The decisions about what kinds of commodities to be produced and in what quantity are vested in managers and consultants within big corporations in cooperation with organized labor. Governments, in addition to setting the rules of the game, protection of property rights, and the resolution of conflicts among groups, own resources and produce or allocate several commodities, such as health, education, and defense. This is not to suggest that the individual decisions and the market mechanism have no role to play in a mixed system. The market mechanism still exists as a coordinating force among firms, but its functions are, in many cases, subject to the control of a few corporations, unions, and government departments. In that case, what is to be produced is very much determined by corporate technocrats, who manipulate individual consumer preferences through advertising. Consumers may suddenly switch from donuts to croissants, not because they were dreaming of the latter but because their minds were psychologically stimulated with commercials the night before. The image of consumers guiding the production of goods and services in the market system (consumer sovereignty) may have become obsolete, and reversed (this is what Galbraith has called **reversed sequence**).

Nobody could have confirmed this better than Sony's founder, Akio Morita:

> Our plan is to lead the public with new products rather than ask them what kind of products they want. The public does not know what is possible, but we do. So instead of doing a lot of market research, we refine our thinking on a product and its use and try to create a market for it by educating and communicating with the public (Akio Morita, p. 79).

And as the government interferes more and more in economic matters, consumer sovereignty is giving away to corporate and government paternalism.

For Whom and How to Produce

The distribution of income and commodities among individuals is the result of the interplay between the various players mentioned above, i.e., large corporations, labor unions, consumer associations, and government. The domination of a market by a few large corporations means market control resulting in higher prices for the consumers who buy the product of that sector. Powerful unions, for example, in a particular industry, means relatively high income for the workers working in that industry. A strong consumer association means lower prices for the consumers who have joined the association. Government intervention can re-allocate income and commodities in favor of a certain group at the expense of others.

2.3 Economic Systems and Economies

Economies are more complicated than economic systems. They include, in addition, institutional arrangements which legitimize and support an economic system. For example, the U.S. Constitution legitimizes individual, business and government property, preventing arbitrary nationalization and socialization. Similarly, the former Soviet constitution legitimizes state ownership of business, while the Yugoslav constitution legitimizes the power of labor councils to make production decisions.

Exhibit 2.1
The Circular Flow of a Market Economy

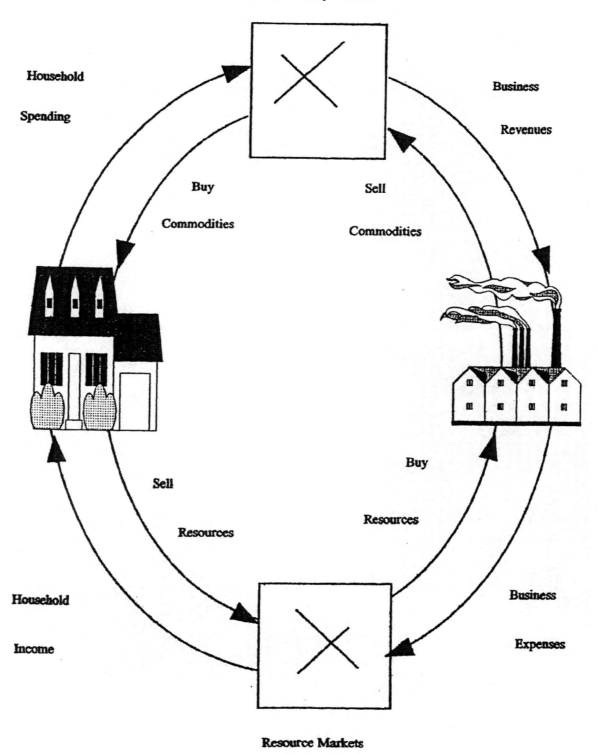

Commodity Market

Household Spending

Business Revenues

Buy Commodities

Sell Commodities

Sell Resources

Buy Resources

Household Income

Business Expenses

Resource Markets

From One System to Another: How Painful Is the Transition?

For years critics of the market system were searching for alternative economic systems. Some were looking at the command system of the former Soviet Union as an alternative. Others were looking at the market socialism of the former Yugoslavia. But how it could be done? What kind of changes were necessary? Some argued for radical measures. Others were taking a more gradual approach. But as these systems collapsed in the late eighties, critics of the command and market socialism systems are looking to the market system as the sole viable alternative, and they are devising ways to get there. Once again, some have argued for a radical, "shock therapy" treatment, that transforms institutions in one strike. Others have argued for a less radical, gradual approach. Poland, the Czech, and the Slovak Republics have adapted the former approach, while Russia, Ukraine, Romania, and Bulgaria have followed the latter.

Irrespective of the road chosen, the transition from one system to another is a long and painful process during which things turn worse before they turn better. In the short run, for instance, the privatization of governmentally owned enterprises is followed by a sharp decline in output and employment, an acceleration of inflation and a decline in real incomes. Indeed, every country of Central and Eastern Europe and the former Soviet Republics has gone through a sharp decline in real output, double digit unemployment rates, monthly double-digit inflation, and declining real incomes.

A Bad and Dangerous Cocktail: How China Blends Capitalism with Socialism

It is time to prosper. China has been poor for 1,000 years.
—Deng Xiaoping

By PANOS MOURDOUKOUTAS—Visiting the Great Wall of China from downtown Beijing on a Saturday morning would be an easy one-hour ride, according to our guide. Unfortunately, the ride took a little over three hours, with another hour to find an empty parking spot. The reason, as any driver would have guessed, was road construction during rush hour. The region's farmers—rather than experienced and professional contractors—paved the road a small lot at a time, slowly and with little supervision, if any. The absence of any traffic patrol to ease the traffic jams on the highway and at the Great Wall parking lot compounded the problem.

The absence of government is not confined to the supervision of highway construction and the patrolling of traffic to ease jams. It extends to other parts of Chinese life, such as the protection of the environment and public health. For years, the government has failed to protect its Henan Prefecture citizens from industrial pollution that has contaminated drinking and irrigation water. Chinese people in every major city breathe contaminated air from outdated coal factories releasing millions of tons of sulfur dioxide, the major cause of acid rain. Earlier this year, the government failed to protect its Fuyang region citizens from substandard milk powder that led to the deaths of at least 12 infants. The government has further failed to protect its citizens from financial fraud, and in some cases officials have become accessories to such fraud. A recent example is the case in a Fujian prefecture. A local government representative known as the "credit queen" ran an illegal investment find and disappeared with the life savings of numerous villagers.

In the case of China, the magnitude, frequency, and locations of these incidents make them systemic rather than accidental, revealing an interesting paradox about the role of government in the country's emerging economic regime. In public places, where citizens of most democratic societies would expect a government presence, it is absent and inactive. Government is present and active in private places, in ways that may startle people from free-market democracies.

The government is present in the State Owned Enterprises (SOEs) and Town Village Enterprises (TVEs) as owner, entrepreneur, and manager, producing everything from steel to laundry powder, aluminum to toilet paper. The government is present in "privatized" enterprises and owns sufficient shares to control their management. The government is present in the banking industry, controlling almost every major bank, rationing credit by political fiat rather than by market forces. The government owns and operates almost every major restaurant in town, choosing the menu for its captive patrons. The government is even present in private enterprises and joint ventures, as a financier and as the sole landlord, breaking leases any time it deems appropriate.

The government is also present in citizens' private lives. It searches hotel rooms without search warrants, arrests its political opponents for violating prostitution laws and sentences them to "labor education" without a trial by jury, as illustrated by the case of a Hong Kong democratic politician in Shenzen. The government prevents people from exercising their religious faith, prosecuting, detaining, and sentencing religious leaders. The government is also present in the publishing industry, banning the publication and circulation of books that criticize its past policies and practices, as in the case of an investigative report that exposed government atrocities against farmers. The government is present in cyberspace, filtering Internet content from communicating words such as "democracy," "human rights," and "religion."

By removing itself from activities that are considered its domain in most democratic, market oriented societies and meddling in those activities that are not, China attempts to combine and compromise the very premises of the two opposite systems of Capitalism and Communism. The four "cardinal principles" of Communism and central planning—upholding the socialist road to prosperity, the dictatorship of the proletariat, the leadership of the Communist Party and Marxist-Leninist-Maoist ideology—conflict with the four principles of capitalist democracy: individual freedom, protection of individual property rights, freedom of exchange and a limited role of government in addressing market failures.

In attempting to compromise and unite the very premises of these two opposite systems, China creates a bad dangerous cocktail that blends the worst aspects of capitalism and socialism. The absence of government from public places and government's failure to regulate and monitor traffic, environmental pollution, product standards, and fly-by-night operations preying on investors constitute more of a legacy of the Victorian era English and wild-West American capitalism of mid-19th century America than modern-day capitalism. The presence of government in the economy in SOEs as owner, entrepreneur, and manager is a legacy of the discredited Soviet style communist system that has turned SOEs into "units" within a central plan that allocates resources through political and administrative processes, with little responsibility, accountability, and control as to how efficiently and effectively such resources are utilized. Government appointed SOE managers lack the skills, the freedom, and the incentives to adjust inputs and outputs changing market conditions, and to pursue new business opportunities.

Management problems are more acute in state owned banks where bankers are preoccupied with the preservation of the vested interests of national, provincial, and local Communist Party leaders rather than with risk management. Banks extend loans to money-losing SOEs and TVEs—often to pay for wages and benefits to labor in order to maintain the "iron bowl" tradition of the Maoist era-finance infrastructure projects on behalf of the local party leaders and their patrons, and churning assets indiscriminately fuelling a financial bubble that dwarfs that of the 1980s Japan's. Most notably, government's function as a sole landlord writing and breaking leases as it deems appropriate magnifies business risks and uncertainties, and multiplies local official corruption—rampant throughout China.

Above all, the government's meddling in people's private lives, the prosecuting and sentencing citizens without trial by jury is a challenge to the very theory of dialectical materialism that Karl Marx, Vladimir Lenin, and Mao Zedong and their disciplines saw as the root of social revolutions: The breakdown between the economic base and the political superstructure, and the contradictions it breeds between the new emerging economic classes that demand an open-democratic society, and the Communist Party that seeks to preserve a closed-authoritarian regime, at any cost.

The contradictions between the emerging economic classes and the Communist Party are most pronounced when Beijing's economic regime is compared with the country's Special Administrative Region of Hong Kong. By contrast to Beijing, Hong Kong hasn't placed Capitalism and socialism in the blender at least not yet. Hong Kong government closely monitors road construction, traffic, and parking rules, handing heavy fines to those who fail to follow them, but it doesn't meddle in private business. According to the *Index of Economic Freedom* published by the *Wall Street Journal* and the *Heritage Foundation*, Hong Kong occupies the first position among the 30 Asian countries included in the survey, while China follows far behind, occupying the 127 position, behind even Mongolia, India, Sri Lanka, and Bangladesh. Hong government resists Beijing's pressures to crack down on democratic politicians, straining relations between the two parties. In a blow to Beijing tactics to sentence democratic politicians without trial by jury, the Hong Kong Justice Department didn't recognize the conviction of the Hong Kong politician mentioned earlier. Young Hong Kong residents continue to remain skeptical about Beijing's Communist regime. A recent interview of top Hong Kong high school students visiting Beijing revealed that Hong Kong's young people love China, love the city of Beijing, but not the Communist regime.

In its long history, China has missed many chances to grow and prosper. Emperors and bureaucrats have slammed the door to foreign trade, investment, and technology. Professional guilds and special interests prevented inventors from turning their inventions to innovations. Chinese people have served many emperors and party bosses. They have built palaces and the Great Wall, they have dug and carved tombs, and they have stayed poor for far too long. "To get rich is glorious," but the construction and the pavement of the road to get China there must be left to the right institutions and policies: Let genuine entrepreneurs, not government bureaucrats, create wealth, choose what, where, and when to produce goods and services, bearing the risks and the rewards associated with such choice. Let professional managers manage and control the production and distribution of the said goods to ensure that economic resources are allocated efficiently and effectively. Let markets adjust prices to reflect the relative scarcity of economic resources to different uses. Let bankers behave as true bankers, manage bank assets and liabilities according to modern principles of risk management rather than by the outdated and failed principles of central planning. Let the government create a business friendly regime, defining, and protecting property rights, and develop a fair, just, and transparent tax system that amasses sufficient revenues to address market failures, in partnership with business and civic groups. And above all, keep government away from people's private lives suppressing and inhibiting the ingenuity and creativity of the Chinese people, the most important resource for China's sustainable growth in a global economy.

2.4 The U.S. Economy: An Overview

Where does the U.S. economy fit in? The above discussion suggests two possibilities, the possibility of a market economy and the possibility of a mixed economy. Which model represents the U.S. economy better? The answer depends on what characteristics one places emphasis on.

Many economists, emphasizing the fact that economic resources are, primarily, privately owned and allocated through the market classify the U.S. economy as a market economy. Others, emphasizing the fact that (i) many sectors of the U.S. economy are dominated by a few large corporations; (ii) millions of American laborers have joined powerful unions as well as consumer associations; and (iii) the government allocates almost one-third of the Gross National Product, and owns and manages resources, especially at the local level, classify the American economy as a mixed economy. Again, siding with either group is a matter of focus. Historically speaking, the U.S. economy was more of a market economy in the nineteenth century when firms were small and the role of government limited, and is more of a mixed economy in the twenty-first century when firms are large and the role of local governments more extensive.

Basic Characteristics of the U.S. Economy

(A) As in any free enterprise system, the U.S. free enterprise system allows Americans to enjoy a number of benefits as consumers and producers.

Individual consumers have the right to own property, including a home, because of the free enterprise system. Homeownership, for instance, allows people to have a stable residence where they can start and grow a family, and become an integral part of the local community. In the U.S., homeownership allows people to borrow against their homes and use the funds to improve these homes, to educate their children, and to pursue business opportunities. This is in sharp contrast to command systems where people do not own their homes; and to a number of free enterprise economies where property rights are not well defined—as in most Latin American countries.

Individual consumers have the incentives and the freedom to act for their own benefit: shop around for the best product at the best prices, "voting" with their dollars for different products, while competition among sellers and limited government interference assure that consumers acquire these products at the lowest prices. This is not the case in a command system, however, where consumers have limited shopping choices, if any.

Producers are free to make choices because of the free enterprise system. Producers are usually business owners and managers. Economic freedom and incentives allow producers to decide what to produce and where and when to produce it; and to acquire the necessary economic resources. Again, this principle is different than in command systems where businesses are owned by the government, and managers lack the freedom and the incentives to produce what they want and where and when they deem appropriate.

Competition among producers provides consumers a variety of choice as to what types of goods and services to buy and where and when to buy them; limits the prospect that one producer or a group of producers will assume control of the market; ensures that producers will allocate economic resources efficiently and effectively.

A limited role of government allows producers to assume the risks and rewards from the discovery and exploitation of new business opportunities. The late nineteenth century U.S. history provides plenty of examples that confirm the magic force of incentives in unleashing the "Yankee ingenuity" in the pursuit of new business opportunities that created wealth in the process. In the late twentieth century, the pursuit of new business opportunities in the biotechnology industry produced blockbuster drugs from companies like Pfizer and Amgen that help people live healthier and longer. In the high technology areas and the pursuit of new business opportunities, industries gave rise to pioneering companies like Microsoft, Apple Computers, and Corning (the inventor of the fiber optic cable) that changed the way people live and work.

(B) In the last thirty years, the basic characteristics of the free enterprise system have been changing, adapting and adopting to emerging social, technological, and ideological trends.

In the 1980s and the 1990s, the spread of globalization, the increasing integration and interdependence of local, domestic, and international markets, the diffusion of technological, financial, and organizational innovations, and the spread of pro-market ideologies have broadened and strengthened the basic characteristics of the free enterprise system.

In the household and business sectors, financial and organizational innovation expanded and broadened private property among the members of society, as more people had the opportunity to become homeowners and business owners, either individually or collectively. In the U.S., for instance, the introduction of securitization, a form of financial innovation that lowered the cost of borrowing, allowed more people to live in their own homes, while the spread and diffusion of an organizational innovation known as Employee Stock Ownership Plans (ESOPs) has allowed more people to participate in the ownership of business.

The broadening of private ownership, in turn, strengthened another characteristic of the free enterprise system, incentives. The diffusion of homeownership, for instance, allowed some households to borrow funds against their homes to pursue new business opportunities, creating wealth for themselves and their fellow citizens. The diffusion of ESOPs has aligned the interests of employees with those of the company stockholders fostering higher productivity and innovation.

The strengthening of incentives was supported and re-enforced by an expansion of economic freedom driven by the spread of globalization and the Internet that strengthened competition, which in turn, broadened consumer and business opportunities. Globalization, for instance, allowed consumers to have access to a broader variety of products at more affordable prices, while the Internet allowed consumers to find almost instantly who sells what and at what price. Technology from TiVo allowed consumers to choose what shows to see without commercial interruptions, turning "Prime Time" into "My Time." Globalization allowed businesses to broaden their overseas opportunities, while the Internet allowed business to communicate efficiently and effectively with their suppliers, partners, and customers.

The expansion of economic freedoms and the spread of globalization were accommodated by economic policies that have limited the presence of government in certain sectors of the economy. In the U.S. utilities and the telecommunication sectors, for instance, the governments have lifted regulations encouraging the entry of new competitors, breaking decades-old monopolies.

While some of these trends continued to strengthen the basic characteristics of the free enterprise system in 2000s, others undermined them. The spread of the Internet, for instance, continued to strengthen the freedom of consumers to shop around for the best value for their budget, and the freedom of producers to find ways to cut costs and develop new products. The spread of globalization, however, began to have mixed results on other social groups. In the U.S., for instance, globalization and outsourcing affected adversely small local business and labor that couldn't compete against their overseas low-cost counterparts. The uncontrolled and unregulated growth of securitization that helped more people purchase homes, ended up undermining both private property and incentives, as some people bought homes they could not afford, and eventually lost. Securitization further undermined private property, as titles to these homes were transferred from the nearby eponymous local bank that financed the loan to the distant anonymous investor who purchased the loan—the cause of the foreclosure mess that spread in late 2010.

In the aftermath of the Great Recession (2008–2009), the role of government has been extended beyond the determination of the rules of the game for market participants, to the ownership and management of banks and automobile and insurance companies, restricting economic freedom through mandates, as has been the case in the healthcare industry. At the same time, the extension of unemployment insurance from the usual 26 weeks time period to the two-year period has discouraged some people from actively searching, finding, and accepting job.

Government's extensive presence in the economy doesn't necessarily signal a radical shift in its role in the economy. In past recessions and depressions, the U.S. government extended its presence in the economy, only to scale back once the economy recovered. In the aftermath of the Great Depression of the 1930s, for instance, the government launched a massive public works program, and expanded regulation of financial institutions, but it rolled these policies back once the economy returned to normal. In the aftermath of the severe recession of the early 1980s, the government took over Chrysler, but turned it back to the private hands once the economy had fully recovered.

2.5 Review

1. The major economic problems of any society at any time are: What commodities should be produced? How much of each commodity should be produced? How should commodities be produced? For whom should commodities be produced?

2. The major economic systems designed to solve these problems are: the Planned or Command System, the Self-Managed System, the Market System, the Mixed System.

The Command System is a system of central planning and control. The government owns economic resources, has command over them, and provides solutions to the four fundamental economic problems.

The Self-Managed System is a system of government ownership of the means of production but decisions on what, how, where, and for whom production will take place are vested both in workers' councils, existing in each company, and the government authorities, with the market still playing an important role as a coordinating force among firms.

The Market System is a system of private ownership of the means of production, individual decision making, and the exchange of goods and services, with the market system being the coordinating force among individual decisions. Consumer sovereignty is the guiding principle of what and how much to be produced, while competition among firms assures that production of such goods and services remains efficient.

The Mixed System is a combination of all of the above systems. Resources are owned both privately and socially. Individual decision making is substituted by group decision making. Unions sustain control over the resource markets while firms exercise their control over the commodity markets, both being subject to government intervention in several capacities within the economy.

3. Economies are broader than economic systems. Economies, in addition to economic systems, include all the institutions needed to support their existence.

4. The U.S. economy is a mixed economy. Many sectors of the economy are dominated by large corporations controlling a large percentage of the market. Millions of American laborers have joined powerful unions as well as consumer associations. The government allocates almost one third of the Gross Domestic Product.

5. In 2008 there were 61,244 thousand households compared to 43,554 in 1950. In the same period, the average household size has declined from 3.37 to 2.69 persons. Households derive their income mainly from labor (73.5 percent) and they spend most of it on services, food, shelter, motor vehicles and parts.

6. In 2006, there were 22,075,000 proprietorships, 2,947,000 partnerships, and 5,841,000 corporations. Although corporations are relatively fewer than proprietorships, nevertheless due to their size, they control a large part of the commodity markets. In 2009, the 100 largest corporations held 53 percent of assets, while the 200 largest corporations held 58 percent of assets.

7. By 2009, about 12 percent of the labor force had joined labor unions, a lower percentage as compared to about 24 percent in 1947. Notice that, contrary to corporate market control which has been increasing over time, union control has diminished. Nevertheless, although only 12 percent of the labor force is organized, negotiations taking place in the unionized sectors of the economy set the guidelines for the rest of the economy.

8. In any modern mixed economy the government carries out the following five functions: The legitimation function, the allocation function, the distribution function, the stabilization function and the regulation function.

The legitimation function is the process which secures the property rights of commodities vested in members of society and the transfer of those rights from one party to another. The allocation function is the process of deciding what kinds of public commodities should be produced and at what quantity. The distribution function is the process of transferring resources from the upper and middle classes to the lower classes in order to smooth out income inequalities across the society. The stabilization function is the process of smoothing out cyclical variations in economic activity which often give rise to unemployment and inflation. The regulation function is the process of mitigating conflicts between individual interests, which may arise in the production and consumption of commodities. Governments fulfill these functions by the allocation of resources, obtained mainly through taxation.

Real World Link 4: American Cities Shouldn't Tell Chipotle and McDonald's How to Run Their Businesses

Key Concept:

- Socialism Spreads in American Cities

City governments need to cut back on their mandates over how national franchises like Chipotle, McDonald's, and Shake Shack do business. At the very least, they should leave it up to them to decide how they manage work schedules, and align work requirements with customer demands.

That's one of the fundamentals of an effective business strategy; and at the core of the free enterprise system America claims to operate under.

Letting private companies decide how to run their day-to-day operations is one of the many things that separates the American system from socialist countries such as Cuba and Venezuela; countries where too much restriction on the market has created some serious problems.

It seems like local governments are determined to push America towards a more socialist ideal through passing legislation that mandates work schedules and labour pay, among other things. In particular, the New York City government passed minimum wage hikes with the intention of creating a "living wage" and the "Fair Workweek Laws." These laws force food service providers such as Shake Shack, McDonald's and Chipotle to prepare working schedules ahead of time.

The problem is that it takes a great deal of guessing of market conditions to prepare these schedules in advance, in some franchise segments.

And a good luck to enforce them.

Even so, New York City has been forceful in their approach to the laws and has gone after companies such as Chipotle. Wall Street didn't respond too well, with shares in companies like Chipotle and other food service franchises dipping a couple of week ago, following the news.

"The main reason behind Chipotle's price decline was a report that the City of New York is suing Chipotle for violation of the recently enacted Fair Workweek Law," says equity analyst John Zolidis. "This law is intended to protect hourly workers by prohibiting companies from excessively changing their schedules at short notice."

These laws impose a serious burden on the sector. "Our understanding is that this new regulation both makes staffing more cumbersome for companies but also requires increased costs related to compliance, Zolidis adds. "The City of New York's action virtually ensures that Chipotle's operating costs related to staffing and compliance are going up."

The news about Chipotle spread and started to affect other fast food service providers. Shake Shack also had their stock value drop, following the news that NYC is after Chipotle. Shake Shack, much like Chipotle, employs hour employees in New York City and so they would need to spend more on compliance and staffing too.

Still, Jeff Kreisler, the Editor-In-Chief of Peoplescience.com's, believes that providing advance scheduling is a good idea. "Providing an advanced scheduling and some sense of income and employment certainty is a fantastic, *low-cost* way to alleviate the financial stress and concern faced by frontline employees which causes issues of low productivity and workplace safety," he says. "Financial precarity is now recognized as a real concern for workers of all income level and the impact on organizations affects their bottom lines as much as health and wellness. "

But it should be left up to the companies to do so, rather than mandated by law. "It would be better if organizations just choose to be better—for their employees and their shareholders—but . . . not all have done so *yet*," he says.

Source: *Forbes Magazine*

Review Questions

1. What is an economic system?
2. Which criteria do economists apply to evaluate an economic system?
3. What are the advantages and disadvantages of a command system?
4. What is consumer sovereignty? What is reverse sequence?
5. Is the U.S. a market economy?
6. What is the largest source of income for American households?
7. What are the functions of government in a mixed economy?
8. What are some of the problems of transition from a command to a market system? What are the alternative approaches?
9. What are the benefits of the free enterprise system on U.S. consumers and producers?
10. How has the Internet affected economic freedom of U.S. consumers and producers?
11. Why are some of the recent changes in the basic characteristics of the U.S. economy?
12. How can government policies undermine people's incentives to save, invest, and work?

Homework 2

1. What are the fundamental problems of every society?

2. What is an economic system?

3. What is a command or a central planning system?

4. What is a self-managed system?

5. What is a market system?

6. What is Consumer sovereignty?

7. What is a mixed system?

8. What are the functions of the government in a mixed market system?

9. How would you classify the American economy?

10. Which sector provides most of the jobs in the U.S.?

11. Why did the Soviet system collapse?

Chapter Three

THE MARKET FOR A COMMODITY

Preview

Preview

In a competitive market system, the price and the quantity of commodities are determined by markets. The market for a commodity is a mechanism that brings the buyers and sellers of that commodity together. A market is defined within a local, national, or international area and has two sides, demand and supply. The two sides jointly determine the equilibrium price and quantity. Changes in equilibrium price and quantity reflect changes in demand and supply. An introduction into the mechanics of demand and supply, this chapter defines the concepts of demand and supply and explains how they determine the price of a commodity.

3.1 Introduction

In the fall of 1973, the price of crude oil skyrocketed, from $3.5 a barrel to more than $10 by the late spring of 1974. In 2020, during the COVID-19 pandemic, oil traded as low as $11.25 and as high as $63.27. In the summer of 1988, the price of wheat, corn, soybeans, and other agricultural commodities skyrocketed (see exhibit at the end of the chapter). In 1989, beef was selling at a $1.50 per pound, butter at $1.30 a pound, and eggs at $.84 a pound. More than 30 years later, beef is selling at $4.50 a pound, eggs at $1.62 a dozen, and butter at $1.81 a pound (see Exhibit 3.1). Crude oil and agricultural commodities are not the only items subject to price fluctuations; every commodity may fluctuate in price. What determines the price of a commodity? Why do some commodities sell at a higher price than others? Why do commodity prices fluctuate?

Not only do commodities fluctuate in price, they also fluctuate in sales and production. Some industries are in temporary or secular expansion while others are in a secular decline. The production of black and white television sets, for instance, has faded away in the U.S. By contrast, the production of smartphones is on the rise, reaching 1,535.21 millions in 2021. Why are some industries expanding and others declining?

Questions about the determination of the price and the quantity of a commodity are very old and can be traced all the way to the classical school of economics, to economists like Adam Smith and David Ricardo who claim that production costs determine the price of a commodity. The search goes on to the utilitarian school of economics, to economists like Jules Dupuit and William S. Jevons who claim that demand determines the price of a commodity. The search ended with the neoclassical synthesis, with Alfred Marshall who claims that demand and supply jointly determine commodity price and quantity.

Exhibit 3.1

A. Cash Prices for Selected Commodities
Friday, October 20, 1989; Friday, May 7, 1993;
Wednesday, May 30, 2001; and Wednesday, May 30, 2021

	1989	1993	2001	2021
Beef lb.	1.50	2.78	1.40	4.50
Butter AA lb.	1.30	.76	1.91	1.81
Eggs large doz.	.84	.66	.56	1.62
Flour lb.	.22	.11	.20	0.44
Coffee beans lb.	.69	.55	.67	1.68
Cocoa beans lb.	.45	.25	1.29	2.10

Source: Adapted from *The New York Times*, Saturday, October 21, 1989, and Saturday, May 8, 1993, and *Wall Street Journal*, May 30, 2001, and April 14, 2010, and FRED Economic Data, May 30, 2021.

Markets may be examined from various perspectives. From the legal perspective, a market is the process which facilitates the transfer of property rights from sellers to buyers. From the sociological perspective, a market is a set of institutions that facilitate the exchange of goods and services. From the economic perspective, a market is the mechanism that brings buyers and sellers together. This mechanism includes two components, the demand side which reflects consumers' plans to buy a particular commodity and the supply side which represents sellers' plans to sell that commodity.

But how are the price and the quantity of a commodity determined? Does demand and supply always do the job? Depending on the number of sellers, the entry restrictions and the type of the commodities to be sold, markets are classified in three major categories, perfect competition, monopoly, and imperfect competition (see chapter four of the microeconomics volume). In monopoly and imperfect competition, suppliers normally have more power than consumers in determining either the price or the quantity of the commodity. In perfect competition, neither of the two sides has control over the market and price. A large number of well-informed consumers and a large number of sellers of a homogeneous commodity, with unrestricted entry makes it impossible for either of the two sides to control the market; the two sides jointly determine what economists call equilibrium (market) price and the equilibrium (market) quantity (see Exhibit 3.2).

Adopting this theoretical framework, this chapter discusses the following questions: What determines consumers' plans to buy a particular commodity and what determines sellers' plans to sell that commodity? How does the interaction between the two sides determine the equilibrium price and quantity of that commodity? Why might the equilibrium price and quantity of the commodity change?

The remainder of the chapter is in five sections: the second section discusses the demand side of the commodity market; the third section the supply of the commodity market; the fourth section discusses how the two sides jointly determine the equilibrium price and quantity of the commodity; and the fifth section discusses fluctuations in the equilibrium price and quantity. The chapter ends with a review of the key concepts, applications of the demand and supply model, and a mathematical appendix.

Exhibit 3.2
The Two Sides of the Commodity Market

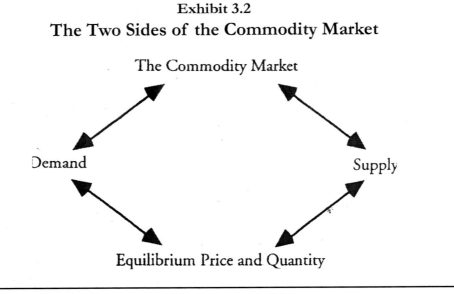

3.2 The Demand Side: Consumers

Everywhere around the world, commodity producers spend billions of dollars to identify the factors that influence consumers' decisions to allocate their budgets over a variety of commodities, and even more billions are spent for the forecasting of consumer demand. How do consumers make their choices? What are their options and limitations? To answer these questions, economists view consumer decisions as a two-step process.

In the first step, consumers decide whether to include a particular commodity in their shopping lists. In the second step, consumers decide on the quantity of that commodity that they would like to buy. Corresponding to this two step decision process economists have developed two concepts, the concept of **demand** and the concept of **quantity demanded**.

Demand and Quantity Demanded

Every month, Mrs. Smith receives her pension check and makes her shopping list. In most cases, the list consists of necessities such as milk, sugar, eggs, vegetables, fruits, bread, and meat. In other cases, looking over store circulars, she discovers bargains that she cannot resist. Last month, chicken was on sale and she got three packages, enough for two months. This month cereals are on sale and she plans to buy and store a few boxes. She is also looking for a bargain in orange juice, the price has been too high for her in the last couple of months. As she is going through the last page of the circular, she discovers that pork chops are on sale, but she does not even bother to check the price. Eating pork is prohibited by her religion. Besides, pork is high in cholesterol and her doctor has placed it on a restricted list.

Mrs. Smith's shopping list is not always confined to groceries, it often includes clothing and occasionally home furnishings. These days, she is thinking of buying a new car, but she does not have enough savings for the down payment. She has also been talking with her friends about a trip to Paris, but she does not have the savings for that either. Besides, Paris is too expensive this season and she may have to wait for a better deal.

Mrs. Smith is not the only consumer that has to prepare a shopping list. Every day, millions of consumers must go through the same exercise. And although they may have different preferences and constraints, they are faced with the same problem, which commodities to choose and at what quantity.

Demand is consumers' *willingness* to buy a particular commodity, i.e., the desire and the ability to buy one commodity over another. In this way economists talk about the demand for apples, oranges, television sets, microwave ovens, personal computers, and private jet planes.

Note that the term "demand" means willingness to buy a specific commodity, i.e., preference and ability to buy that commodity, and should not be confused with the term "purchase" that also depends on the availability of the commodity. Such terms can be discussed only after we put the two sides of the market together.

Quantity demanded is the amount of a commodity consumers are *willing* to buy, i.e., pounds of apples, oranges, number of television sets, and personal computers.

Which factors affect demand and quantity demanded? Mrs. Smith's story has already revealed some of the factors that determine the demand for a commodity. Called "demand factors," these factors include the following:

- Tastes or Preferences
- Income/Wealth
- Prices of Other Commodities
- Number of Consumers in the Market
- Expectations about Future Prices

Once consumers decide to include a commodity in their shopping list, they must also decide about the quantity of the commodity they would like to buy which is determined by the price of the commodity. In what is known as the **law of demand**, economists argue that, with the demand factors staying the same, price and quantity demanded are inversely related: As the price increases quantity demanded decreases. To illustrate the law of demand, economists use numerical examples and graphics (see Exhibit 3.3). An example of such exhibits is given in the following case, the case of the demand for apples, at a market called "Garden Market" during a typical month.

To sum up, the law of demand states that, other things being equal, as the price of a commodity increases, quantity demanded decreases and vice versa. This inverse relationship between price and quantity demanded is reflected in the shape of the demand curve that is negatively sloped. But what are the explanations of the law of demand?

Exhibit 3.3
Exhibits of the Demand Schedule and the Demand Curve
for Apples at the Garden Market in a Typical Month

A. The Demand Schedule

Price of Apples (cents/pound)	Quantity Demanded (pounds)
50	130
60	115
70	109
80	104
90	100

The first column of this exhibit gives the price of apples, displayed at the window of the Garden Market, in a typical month. The second column gives the quantity of apples demanded by consumers during the same month. As the price declines the quantity demanded increases.

B. The Demand Curve

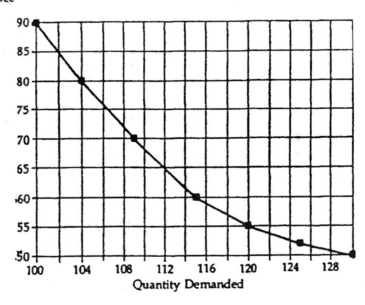

Exhibit 3.3B is an illustration of the law of demand. The vertical axis gives the price of apples, while the horizontal axis gives the quantity demanded. The DD shows the inverse relationship between price and quantity demanded. As the price of apples decreases, the quantity demanded increases.

Explanations of the Law of Demand

As you may recall, the law of demand applies only as long as the "demand factors" remain the same. As the price of the commodity changes, consumers make adjustments in the quantity demanded that reflect three simultaneous effects

- Diminishing Satisfaction
- The Income Effect
- The Substitution Effect

The Law of Diminishing Satisfaction

An old explanation of the law of demand that dates back to the writings of Jules Dupuit and William S. Jevons, the law of diminishing satisfaction states that successive units of the same commodity give consumers diminishing satisfaction. The second apple gives less satisfaction than the first, and the third apple less than the second. If satisfaction is diminishing, it takes a lower price to convince consumers to buy more units of the commodity.

The Income Effect

A more recent explanation, the income effect, states that consumers can afford to purchase a larger quantity of the commodity of which the price has dropped, with the same income. As the price of apples drops from 80 cents to 50 cents, for instance, a consumer who plans to spend $1.60 on apples can purchase only 2 pounds when the price is 80 cents, but 3.2 pounds when the price is 50 cents.

The Substitution Effect

Consumers like apples, but apples are not the only fruits which exist in the market. Oranges, grapefruits, bananas, and pears are all substitutes for apples. As the price of apples drops, apples become relatively less expensive compared to the substitute commodities. To understand this, assume that both apples and oranges sell at 80 cents. As the price of apples drops, say to 50 cents, while the price of oranges stays the same at 80 cents, a pound of oranges is worth 1.6 pounds of apples. At a lower price, some consumers will find apples more price appealing and demand a larger quantity.

To sum up, as satisfaction diminishes with larger consumption, consumers are willing to buy a larger quantity of the commodity only if the price of that commodity declines. In addition, a lower price makes the commodity more affordable compared to substitute commodities and further boosts quantity demanded. But what happens to the demand for the commodity if any one of the demand factors change?

Changes in the Demand Factors: Shifts of the Whole Demand Curve

To distinguish the impact of changes in the price of the commodity versus changes in "demand factors" on consumers' plans, economists have developed two new concepts: change in the quantity demanded versus change in demand.

Changes in the quantity demanded defines the impact of the price change on the quantity of a commodity when the "demand factors" remain the same. When the price of the commodity changes, consumers adjust their quantities "moving" along the same demand curve. When the price of apples decreased, for instance, from 80 cents to 70 cents, the quantity demanded increased from 104 to 109; consumers "move" from point A to point B (see Exhibit 3.4A).

Changes in Demand defines the impact of a change in any of the "demand factors" on the demand for a commodity. When one of the demand factors changes, the demand curve shifts from one position to another. A change in a factor that has a positive impact on demand shifts the demand curve to the right. When income, for instance, increases, the demand for apples shifts to the right; consumers are willing to buy larger quantities at each price (see Exhibit 3.4B). But let us discuss how each of the demand factors may affect the demand curve in more detail.

Change in Demand vs. Change in Quantity Demanded

	Increase In	Decrease In
Quantity Demanded	move along the same curve to the right	move along the same curve to the left
Demand	shift the whole curve to the right	shift the whole curve to the left

Tastes or Preferences

Consumers' tastes or preferences are one of the most important factors of consumer demand. Each consumer has his/her own preferences. Some consumers like apples while others are allergic to them. Some consumers love smoking; others hate it. Some consumers love pork chops while others do not even want to try pork chops.

Determined by cultural, environmental, and health considerations, tastes may differ from one society to another. Muslims, for instance, do not eat pork and Jews do not eat certain preserved meats. People who live in cold climates have a strong taste for a hot food diet and people in warm climates have a strong taste for a cold food diet. And health conscious consumers have a strong taste for a low calorie/low cholesterol diet. Mrs. Smith, for instance, must be careful with high-cholesterol items that are bad for her health. Not only that, as consumers learn more about a product, they may change their tastes. News, for instance, that apples contain a vitamin that may strengthen one's immune system, may raise the demand for apples: the demand curve shifts to the right (see Exhibit 3.4B).

Though consumers may have a taste for many commodities, only those that are affordable make their shopping lists; affordability is determined by income and wealth.

Income/Wealth

At any given commodity price, consumers' purchasing power is determined by income and wealth; it increases with income and wealth and decreases along with them. With a higher purchasing power, consumers can afford larger quantities of the commodity at each price: the demand for the commodity increases, i.e., the whole curve shifts to the right (see Exhibit 3.3B). Conversely, with a lower purchasing power, the demand decreases, i.e., shifts to the left. You should notice, however, that the direction in which the demand curve shifts as income increases may not always be the same. It depends on consumer status. Low-income consumers may not be in a position to afford even such essential items as fruits, and a higher income allows them to demand more apples. By contrast, high-income consumers may have enough apples already and a higher income may allow them to switch to more expensive substitutes and, therefore, demand fewer apples. But what happens if the price of the substitutes of a commodity change?

Prices of Other Commodities

As we explained earlier, consumers can substitute commodities, one for another. Also, they can consume commodities jointly. Oranges, for instance, may be substituted for apples, and honey and butter may be consumed jointly. Therefore, a change in the price of the one commodity may cause a shift in the demand curve for the other.

When two commodities are substitutes, an increase in the price of the one commodity increases the demand for the other. An increase in the price of oranges, for instance, increases the demand for apples: the demand curve for apples shifts to the right. By contrast, when two commodities are complementary, an increase in the price of one commodity decreases the demand for the other. An increase in the price of honey, for instance, decreases the demand for butter. The demand curve shifts to the left.

Exhibit 3.4

Movements Along the Demand Curve versus Shifts of the Demand Curve at the Garden Market in a Typical Month

A. Movements Along the Demand Curve: Changes in Prices While Demand Factors Remain the Same

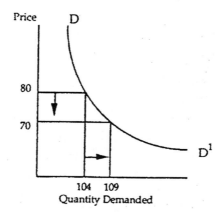

This exhibit depicts the inverse relationship between price and quantity demanded. As the price of a commodity drops, the quantity demanded increases. Consumers "move" along the points of the same demand curve.

B. Shifts in the Whole Demand Curve for Apples: An Increase in Consumers' Income

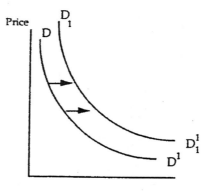

Comparing this exhibit with the previous one, we observe that at any price, consumers demanded more pounds of apples because they have a higher income. For example, at 80 cents, consumers now demand 160 pounds of apples as compared to 100 in the previous exhibit.

Number of Consumers

The demand for a commodity represents the quantities that consumers are willing to buy at different prices. A larger number of consumers, therefore, means a larger demand: the whole demand curve shifts to the right. A smaller number of consumers means a smaller demand; the whole demand curve shifts to the left. The demand for apples, for instance, in the Garden Market may increase if more consumers arrive in the town and decrease if some consumers leave the town.

Expectations about Future Prices

Talking about the demand curve, we focused on the relationship between current price and quantity demanded. What about expected prices? How do they affect the demand curve? If consumers expect a lower commodity price in the near future, they will postpone their demands. In such a case, the whole demand curve shifts to the left. Conversely, if consumers expect a higher commodity price, they will rush to buy today, and the whole demand curve shifts to the right. Actually, the importance of future prices on the demand for a commodity depends on whether the consumer can store the commodity. Future prices are more important for consumer durables and less important for perishable commodities.

To sum up, this section looks at the market through consumers' lenses. When preparing their shopping lists, consumers decide about the demand for a commodity and the quantity demanded. The demand for a commodity depends upon several "demand factors," tastes, income, price of other commodities and the number of consumers in the market. The quantity demanded depends upon the price of the commodity. With the "demand factors" remaining the same, the relationship between price and quantity demanded is described by the law of demand. The law of demand is described by the demand curve. Thus, changes in the commodity price are followed by changes in the quantity demanded along the same demand curve. Changes in the "demand factors" are followed by shifts of the demand curve from one position to another. But how do suppliers view the market? How do they make their decisions in supplying a commodity?

3.3 The Supply Side: Firms

Consumers cannot buy commodities unless they are made available to them. In a market economy, the production of commodities is organized by individual firms and corporations in anticipation of profit. With this motive taken for granted, firms make decisions about the types and the quantities of the commodities they would like to include in their production plans. As we assumed in the analysis of the demand side of the market, producers make supply decisions in two steps. In the first step, they decide the kind of commodity they would like to supply, and in the second step the amount of the commodity they would like to supply.

Supply and Quantity Supplied

Mr. Brown is a vendor in the Garden Market. Every month he makes his plans as to what commodities he will bring to the market. In most cases, he brings oranges; but this month, due to a frost in Florida, he did not receive any shipment so he thought of bringing apples. One of his friends told him that apples have been rising in price and he plans to bring a larger load to the market next time.

Choosing which commodity to bring to the market is not Mr. Brown's only problem. He needs an assistant to help him load and unload the merchandise and good help is hard to find these days at reasonable wages. Fuel is also going up and his truck is too small to carry all the merchandise he needs. Perhaps, if interest rates drop, he will get a loan and buy a bigger truck. Mr. Brown is not the only vendor in the Garden Market, so many other vendors are faced with the problem of what to supply and how much to supply.

Supply is the *willingness*, i.e., the desire and the capability of firms to provide a commodity to consumers.

Note that the concept of supply refers to what firms are willing to sell, i.e., an intention to sell a commodity rather than an actual sale. Actual sales can only be discussed when we put demand and supply together, in the next section.

Quantity supplied is the amount of a commodity firms are *willing* to sell to consumers, i.e., how many pounds of apples, oranges, and television sets. Which factors determine "supply" and "quantity supplied"? Following Mr. Brown's story, we can identify a few of the many factors that determine the supply of a commodity. Called "supply factors," these factors include the following:

- Input Prices
- Technology
- The Number of Firms in the Market
- Expectations about Future Prices

Quantity supplied is determined by the price of the commodity. In what is known as the **law of supply**, economists argue that price and quantity supplied are directly related: with the "supply factors" remaining the same, as the price of the commodity increases, firms are expected to supply a larger quantity to the market. The law of supply can be illustrated with the supply curve which gives the quantities that firms are willing to sell at different prices. To understand the supply curve, let us turn to our familiar market of apples. As the price of apples increases from 50 to 90 cents, the quantity of apples supplied increases from 80 to 120 pounds (see Exhibit 3.5).

To sum up, the law of supply states that the direct relationship between price and quantity supplied, when all "supply factors" remain the same. Reflecting this direct relationship, the supply curve is positively sloped. But what can explain the law of supply?

Explanations of the Law of Supply

Why do firms supply larger quantities of a commodity, as the commodity's price increases? They supply larger quantities of a commodity because of the limitations of short-term production that make the production cost of additional units of a commodity more expensive.

In a market economy, firms organize production and supply of commodities in anticipation of profits, the difference between revenues and costs. Each unit of output is assigned a price which represents the potential revenue from that unit in the market. Also, each unit has a cost, whatever the firm has expended to make the commodity available to consumers. The difference between the price a commodity could be sold in the market and the cost of that unit is the expected profit of the firm. As will be discussed in a future chapter, not all units of the commodity cost the same to the firm. In the short term, as firms try to expand production with more labor but with the same number of machines, the productivity of labor decreases and the cost of production increases: additional units cost more and firms are willing to supply them only if they expect to receive higher prices.

To sum up, the production and supply of commodities is organized by firms in anticipation of profits. With "supply factors" remaining the same, firms are willing to sell a larger quantity at a larger price. But as production of a commodity increases, so do costs; firms are willing to raise production and supply only at higher prices. This is true even with the assumption of fixed input prices. But what happens when those prices change? The supply curve shifts from one position to another.

Exhibit 3.5

The Supply Schedule and the Supply Curve of Apples at the Garden Market in a Typical Month

A. The Supply Schedule

Price of Apples (cents/pound)	Quantity Supplied (pounds)
50	80
60	100
70	109
80	115
90	120

This exhibit shows that as the price of apples drops gradually from 90 cents down to 70 cents, to 50 cents, the quantity supplied of apples gradually drops from 120 pounds down to 109, to 80 pounds.

B. The Supply Curve

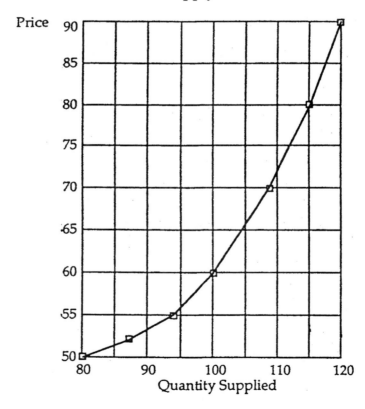

This exhibit illustrates the law of supply. As price increases, a larger quantity is supplied. For instance, as the price increases from 50 cents to 60 cents, the quantity supplied increases from 80 pounds to 100 pounds.

A Change in the Supply Factors: Shifts in the Whole Supply

As with the discussion of the demand side, economists distinguish between two concepts, change in the quantity supplied and changes in supply.

Changes in the Quantity Supplied emphasizes the law of supply, the relationship between price and quantity supplied, when the "supply factors" remain the same. Any time the commodity price changes, suppliers "move" along the same supply curve. A higher price, for instance, induces suppliers to supply a larger quantity of the commodity. Consumers move from point B to point C on the same supply curve (see Exhibit 3.6A).

Changes in Supply emphasizes the impact of a change in the "supply factors" on the supply curve. A change in any of those factors results in a shift of the whole curve from one position to another. Technological advances, for instance, increase the supply of a commodity: the supply curve shifts to the right (see Exhibit 3.6B). But let us discuss the impact of each "supply factor" on the supply curve in more detail.

Exhibit 3.6
Movement Along the Supply Curve versus Shifts of the Supply Curve of Apples at the Garden Market

A. Movements Along the Supply Curve: Changes in the Price of Apples (Supply Factors Remain the Same)

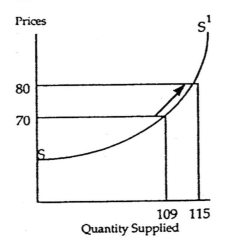

This exhibit is similar to Exhibit 3.4A. Again, it shows the direct relationship between price and quantity supplied. As the price of a commodity drops, the quantity also drops. Firms "move" along the points of the supply curve.

Exhibit 3.6
B. Shifts of the Supply Curve of Apples: Changes in the Supply Factors

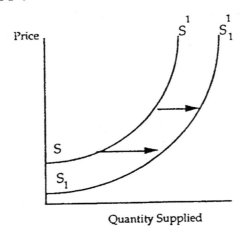

This exhibit depicts the effect of a decrease in the price of inputs used in the production of apples. Comparing this exhibit with the previous one, we observe that at any price, firms supply more pounds of apples because they must pay lower prices for the inputs used in the production of those apples. For example, at 50 cents, firms now supply 140 pounds of apples as compared to 90 in the previous exhibit.

Input Prices

Firms produce commodities with the use of human and nonhuman resources (inputs) which they buy in resource markets. Changes in the price of any input affects the cost and the supply of commodities. An increase in the wage of farm workers, for instance, raises the cost of picking apples. Faced with higher labor costs, apple producers may not hire enough workers to pick all the harvest, and, therefore, the supply of apples declines: the supply curve of apples shifts to the left. By contrast, lower wages shifts the supply curve to the right. Similar arguments can be made for higher or lower prices for other inputs. But what if technology improves?

Change in Supply vs. Change in Quantity Supplied

	Increase In	Decrease In
Quantity Supplied	move along the same curve to the right	move along the same curve to the left
Supply	shift the whole curve to the right	shift the whole curve to the left

Technology

Technology is an important factor in the production of every commodity, including what they are called: high technology products, like computer chips and cellular phones. Among other things, changes in technology results in a better utilization of inputs and, consequently, lowers the cost of production of the commodity. Faced with lower costs firms expand production and supply, i.e., the whole supply curve will shift to the right.

Number of Firms in the Market

As in competitive markets, firms are assumed to be of the same size, the number of firms in the market is one of the factors that determine supply. A larger number of firms implies that a larger quantity is supplied to consumers at each price, i.e., the whole supply curve shifts to the right. On the contrary, a smaller number of firms in the market would imply that a smaller quantity is supplied to consumers at each price, i.e., the whole supply curve shifts to the left.

Expectations about Future Prices

In most cases, the production of a commodity takes time to be completed. In those cases, firms are interested not so much in the current price of the commodity but in the future price, the price at the time the commodity will be available to the market. Expectations for higher prices will induce firms to step up production and supply: The supply curve shifts to the right. Conversely, expectations of lower prices will induce firms to scale back production and supply. The supply curve will shift to the left.

To sum up, in this section we looked at the market through the suppliers' lenses. With "supply factors" remaining the same, sellers are willing to sell larger quantities at higher prices. But at higher prices consumers are willing to buy smaller quantities. How do the two sides come to an agreement?

3.4 Putting Demand and Supply Together: The Equilibrium Price and Quantity

Demand and supply are the two components of the same mechanism, the market mechanism. The basic function of this mechanism is to bring the two sides together and iron out any differences between them. In doing so, the market mechanism determines the equilibrium price or market price, i.e., the price which sets quantity demanded equal to quantity supplied: It also determines the equilibrium quantity, i.e., the quantity that corresponds to the equilibrium price and clears the market. To understand how this happens, let us return to our example of the market for apples (see Exhibit 3.7).

Exhibit 3.7
Demand, Supply, and Equilibrium Price for Apples at the Garden Market in a Typical Month

A. The Demand and the Supply Schedules Together: Equilibrium Price and Quantity

Price of Apples (cents/pound)	Quantity Demanded (pounds)	Quantity Supplied (pounds)
50	130	80
60	115	100
70	109	109
80	104	115
90	100	120

This exhibit brings the demand and supply schedules together. You should notice that quantity demanded and quantity supplied are equal only at the price of 70 cents, which is called the equilibrium price.

Exhibit 3.7
B. The Demand and the Supply Curves Together:
Equilibrium Price and Quantity

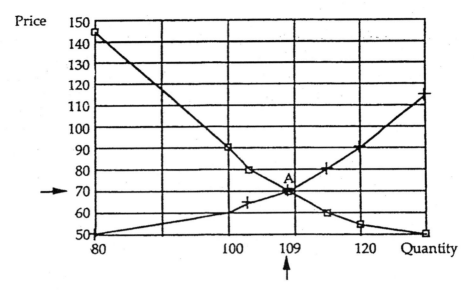

It is important to note that the demand and supply curves intersect at point A, which corresponds to a price of 70 cents (equilibrium price) and to a quantity of 109 pounds (equilibrium quantity).

As can be seen in both Exhibits 3.7A and 3.7B, at the price of 70 cents consumers demand 109 pounds of apples while firms supply exactly as much. This price, which sets quantity demanded equal to quantity supplied, is called **equilibrium price**, a price that allows for the plans of both consumers and firms to be realized; the quantity that corresponds to the equilibrium price, 109, is called equilibrium quantity.

What happens at a price other than the equilibrium price? There is an imbalance between demand and supply. At a price above 70 cents there is a **surplus** of the commodity. At 90 and 80 cents consumers plan to buy 100 and 104 pounds respectively, while firms plan to sell 120 and 115 pounds respectively. By contrast, at a price below 70 cents there is a **shortage**; at a price of 50 cents, consumers are willing to buy 130 pounds of apples, while firms are willing to supply only 80 pounds.

Another way of understanding how the product market works would be to think of demand and supply as lists of quantities consumers and firms make **independently**. Consumers plan to purchase larger quantities as the price drops, while firms plan to supply smaller quantities as the price drops. Because of the independence in consumers' and firms' plans, and because of the asymmetry in the way each party responds to price variations, there is no guarantee that those plans will look alike when they are put together. As it turns out, there is only one price at which both plans look alike and that is the price of 70 cents which ultimately prevails in the market and satisfies both parties.

At any other price, the plans look different and this will make the sellers unhappy, if the price is above the equilibrium level, and consumers unhappy, if the price is below the equilibrium level. Although trades may take place under conditions of surpluses or shortages, the two sides have the incentive to gradually reach and trade at the equilibrium price. In the case of a surplus, firms are willing to accept a lower price in order to get rid of excess quantity of the commodity. In the case of a shortage, consumers are willing to accept a higher price to see some apples available on the supermarkets' counters. In other words, there is a way for both consumers and firms to make their lists alike and that works through increases and decreases in the commodity's price until the equilibrium price is reached. Though simple, the process of adjustment from disequilibrium to equilibrium is not always smooth and speedy. Real world markets are far more complicated than our model and institutional imperfections may impede or even derail market adjustment.

3.5 The Market Model, Institutions, and Price Stability

So far, we have developed a model of price determination that should guide one's thinking when looking at real world markets that are much more complicated than our model. The assumption of competition, for instance, may not apply in many real world markets. Besides, in the real world, supply and demand for a commodity may not always be well defined. Trade may not take place in well-defined geographical areas; markets may also be subject to federal, state, and community laws and regulations that both parties must follow. For instance, it is illegal to sell stolen commodities, or commodities that society has declared illegal. And you must get government approval to sell commodities that may be hazardous to consumers' health or to the environment. You must, therefore, have knowledge of the market institutions and constructive imagination, in order to successfully apply the market model to the real world.

Another important issue that one may raise regarding real world markets is the process that adjusts price and quantity to the equilibrium levels. In some markets this is done through auctions, like those held by the Federal government for confiscated property. In other cases, it is done through pit trade or computerized trade, like the ones held for publicly traded stocks. In some markets, suppliers may control the market and fix the prices. In others the government may set the price. In other markets, this is done through a trial-and-error process. Take for example the market for any grocery product. For practical purposes, supermarkets cannot hold auctions for that product. Neither can they adjust the price every hour or every day. That would cost money (stamping new prices) and uncertainty for consumers. Instead, they choose a price at which they would like to sell the product and watch to see how consumers respond. As our model suggests, that price may be above the equilibrium price, below the equilibrium price, or equal to the equilibrium price. Corresponding to these three prices, supermarkets will experience a surplus in the first case, a shortage in the second case, and neither surplus nor shortage in the third case. All they have to do, therefore, is look at their counters and adjust the price accordingly. Lower the price if there is a surplus; raise the price if there is a shortage.

To sum up, real world markets are far more complicated than the fiction of our model. A knowledge of the legal, political, and social context in which the tools of demand and supply are applied, and the way this context may impede price or quantity adjustments is essential. But let us apply the market model to explain another important subject: changes in the price of a commodity.

3.6 Changes in the Equilibrium Price and Quantity

Commodity prices do not stay still. Rather, they change to reflect changes in market conditions, i.e., changes (shifts) in demand and supply. Such changes can, in turn, be attributed to changes in the underlying factors that determine demand and supply; changes in consumer preferences, income, expectations, etc.; changes in input prices, technology, producers' expectations, etc. We can distinguish among three cases of price changes, those due to demand shifts, those due to supply shifts, and those due to a combination of both demand and supply.

Changes Due to Shifts in Demand

As we discussed earlier, a change in any one of the factors that determine the demand for a commodity will shift the whole demand curve. For instance, an increase in the income of consumers who participate in the Garden Market will shift the demand for apples. This means that as income increases, consumers are willing to buy a larger quantity of apples at each posted price. Assuming that the supply curve of apples doesn't change, the equilibrium price and the equilibrium quantity will increase (see Exhibit 3.8). Similarly, a decrease in consumers' income will result in a downward shift in the demand for apples and a lower equilibrium price and quantity (could you draw the graph for this case?).

Exhibit 3.8
An Increase in the Demand for Apples Will Result in a Higher Equilibrium Price and Quantity

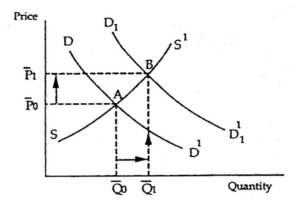

Exhibit 3.8 shows that an increase in the demand for apples (a shift of the whole curve to the right), caused by an increase in consumers' income, will result in a higher equilibrium price, and also in a higher equilibrium quantity.

Exhibit 3.9
An Increase in the Supply of Apples Will Result in a Lower Equilibrium Price and a Higher Quantity

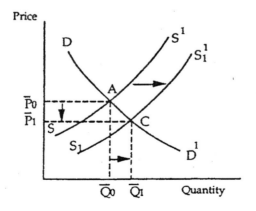

Technological advances in apple-picking technology will result in a larger supply of apples. With a given demand curve, a larger supply means a lower equilibrium price and a higher equilibrium quantity.

Changes Due to Shifts in Supply

Changes in the factors that determine the supply side of the market are reflected in shifts in the supply curve. Advances in the apple-picking technology, for instance, will allow apple suppliers to harvest the largest quantities of apples: the whole supply curve of apples shifts to the right. Given the demand curve for apples, the equilibrium price of apples will decrease and the equilibrium quantity will increase (see Exhibit 3.9). Conversely, an increase in the cost of production of apples, say due to higher wages, will result in a shift of supply curve to the left. Assuming, again, that the demand curve remains unchanged the equilibrium price will increase and the equilibrium quantity will decrease (could you draw the graph?).

Changes Due to Shifts in Demand and Supply

Demand and supply may shift simultaneously. For instance, an increase in consumer income, and a technological advancement in picking apples will result in a simultaneous shift of the demand and the supply curves that may determine a new equilibrium price and quantity (see Exhibit 3.10).

Exhibit 3.10
A Combined Increase in Demand and Supply of Apples
Results in a New Equilibrium Price and Quantity

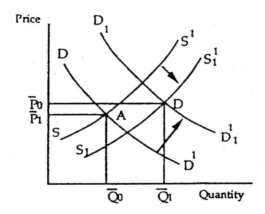

A simultaneous increase in demand for, and the supply of, apples results in a higher equilibrium price and quantity, assuming that demand increases out race supply increases.

Note, unlike the previous two cases where we have a clear-cut direction in the equilibrium price and quantity, in this case things are not clear. We must further make assumptions about the relative pace of the demand-and-supply increases: (1) if the demand increase out races the supply increase both equilibrium price and quantity will be higher; (2) if supply increase out races the demand increase, the equilibrium price will be lower and the equilibrium quantity will be higher; (3) if demand increases exactly like the supply increases, the equilibrium price will remain the same and the equilibrium quantity will increase (could you draw a graph for each of these three cases?).

To sum up, a change in any of the factors which affect the demand for a commodity will result in a higher or a lower equilibrium price, depending on whether that factor causes a right or a left shift in the demand curve for that commodity. Similarly, a change in any of the factors which affect supply, except price, will result in a higher or a lower equilibrium price, depending on whether that factor causes a left or a right shift in the supply curve. Also, a shift of both curves, at the same time, will cause a change in the equilibrium price and quantity of the commodity which will depend on the direction and the relative size of the shifts in the two curves. (The impact of shifts in demand and supply are summarized in Exhibit 3.11).

Exhibit 3.11
How Changes in Demand and Supply Affect
Equilibrium Price and Quantity

		Affect On	
Changes In		Equilibrium Price	Equilibrium Quantity
Demand	Increase	Increases	Increases
	Decrease	Decreases	Decreases
Supply	Increase	Decreases	Increases
	Decrease	Increases	Decreases
Both	Increase	Not clear*	Increases
	Decrease	Not clear*	Decreases

*More information is needed regarding the relative size of the changes in demand and supply.

In conclusion, in a competitive market, the equilibrium price and quantity of a commodity are determined by demand and supply. And changes in the equilibrium price and quantity reflect changes in demand and supply and the underlying factors that determine them. The following sections close the chapter with a review of the main points and concepts, and with an application designed to help the reader understand how demand and supply are used in economics and business.

Price Controls

Markets are not just price setting mechanisms. They are income distribution mechanisms, too. For consumers, commodity prices determine their living standards, the things they can and cannot afford to buy. Too high wheat prices, for instance, may mean bread is not affordable for low income consumers. For sellers, commodity prices determine the income they receive from selling their produce. Too low prices, for instance, may mean wheat farmers cannot earn a good living. What's the solution?

For some politicians, the solution is price controls, the setting of commodity prices by government bureaucrats rather than markets.

Price controls come in two types: price ceilings and price floors. Price ceilings are the maximum price that sellers can charge for a commodity, while price floors are the minimum price sellers can charge for a commodity; price ceilings are set below the equilibrium price, while price floors are set above the equilibrium price (see Exhibits 3.12 and 3.13). As can be inferred from these graphs, price ceilings create shortages, while price floors create surpluses, which may eventually have the opposite effects on consumers and producers than those intended by politicians. Shortages, for instance, create long shopping lines and may give rise to underground markets, rather than lowering the prices that consumers pay for commodities. That's why economists are skeptical about price controls.

Exhibit 3.12
A Price Ceiling of $2 Results in a Shortage of Four Units

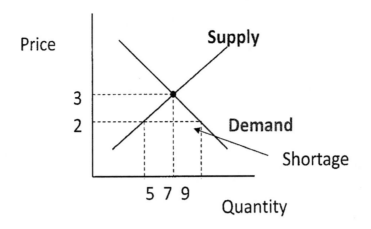

Exhibit 3.13
A Price Floor of $5 Results in a Surplus of Two Units

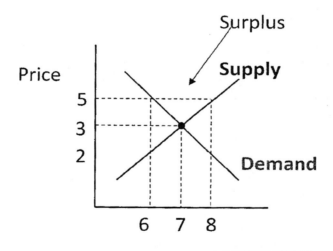

Market Failures and Regulation

Economic progress has "side effects," like pollution. A report published by U.N. Intergovernmental Panel on Climate Change (IPCC) on November 17, 2007 confirmed what many people have suspected in recent years. More than 250 years of economic growth has brought prosperity, but has put our environment, and most notably our climate, at risk. Increased pollution caused by the growing concentration of carbon dioxide and other chemicals in the atmosphere due to the extensive use of fossil fuels for the powering of factories and automobiles is fueling a Global Warming with far reaching consequences for life in our planet.

In market economies, environmental pollution is a typical example of "market failures," situations whereby the economic actions of one individual have negative consequences on the well-being of other individuals, and the society at large. The actions of corporations that run factories that release carbon dioxide have negative consequences on their surroundings and the world community, as have the actions of motorists who drive gas- and diesel-fueled engine vehicles. This means that the social costs of production are not factored into the dollar cost of production.

Addressing market failures is a difficult issue. Measuring social costs and coming up with practical solutions to lower or even eliminating them is a difficult economic and political issue. This has not stopped economists from coming up with a number of policies to deal with market failures.

Taxation: As the society as a whole pays the social costs, one way to add the social costs into the cost of production or consumption is through taxation. Taxes raise the price of polluting products, and therefore, limit its consumption. A good example of such a tax is a gasoline tax that raises the price of gasoline, thereby discouraging unnecessary driving, and consequently, reducing gas emissions.

Sanctions: Another policy is the use sanctions and incentives to discourage market participants from engaging in a polluting behavior. Sanctions further include penalties that raise the cost of producing polluting products. Under the Federal Water Pollution Act, for instance, the U.S. Government can prosecute environmental polluters.

Regulation: Governments may impose production standards and output limits to polluting industries. Governments, for instance, may impose a certain maximum number of pollutants per factory; and may further require that factories substitute old technologies with new less-polluting technologies. Another example of regulation is the creation of "pollution rights" or "emission reduction credits," whereby corporations that exceed certain pollution limits may buy the right to do so from corporations that stay below these limits.

Incentives: Incentives include government subsidies that lower the price of alternative products that limit or eliminate pollution. Both European and American governments, for instance, subsidize the use of solar and wind technologies for the production of energy as an alternative to conventional oil and coal producing technologies. The American government further subsidizes the purchase of hybrid cars that run on both gas and batteries, while the government of Iceland subsidizes the purchase of hydrogen cars.

Each policy has its own advantages and disadvantages. Outright regulations, for instance, are hard to monitor and may end up creating red tape that discourages entrepreneurial activity. Markets for pollution rights may be too small to be viable, especially in industries where the pollution firms are small and too few to foster sufficient number of buyers and sellers for pollution rights. Incentives for the use of alternative technologies create additional fiscal responsibilities for governments; and may create environmental problems of their own, e.g., interfere with wildlife.

As is the case with common medicine, the side effects of economic growth cannot be ignored for too long. Environmental pollution has reached to the point that may undermine or even outweigh the gains in economic growth. Reducing or even eliminating pollution will be one of the most important challenges of the future.

3.7 Review

1. This chapter discusses the model of the market for a commodity. This model separates the market for a commodity in two sides: the demand side and the supply side. The demand side of the market, represented by the demand curve, includes all consumers that are willing to buy the commodity at different prices. The higher the price, the lower the quantity demanded.

2. Reflecting changes in any of the "demand factors," the demand curve may shift from one position to another. Higher income, for instance, shifts the demand for a commodity to the right.

3. The supply side of the market, represented by the supply curve, includes all the firms that are willing to sell a commodity at different prices. The higher the price, the higher the quantity of the commodity firms are willing to supply.

4. Reflecting changes in "supply factors," the supply curve shifts from one position to another. Technological advances, for instance, expand the supply of a commodity. They shift the whole supply curve to the right.

5. The demand and supply curve jointly determine the equilibrium price and quantity of the commodity. The equilibrium price is the price that sets quantity demanded equal to quantity supplied. Equilibrium quantity is the quantity that corresponds to the equilibrium price.

6. Fluctuations in the equilibrium price and quantity reflect changes (shifts) in the demand and the supply of the commodity. With a fixed supply, for instance, an increase in demand results in higher equilibrium price and quantity. Demand-and-supply shifts, in turn, are caused by changes in the underlying "demand-and-supply factors."

Review Questions and Problems

1. What is the difference between demand and quantity demanded?
2. Which factors affect demand and quantity demanded?
3. How do changes in income affect the demand for a commodity?
4. Which factors affect the supply of a commodity?
5. How do technological advances affect the supply of a commodity?
6. Based on the following figures, draw the demand and the supply curve and find the equilibrium price and quantity:

P:	20	30	40	50	60
Q_d	200	160	120	80	40
Q_s	60	90	120	150	180

7. Draw a graph to show how higher income affects the demand for automobiles.
8. Draw a graph to show how a weather frost can affect the price of orange juice.
9. Draw a graph to explain how an economic expansion will affect the automobile market.
10. Draw a graph to explain how another oil shock will affect the oil market.
11. Draw a graph to explain how a California hurricane will affect the price of vegetables.
12. Why is water cheaper than diamonds?
13. Why is playing golf so expensive in Japan?
14. How will a sales tax on energy affect the price of energy?

15. Appendix A

Nowadays, many economists present the model of aggregate demand with a system of two equations, one for the demand side and another for the supply side.

To understand how this system works, let us assume the following:

P:	Price
Q_d:	Quantity demanded
Q_s:	Quantity supplied
a, b, γ, δ:	Parameters

The demand side of the market is given by the following equation:

$$Q_d = a - b * P: \text{ where } a,b > 0 \qquad (1)$$

The supply side of the market is given by the equation:

$$Q_s = γ + δ * P: \text{ where } γ,δ > 0 \qquad (2)$$

To find the equilibrium price and quantity we must solve the system of equations (1) and (2):

$$Q_d = a - b * P$$
$$Q_s = γ + δ * P$$

At Equilibrium $Q_d = Q_s$, so:

$$a - b * P = γ + δ * P$$
$$\rightarrow \quad -b * P - δ * P = γ - a$$
$$\rightarrow \quad -(b + δ) * P = γ - a$$
$$P = \frac{γ - a}{-(b + δ)} = \frac{a - γ}{b + δ} \qquad (3)$$

Equation (3) gives us true equilibrium price. If (3) is substituted to either equation (1) or (2), is gives us the equilibrium quantity:

$$Q_d = a - b\left(\frac{γ - a}{δ - δ}\right)$$

Example:

Let:

$Q_d = 400 - 2P$	(1) and
$Q_s = 160 + 4P$	(2) Find the equilibrium price and quantity.

By definition at equilibrium: $Q_d = Q_s$, so:

$$400 - 2P = 160 + 4P$$
$$\rightarrow \quad -2P - 4P = -400 + 160$$
$$\rightarrow \quad -6P = -240$$
$$\rightarrow \quad P = 240/6 = 40$$
$$\rightarrow \quad P = 40$$

Substituting the equilibrium price into equation (1) we find the equilibrium quantity:

$$Q_d = 400 - 2(40) = 320$$
$$\text{so, } Q = 320$$

Real World Link 5: The Impact of Summer 1988 Drought on the Price of Soybeans

Agricultural production is at the mercy of the weather. Any adverse weather conditions can substantially diminish the supply of agriculture products. A fall frost in Florida is followed by a smaller supply of oranges. A summer drought in the midwest states is followed by a smaller supply of wheat, corn, and soybeans. How do adverse weather conditions affect the price of a commodity? Assuming a fixed demand for the commodity, a smaller supply results in a higher price (see Exhibit 3.14A and 3.14B).

Exhibit 3.14

A. The Market for Soybeans in the Face of a Summer Drought

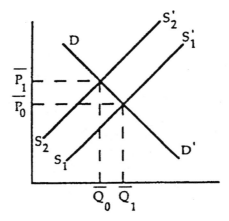

Evidence on the price of soybeans and weather temperature confirms the direct relationship between hot weather on the price of soybeans (see following exhibit).

B. The Market for Soybeans in the Face of a Summer Drought

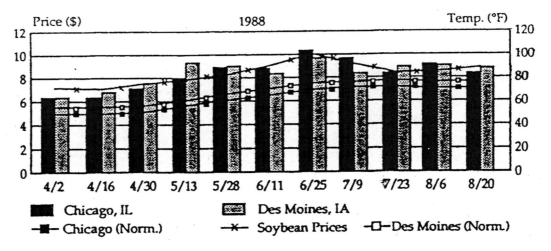

As illustrated in this exhibit, soybean prices are directly related to weather conditions, the latter displaying much higher than normal temperatures for the midwest region (Illinois and Iowa are the largest producers of soybeans; statistics on normal temperatures are averages for the period 1951–80). The hot weather and the lack of rainfall was followed by crop failure and shortages that drove soybean prices higher.

Real World Link 6: Why New York State May Be Running Out of Milk

New York, the country's third largest milk producer, doesn't have enough cows to raise the supply of milk needed to accommodate the soaring demand.

The reason? Rapid growth of the Greek yogurt industry in New York, combined with environmental regulations that prevent farmers from raising more cows to produce more milk. It's a typical demand/supply imbalance that pushes the price of milk higher, hurting both milk consumers and yogurt producers.

The rapid growth of the Greek yogurt industry at a time when growth is hard to come by highlights the importance of entrepreneurship in revitalizing the country. As discussed in a previous piece, Greek yogurt was brought to New York by Costas Mastoras, owner and founder of Optima and Titan Foods in Astoria, Queens. Costas is the man who discovered FAGE, the first Greek company that mass-produced the centuries-old strained yogurt, and imported it in America.

In the beginning, FAGE yogurt was selling at Titan Foods only, to Greek American customers. Eventually, word of mouth spread the news, and demand expanded among Titan's American customers in Manhattan and Long Island. The turning point, however, came when Trader Joe's and Whole Foods decided to carry the product, and sales jumped from $4 to 40 million.

Now, FAGE doesn't have enough capacity to supply the U.S. market. Besides, what is the point of bringing yogurt from Greece when milk is less expensive in New York?

Eventually, FAGE opened its owned factory in upstate New York. Efratis, a feta cheese company, followed suit shortly after with the brand name "Chobani," which ended up dominating the market.

According to a CNBC documentary, Chobani saw its sales soar, from nothing in 2007 to $500 million by 2011, leaving traditional yogurt makers like General Mills and Kraft striving to catch up.

The rest is history—in 2010, New York state produced 368 million pounds of yogurt, 60 percent more than five years earlier, straining the state's milk supplies, as Greek yogurt contains more milk than traditional American yogurt.

But there is one more question to be addressed: will regulations kill another vibrant industry, hurting consumers and producers?

Source: *Forbes Magazine*

Homework 3

1. What is the difference between demand and quantity demanded?

2. State and explain the law of demand.

3. What is the difference between changes in demand and changes in quantity demanded?

4. What is the difference between supply and quantity supplied?

5. State and explain the law of supply.

6. What is the difference between changes in supply and changes in quantity supplied?

7. Define and explain the concepts of equilibrium price and quantity.

8. How does a price ceiling affect the price of a product?

9. How does a price floor affect the price of a commodity?

10. How do technological improvements affect the price of a product?

Chapter 4

MICROECONOMIC ISSUES AND CONCEPTS

Preview

The first three chapters provided an overview of economic methods, economic concepts and economic problems. This chapter continues the discussion, focusing on the distinction between macroeconomics and microeconomics and reviewing the concepts of corporate organization, industry, and market structure. Some of the questions to be addressed are: What determines corporate and industry performance? What is corporate organization? What are the corporate objectives and internal structure? What is the relationship between corporation and industry, industry and market? How do markets differ?

Introduction

Japan is a rich country. In some respects, the Japanese economy is even stronger than the U.S. and EU economies. The yen is soaring; manufacturing is still growing; and the Japanese people enjoy a high per capita GDP. But are Japanese people rich? Are Japanese consumers better off than their U.S. and EU counterparts? The answer is no. Japanese people work longer hours than their counterparts and earn more, but their income does not buy much. Life in Japan is far more expensive than in the U.S. and EU. In 2010, for instance, rice cost $2.55 per pound in Tokyo but only $.79 in New York, and a movie ticket cost $19.00 in Tokyo but only $12.00 in New York. Why are commodity prices so high in Japan? One reason, perhaps, is that Japan is poor in natural resources and that makes production and storage of commodities costly. But in a global economy where resources can be purchased in foreign markets at competitive prices, resource scarcity alone cannot explain the high prices in Japan. Another reason is protectionism and regulation that restricts competition and keeps prices high. But what is competition? How can competition be restricted? How does competition affect consumer and social welfare?

Speaking of competition, what determines industry and company performance? Why do some industries and companies grow faster than others? Why do some industries and companies make profits and others lose money? According to data published by Statista in 2019, Saudi Aramco, Apple, and Microsoft were among the most profitable companies (see Exhibit 4.1).

Economists attribute business performance to macroeconomic factors such as business cycles, fluctuations in interest rates and exchange rates, monetary and fiscal policies, and to microeconomic factors, such as corporate organization, market structure, productivity, costs, product, and resource pricing. Addressing some of the microeconomic factors that affect company, industry, and country performance, this chapter is an introduction to microeconomics. The remainder of the chapter is in six parts. The first part discusses the distinction between macroeconomics and microeconomics. The second section discusses the issue of resource allocation and organization. The third and the fourth sections discuss the concepts of the firm, industry, and market. The fifth section is a discussion of the relationship between market structures and welfare. The sixth chapter is an overview of microeconomics, and the seventh is a review of the chapter.

4.1 Macroeconomics versus Microeconomics

As discussed in Chapter One, today's economies are much too complicated to study and understand in one session. In fact, the same economies may be studied from different perspectives. One perspective would be to focus on the functioning of the economy as a whole. Another perspective would be to focus on the studying of the economy taken in separate units. Conventionally, and in order to handle the difficulties and specificities associated with the study of various problems of an economy, economists have distinguished between two major fields of concentration: macroeconomics and microeconomics.

Macroeconomics is the study of an economy taken as one single unit. In macroeconomics, economists focus on aggregate decision-making: how GDP and its components are determined; the causes of government and trade deficits; the causes of economic expansions and contractions; the causes of inflation, unemployment, and stagflation; and the policies that can be applied to deal with such problems.

Exhibit 4.1

The Most Profitable Companies in the World

2019 net income of publicly listed companies (in billion U.S. dollars)

Saudi Aramco — 88.2
Berkshire Hathaway — 81.4
Apple — 55.3
ICBC — 45.2
Microsoft — 39.2
China Construction Bank — 38.6
JPMorgan Chase — 36.4
Alphabet — 34.3

Source: Fortune Global 500

IBT statista

Microeconomics is the study of an economy taken as separate units, consumers, workers, investors, and corporations. In microeconomics economists focus on the decision making of such units and the ways they interact with each other: how consumers allocate their income on various commodities; how individuals allocate their time between market and non-market activities; how firms organize production, and how they deal with questions of costs and product development; how firms and consumers interact in the commodity markets; and how firms and the owners of economic resources interact in the resource market.

4.2 Resource Allocation and Organization: Corporate Organizations

Entrepreneurship, corporate organization, and industrial structure have always been important factors for capitalist development and economic growth. The entrepreneurial talent of Andrew Carnegie, Henry Ford, and John D. Rockefeller, the emergence of corporations, and the unleashing of competitive forces were major factors contributing to America's manufacturing vigor and global expansion in the latter part of the 19th century; and they still are. Entrepreneurship and organization are still important today. The difference is that the world has become more complicated. But why are corporations necessary? Because the production of commodities requires a variety of resources that are owned by many individuals living in different parts of the economy.

As economic resources are scattered across the economy, producing commodities is a complex operation. Resources must be pulled together and directed to the production of commodities. Producing computer microchips, for instance, requires capital equipment, raw materials, technology, the engineering expertise, etc. The parties that possess these resources may be scattered from Boston to San Francisco, to Miami, and even to foreign countries. Bringing all these resources together, therefore, can be a difficult task that requires organization. IBM, for instance, organizes the production of computers. General Motors organizes the production of automobiles, McDonald's the production of fast food. Once resources are pulled together, production is more efficient inside the corporation, i.e., the outcome of joint efforts exceeds that of individual efforts. But let us look at the firm's functions, objectives, internal structure, and market environment.

The Three Functions of the Firm

In a market economy, firms perform three functions: the social function, the managerial function, and the entrepreneurial function. The social function of the firm defines the very existence of the firm as a social institution: the serving of consumer needs, or social needs—that is, the delivery of goods and services to consumers; the provision of employment and income for labor; the creation of tax revenues for governments; and the provision of charitable funds. The managerial function of the firm is the allocation of scarce resources to the production of goods and services to alternative uses. Management is the "brain" of the enterprise that gives the directives of how resources should be allocated to alternative uses, and how different tasks will be performed. The entrepreneurial function is the discovery and exploitations of new business opportunities. Entrepreneurship is the soul of the firm that keeps it alive for decades, even centuries.

The three functions aren't independent from each other. To perform its social function efficiently and effectively, for instance, the firm must be profitable, and that assumes that it performs its managerial and entrepreneurial functions well. To execute its vision, to deliver value to consumers and to contribute to the society through charitable donations, the firm must produce and deliver high quality innovative products and services. Conversely, to perform its entrepreneurial and managerial functions well, it must enjoy harmonious internal and external relations, which assumes that it performs its social function well. To perform its entrepreneurial function, the firm must perform its managerial and social functions well. The production and delivery of new products and services requires the control of both the costs and quality.

Corporate Objectives

What are the objectives of a corporation? To maximize stockholders' value? To maximize sales? To maximize market share? To promote managers' welfare? To maximize workers' income? To enhance a public image? It depends on who is faced with the question. Serving the consumer, serving society, and serving the community are some of the objectives that appear on top of the list of goals found in corporate charters and reports. Matsushita's corporate report, for instance, states that the objective of the company is "to foster progress, to promote the general welfare of society, and to devote ourselves to the further development of a world culture." From an economist's perspective, however, corporate objectives depend on several factors including the market environment, labor/management relations, and the financial constraints on the company.

In competitive markets, where managers serve stockholder interests, firms maximize stockholder value. In oligopoly markets, where managers may not necessarily share the stockholder interests and workers and corporate creditors have considerable power, firms maximize sales and market shares. Actually, different corporate objectives may not be mutually exclusive. In fact, profit maximization may be a short-term goal while sales growth and market share are long-term goals. Corporate goals must, therefore, be ranked according to their priority for the mission of an organization. In a relevant survey published in the *New York Times*, 300 executives at medium and large companies rank customer satisfaction, financial performance (profit), product and service quality, and competitiveness (market share) as their top four priorities.[1] But let us turn our discussion to different corporate structures.

Corporate Structure: Centralized and Decentralized Corporations

From an organizational perspective, a corporation can be viewed as the matrix of three distinct structures: the decision structure, the information structure, and the motivation structure. The decision structure facilitates the allocation of authority among the members of the corporate organization. The information structure facilitates the flow of information among the members of the organization, i.e., provides for the communication network. The motivation structure provides for the incentives that induce the members to pursue the objectives of the organization.

Corporate structures may be hierarchical and centralized or non-hierarchical and decentralized. Hierarchical structures allocate most of the authority at the top. Decisions are made at the top and transmitted to lower echelons of hierarchy through vertical channels of information, passing from superior to subordinate. Horizontal communication is not permitted, and lower echelons of management cannot communicate with each other. Subordinates in various departments can communicate only through their superiors.

The advantage of hierarchical organizations is the tight control of the top leadership over the organization. The top management sets up the goals of the organization and allocates organization resources accordingly. The disadvantages of hierarchical organizations are lack of motivation, lack of flexibility, and distortion of information. As decisions are made at the top with little or no participation from the lower levels of management, many organization members may feel left out of the decision process and have little or no incentive to pursue organization objectives, especially when rewards are not connected to performance.

While lack of motivation is a serious concern, lack of flexibility is an even more serious one. As economic conditions often change, organizations must respond quickly, a difficult task when lower management has no authority to deal with new economic conditions. Organizational decisions may, therefore, accomplish too little too late, and even impact negatively on performance.

Information distortion is always a problem in a hierarchical organization. As messages flow, back and forth, from superiors to subordinates, and from subordinates to superiors, they may be intentionally or unintentionally distorted. And if the wrong message reaches the top, the wrong decision will be made.

Nonhierarchical or decentralized organizations allocate authority across all levels of the corporate structure. Each member is given the chance to participate in the decision-making process of the organization, and to share the responsibility and the rewards of the organization. Information flows horizontally from member to member, and decisions may be made by lower management and other members of the organization without any reference to top management.

Motivation, flexibility, and clear communication are the advantages of organization decentralization. Responses to change in the economic environment are likely to be timely and accurate. And when organization members participate in decisions and share decision-making, they have reason to pursue organizational objectives with little or no supervision.

In the sixties and the seventies, American corporations were more centralized, which caused them serious problems in competing in world markets, especially during the worldwide slowdown in the seventies. Their market share has been eroding to foreign competitors, especially the Japanese. This situation changed in the eighties, however, when decentralization succeeded centralization. Some corporations have gone even further with decentralization. They have *re-engineered* their operations, bringing down divisions, abolishing traditional job tasks, and organizing production by *process*, rather than by task. Team effort and team evaluation have replaced individual effort and compensation.[2] Much of that movement for re-engineering relates to the conflict between ownership and control and the wave of mergers and acquisitions that took place in the preceding decade.

4.3 Structure of the Corporation: Ownership and Control

From a legal perspective firms are classified into three categories: proprietorships, partnerships, and corporations. It is important to note that in the first two types of business organizations, the owners of the firm are often the managers as well. When this is the case, the objectives of the firm are usually well defined, especially that of profit maximization. In the corporation, however, management may be separated from ownership, and a conflict may arise between the interests of the stockholders, calling for profit maximization, and those of management that call for job security, emoluments, prestige, and power, known as the "principal-agent" problem.

The Principal-Agent Problem

- Separation of ownership and control raises the potential of incentive misalignment between owners and managers known as the "Principal-Agent Problem."
- The incentives of the "agents—" managers may not be aligned with the incentives of the "owners—" stockholders.

Conflicts of interest between management and stockholders are especially problematic for publicly traded corporations where shares of common stock are held by tens of thousands of small investors. RJR Nabisco, for example, owned several jet planes to carry management around, and this is but one of a few cases that one could mention. Fortunately for the stockholders of RJR Nabisco, corporate raiders took the company private, paying them a hefty premium over the market price. The stockholders of Time, Inc. were not as fortunate, however. To avoid a two hundred dollar-a-share hostile takeover by Paramount Communications, Time, Inc. merged with Warner, Inc. One year later, after the Delaware court ruled that the merger was in the long-term interests of stockholders, the combined company of Time-Warner was trading at less than one hundred dollars a share; lucky stockholders!

While the corporate world was shaken by the flurry of corporate takeovers in the eighties, well justified in many cases, some economists are skeptical whether all corporate takeovers are beneficial for stockholders and to the economy as a whole. Fearing a takeover, it is argued that management opts for short-term rather than long-term strategies. As a result, American companies may fall behind foreign competitors that adopt a long-term strategy.

This discussion suggests two things. First, in large corporations where ownership is separated from control, corporate objectives may not be well defined. They may be in conflict with each other. Second, large corporations may be run inefficiently. Economic resources may be diverted to all kinds of activities with little relation to the production content of the corporation. But let us now turn to the external environment of the firm, i.e., examine the relation of the corporation to the industry and to the market.

The Corporation and the Industry

In today's world where each firm sells hundreds or even thousands of products in many markets, it becomes more and more difficult to come up with a universal classification of firms into industries. For instance, where would you classify Procter and Gamble? Philip Morris, CPC International, and Motorola? What criteria would you apply? Most economists classify companies into various industries according to two parameters—similar products and area of supply. All firms that produce the same or similar products within a defined supply region constitute an industry. All computer firms in the U.S. make up the U.S. computer industry. All computer firms in the world make up the world computer industry. Moreover, the computer industry can be divided into hardware and software, industrial applications and consumer applications, etc. Similarly, all aerospace firms make up the aerospace industry, all cellular telephone firms make up the cellular telephone industry, and all firms that produce consumer goods make up the consumer products industry.

While classifying firms into industries is very important, discussing the relation of firms to markets is at least as important.

4.4 The Firm and the Market

An industry cannot exist without consumers that are ready to buy the products that firms have for sale and owners of economic resources that are ready to sell to firms the resources needed to produce commodities. When the supply of commodities is put together with the demand for the commodities, they make up the commodity markets. When the supply of resources is put together with the demand for resources, they make the resource markets.

Commodity and resource markets are the cells of our market economy. Tens of thousands of commodity and resource markets bring together buyers and sellers of commodities and resources and determine prices and the volume traded at those prices. In other words, a market is a process which brings buyers and sellers together at a shopping center, over the telephone, by electronic mail, or at a professional convention.

Not all markets are alike. Commodity and resource markets have their own characteristics and peculiarities. Differences and peculiarities extend even within commodity and resource markets, between a flea market and the stock market, between the market for automobiles and the market for oranges, between the market for lawyers' services and the market for singers' talents. How can commodity and resource markets be classified? Economists apply four criteria: number of sellers and buyers in the market, product homogeneity or nonhomogeneity, entry and exit constraints, and the availability of information. Markets with many sellers of the same product, for instance, open to new sellers, and open to well-informed consumers, are classified as competitive markets. On the other hand, markets with one seller in a position to keep potential sellers (buyers) off the market are classified as monopolies (monopsonies). Markets in between the two extremes are classified as having imperfect competition. Briefly:

I. Commodity Markets

    Perfect Competition

    Monopoly

    Imperfect Competition

        Monopolistic Competition

        Oligopoly

II. Resource Markets

    Perfect Competition

    Monopsony

    Imperfect Competition

What are the characteristics of commodity and resource markets? How do different markets work and impact consumer and social welfare? To answer these questions, the next sections are an overview of the commodity and resource markets. A more detailed discussion will follow in Chapters Seven, Eight, Nine, and Ten.

Commodity Markets

In today's global economy, defining and understanding commodity markets is a rather complicated task. One of the problems is that markets are no longer located in a specific place. With the Internet and other branches of the information highway, the buyer and seller may find one another without ever meeting, and they may complete a transaction via computer without ever leaving their offices. Reflecting this new reality, we could define commodity markets as the process that facilitates the transaction of goods and services. As we have already discussed, commodity markets may be classified in three categories: perfect competition, monopoly, and imperfect competition.

Perfect Competition

For years, the idea of perfect competition has been a popular concept among economists, a benchmark against which one can measure real world markets. Perfect competition is based on four assumptions: a large number of sellers, homogeneous products, unrestricted entry, and perfect information.

A large number of small sellers

This assumption is crucial for competition. The larger the number of sellers, the larger the choice consumers have and the more they can shop around for the best value for their dollars. Even more important, the larger the number of sellers, the more difficult it is for a group of them to get together and corner the market.

Actually, cornering the market is even more difficult if it is further assumed that all sellers are about the same size so no group has an advantage over other groups.

Homogeneous commodities

All sellers sell identical products. This assumption makes competition even more intense. If all sellers sell the same product, consumers do not have to be concerned about the issue of quality and service, and they don't have to be concerned about commercial and market gimmicks, because there are not any. In that case, it does not matter from whom consumers buy the product. They can shop around until they find the seller that offers the product at the lowest price. In other words, consumers are indifferent in terms of choosing a seller from whom to buy. Consumers' choices are based on price alone.

Unrestricted entry and exit

Normally, in the real world, entry or exit to a market incurs a number of costs: licensing, patents, taxes, and investment or liquidation of capital equipment. This is not the case in a perfectly competitive market, however. New sellers can enter the market, and old sellers can leave the market at any time at negligible cost, i.e., economic resources are perfectly mobile across industries. If an industry is profitable, more sellers will enter the market. If the industry is losing money, some sellers will exit the market. Free entry and exit to the market makes it difficult for sellers to corner the market, and therefore reinforces competition.

Perfect Information

Consumers are well aware of prices at which they can purchase the commodity from different sellers. In other words, consumers cannot be fooled by any marketing or advertising gimmicks. They don't have to spend money and time to search around to find out who sells what. Information is at their fingertips, so they can quickly reach the seller who offers the product at the lowest price. But how does this market work? What are the implications of this market for consumer and social welfare?

Implications

A perfect competitive market has a couple of properties that make it appealing: the restrictive assumptions that define this market ensure that price is the sole vehicle of competition. This kind of competition, often called "price competition," is, in general, beneficial for both individual consumers and for society as a whole. For individual consumers, price competition ensures that they get the most out of their dollars, i.e., pay the lowest price for the products they buy. For society, price competition ensures that it gets the most out of the available resources, i.e., ensures that economic resources are allocated efficiently, an issue that is of concern to every society. These implications have made the perfectly competitive model very popular among economists, who use the model as a norm for measuring real-world performance.

Examples

The restrictive assumptions of perfect competition make it difficult to identify any real world market that complies with such requirements. Perhaps the stock market would qualify. There are a large number of stocks within a particular industry, and access is relatively easy to investors (there is a broker's fee, but that is negligible with regard to the volume of transactions). Information about the price of stocks is readily available through computer terminals, newspaper reports, etc. A flea market would be another example that might comply with the perfect competition requirements. There are a large number of vendors of combs, mirrors, toys, etc., and entry to the market for new vendors is easy. Because sellers are next to each other, consumers can easily find out commodity prices. Consumers do not have to search long to find out the commodity price in a monopoly market.

Monopoly

By contrast to perfect competition, monopoly, which is on the other extreme of the market spectrum, is not terribly popular among economists. It is often associated with market control, the limiting of consumer choice, and the inefficient allocation of resources that call for government regulation. The term monopoly comes from ancient Greek, and means a market of only one seller or a group of sellers behaving as one entity. Terms such as "cartels" and "trusts" describe ways that a group of sellers may monopolize a market, and they are often used in a way that is synonymous to monopoly. But how does a seller or a group of sellers control a market? By restricting the entry of potential competitors.

Flea Markets come close to Perfect Competition

Entry to a monopoly market may be blocked through: (a) legal constraints, such as some kind of license granted to only one firm, (b) technical constraints, such as economies of scale, i.e., the production of a particular commodity is profitable only when provided in large quantities (natural monopoly), (c) control over economic resources, i.e., raw materials, (d) the granting of a unique knowledge or a patent that can be exploited exclusively for a certain period of time.

Note: Monopoly power is constrained by the existence of different but substitutable products (i.e., aluminum competes with tin, steel, and plastic), and by consumers' income. Poor consumers, for instance, may not be able to afford even life-saving drugs, if the price is too high.

Implications

Being the only one in the market, a monopoly has no competitive pressures to lower prices, increase sales or improve product quality. Compared to a perfectly competitive market, consumers may get too little of the product at too high a price. In other words, in a monopoly market, consumers do not get the most out of their dollars, and the society does not get the most out of economic resources. The government may, therefore, have to intervene and regulate monopolies in a way that will improve consumer and social welfare.

Examples

Although monopolies are illegal in every developed county, it does not mean that they do not exist. When the sellers of a product get together to corner the market, they do not invite the Federal Trade Commission (FTC) to the party. And even if the FTC, a competitor, or a consumer group invite themselves in and try to make a legal case against them, it may be too hard to prove anything. The FTC, for instance, brought an antitrust suit against the cereal industry but failed to prove that such a trust among cereal sellers had existed. In some cases, monopolies may exist under a certain license, patent, or certain rules made by the government.

For instance, the U.S. Postal Service is a monopoly established through Federal licensing. Amgen, the company that has developed two blockbuster drugs for stimulating red blood cells during chemotherapy, is a monopoly established because of a patent. Long Island Lighting Company (LILCO) is a monopoly established because of economies of scale, but it is regulated by New York State. The same is true of the Long Island Railroad.

Imperfect Competition

Most real world markets do not come close to either perfect competition, or to monopoly, but fall in between. Some markets have many sellers, an element found in perfect competition, but each seller may sell a different product, an element found in monopoly. Other markets are dominated by a few big sellers with substantial control of the market, but still competing with each other. Economists classify all these diverse markets as imperfect competition, which includes several subcategories, the most popular being monopolistic competition and the oligopoly.

Monopolistic Competition

As the term suggests, monopolistic competition is a mix of monopoly and competition. It is competition among many sellers of unique products or services who can exercise limited control over the market. Specifically, monopolistic competition is defined by the following assumptions:

A relatively large number of sellers who exert power over the market. This assumption is less strict than that of perfect competition. Individual sellers may vary in size and be in a position to exert some kind of control over consumers, especially when one looks at the second assumption.

Nonhomogeneous commodities. Nonhomogeneous products or product differentiation is perhaps the most important assumption that distinguishes monopolistic competition from perfect competition. Each seller sells goods and services that differ from those of other sellers. Product differences may be objective or subjective. Objective differences have to do with the way the product is made. One seller, for instance, may have products of superior quality to those of another. Subjective differences have to do with the way consumers perceive the product, differences are in the eye of the beholder. Objective and subjective differences in particular may be subject to a seller's manipulation through advertisement and other marketing instruments that attract consumers to a particular product or brand name. Advertising and the development of brand names are often restrictions that keep potential competitors off the market.

Restricted entry. Advertising and brand name recognition are not the only impediments that may keep competitors off the market. Other restrictions such as licensing and patents may make it costly for new competitors to enter the market. Setting up a professional practice in law, accounting, or medicine, for instance, requires a license and the proper educational qualifications.

Imperfect information. With many sellers selling different products, knowledge about the different products and sellers can become costly for consumers and give an advantage to some sellers over others. When shopping around for the right medical doctor, for instance, consumers may have to make several calls to friends for references, check with medical associations, even visit the offices of various doctors before they make a decision. Such a search may cost consumers both money and time. Better known, more conveniently located sellers may have a competitive advantage over the lesser known, less conveniently located sellers.

Implications. Compared to perfect competition, monopolistic competition is an inferior market in the sense that consumers and the society do not necessarily get the most out of their resources. As different sellers sell different products, they can charge consumers different prices. Sellers that manage to convince consumers that they have superior products can charge premium prices. Advertising and other marketing devices, rather than prices, become the vehicles of competition, vehicles that the consumer ends up paying for in the form of higher prices. Under this kind of competition, consumers do not get the most out of their resources and society does not get the most out of economic resources.

Examples. Many real-world markets are consistent with the assumptions of monopolistic competition. Typical examples are markets for all kinds of professional services, such as lawyers' services, doctors' services, etc., that comply with all of the above assumptions. In any community there is a large number of lawyers, but perhaps not as many as office clerks. This is because of the restrictions imposed on entering this profession, such as a law degree, the BAR examination, and professional practice. The market for real estate brokers' services is another interesting example. First, there are many brokers. In Suffolk County alone, there are 556 realty brokers that belong to the Multiple Listing Service and over 8,000 members of the Long Island Board of Realtors. Brokers list and price houses individually, so two agencies may have the same house listed at different prices, depending upon how fast the owner wants to sell his home. Entry to the real estate business is costly and time consuming. First, prospective brokers must take a 45-hour qualifying course for $175, and then, after successful completion of the course, they must find an agency for which to work. Only after you have found an agent can you take the test for the real estate license. Although entry requirements to monopolistic competition sound strict, entry to oligopoly is even more strict.

Oligopoly

As is the case with monopoly, oligopoly is not a terribly popular concept with economists. Oligopolies are also associated with cartels and trusts, which limit production and raise prices. The term oligopoly, which comes from Greek, means a market of a few sellers. Specifically, an oligopoly is a market defined by the following assumptions.

A few sellers. This means that each seller has a considerable market share and control over the market, and that pricing and output decisions restrict and are restricted by the other sellers.

Homogeneous or nonhomogeneous commodities. This assumption means that there are oligopolies which sell identical products and oligopolies which sell differentiated products.

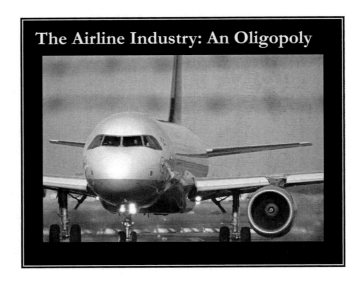

The Airline Industry: An Oligopoly

Restricted Entry. Entry to a market may be restricted by capital, marketing, and technological requirements. Entry to the automobile industry, for instance, may be subject to these requirements, and so is entry to the aerospace and the computer chip industries.

Imperfect information. Consumers may lack information regarding product quality and product prices. Shopping around for the right car or the right computer may be a cumbersome task without an expert.

Implications. Like monopolistic competition, oligopoly is not the best type of market for consumers and society: as price competition among sellers may be limited or even nonexistent, consumers do not get the most out of their dollars, and society does not get the most out of economic resources.

Examples. Many real world markets comply with the requirements of oligopoly. The market for automobiles is often pointed to as a typical case. There are a small number of large automobile companies producing cars that are or at least are perceived to be different. Entry to the market is restricted by capital, technology, and marketing requirements. Similar characteristics are exhibited by steel, aluminum and other heavy metal industries, to mention but a few. The market for groceries on Long Island could also be classified as an oligopoly. Five supermarket chains, A&P (including Waldbaums), Pathmark, Shoprite, Foodtown, and Grand Union control around 60 percent of the market.

In short, commodity markets are classified according to four criteria: number of sellers, type of products, entry restrictions, and available information. Based on these criteria, economists classify markets into three categories: perfect competition, monopoly, and imperfect competition. Imperfect competition includes monopolistic competition and oligopoly (see Exhibit 4.2). But let us turn our attention to the resource markets.

Exhibit 4.2
Commodity Market Structures

Commodity Characteristics

Number of Sellers	Homogenous	Nonhomogenous
Many	Perfect Competition	Monopolistic Competition
Few	Oligopoly	Oligopoly
One	Monopoly	

Resource Markets

In 1994, an explosion in a factory that makes chemicals for semiconductors in central Japan interrupted the worldwide production of semiconductors and pushed their prices way up. In 1974 and 1979, a restriction in the supply of Middle Eastern oil sent a shock wave throughout the world economy. Gasoline, heating oil, and many chemical products skyrocketed, and the world economy entered a recession. These examples demonstrate the importance of resource markets to an economy.

A resource market is the process that facilitates the transaction of economic resources, labor, capital, raw materials, etc., among households and firms. The market for computer engineers, the market for funds needed to purchase capital equipment, and the market for farm land are all part of the resource market. In contrast to commodity markets where firms are the sellers and households are the buyers, in resource markets, firms are the buyers and households are the sellers. Applying the same criteria as with commodity markets, resource markets may be classified into three categories: perfect competition, monopsony, and imperfect competition.

Perfect Competition

Perfect competition in resource markets is a market with a large number of small buyers who buy identical resources. Entry and exit to the market is unrestricted, and sellers are perfectly informed about the price of their services from buyer to buyer. The market for unskilled labor such as for cashiers, waiters, retail salespersons fall into this category; screening, hiring, and laying-off costs are very low, if any, and so are skill differences across workers.

As is the case with perfect competition in commodity markets, perfect competition in resource markets is good for the buyers of resources, firms. Competition among buyers ensures that firms get the most out the dollars they spend on a certain resource. However, this is not the case in the other extreme, monopsony.

Real World Link 7: How Market Barriers Turn Japan into a Rich Country of Poor Consumers

In most western societies, governments are preoccupied with consumer prosperity. But not in Japan, where production comes before consumption, work before leisure, and corporation before family. "Grow or perish," that's how the "Yoshida Doctrine" defined Japan's economic strategy in the post-war era. Indeed, all three economic plans from 1958 to 1970 stated explicitly maximum growth as the most important goal. The Income Doubling Plan of 1959, for instance, called for high savings and investments as the vehicles to achieving rapid technological innovations and high growth; and so did the 1958–62 plan.

Companies, workers, and government all joined forces to achieve this objective. Companies invested heavily in capital equipment and paid little in dividends. Throughout the '60s and the '70s, gross domestic investment accounted for 30–40 percent of the GDP compared to 13–18 percent in the U.S. In 1990, Japanese companies had a layout ratio (the proportion of earnings paid out as dividends) of 30 percent compared to 54 percent of the U.S. companies and 66 percent of British companies. At the same time, companies formed a partnership with labor that promoted worker participation, training, joint consultation, flexible compensation, and decision by consensus. On their part, workers demonstrated discipline and cooperation, worked long hours, and saved a great deal. In the mid-eighties, Japanese workers worked 15–20 percent more than their American counterparts and 25–30 percent more than their Western European counterparts. In 1993, Japan's savings accounted for 14 percent of disposable income compared to Canada's 9.7 percent, France's 12.6 percent, and the U.S.'s 4.9 percent. Joining efforts, the government provided for regulation and protectionism that favored certain relations between manufacturers and distributors, provided for economic visions, offered low interest financing, established research consortia, and reinforced protection of domestic industry from foreign competition.

By the early eighties, the objectives of the "Yoshida Doctrine" had been achieved and even exceeded; Japan had grown and flourished. For the periods 1956–1960 and 1958–1962, Japan's economy grew at 8.8 and 9.7 percent, well above the corresponding 4.9 and 6.5 percent target levels. In the period 1960–73, Japan's economy grew at 6.3 percent while the U.S. economy grew at 2.5 percent and the OECD countries as a group by 4.9 percent; 4–5 percent between 1973 and 1991; followed by the slow-down of 1993–94.

High GDP growth rates accompanied by low inflation and unemployment have allowed Japanese consumers to enjoy a rapid growth in their real income. For the period 1950–1990, real incomes rose from $1,230 (in 1990 prices) to $23,970 (a 7.7 percent average annual growth rate), well ahead of the 1.9 percent growth of the U.S., and 1.0 percent of Great Britain. High economic growth rates, low unemployment, and a high per-capita GDP placed Japan next to developed nations. But as Japanese people paused for a moment to count their blessings, they became disenchanted with what they came to realize. Their economy had delivered growth and jobs, but not prosperity. The size of an average Japanese residence was 881 sq. ft. compared to 1,645 sq. ft. for the U.S., only 3 percent of the Japanese homes had central heating, and 45.4 percent flushing toilets. The corresponding figures for the U.S. were 85 percent and 99.8 percent. Japan's poor housing conditions, long working hours, and a high cost of living place her closer to less developed rather than to most developed nations.

Excessive government regulation and protectionism have created a sanctuary for domestic competitors, and turned Japan into the most expensive place to live. In 111 items compared in a *Business Week* survey, Tokyo was 69 percent more expensive than New York, and 100 percent more expensive than France. In 1993, a pound of rice was selling for $2.71 per pound in Tokyo compared to $0.89 in Manhattan, an apartment was selling for $715.67 per square foot in Tokyo compared to $309.00 in Manhattan, and a Sony walkman $209.92 compared to $39.99. In addition to small houses and a high cost of living, Japanese people are also faced with a poor infrastructure behind those of other industrialized countries. Japan's main sewage system, for instance, serves only 40 percent of the population, compared to 73 percent and 95 percent of the population served by the corresponding U.S. and British sewage systems. The average urban Japanese enjoyed 2.2 square meters of park space compared to 19.2 for the average American living in New York, 30.4 for the average Englishman, and 37.4 for the average German.

Monopsony

A monopsony is a resource market of one buyer. This could be a case where a large company is the main employer in a distant community, such as the textile, mining, and steel industries in nineteenth-century America, automobile companies in Detroit, oil companies in Texas, etc. But even nowadays, Grumman almost has a monopsony in aerospace engineers in Bethpage, Long Island. And the same is true for AT&T for communications consultants in New Jersey. Another example of a monopsony is De Beers; the South African cartel controls about 80 percent of the world demand for raw diamonds. As was the case with monopolies, monopsonies can take advantage of their position as the sole supplier of a resource and raise the price of that resource. In that case, the buyers, firms, do not get the most out of the dollars they allocate to that resource.

Imperfect Competition

Imperfect competition is a resource market between perfect competition and monopsony; i.e., it exhibits a mix of characteristics of both models. The market for software engineers, for instance, could be classified as an imperfectly competitive market; a large number of software engineers with diverse skills; entry restricted by a university degree and relevant experience; firms must undergo a considerable search to identify the right engineers for their projects. Once again, imperfect competition in resource markets implies that buyers, firms, do not get the most out of the dollars they allocate to resources sold by monopsonies.

4.5 Market Structures and Economic Welfare

The brief review of the different markets reveals that how well a society utilizes its resources, and how wealthy the consumers of that society are, depends on the prevailing commodity and resource markets. Societies with few regulations and other market restrictions make better use of their resources and their consumers get the most with their dollars. Societies with many regulations and restrictions to competition do not make good use of their resources, and their consumers do not get the most out of their dollars. It can be argued, therefore, that the higher cost of living in Japan and the European Union has to do with the many more regulations that these societies have compared to the U.S.

4.6 Overview of Microeconomics

As microeconomics is the study of our economy taken in separate units, it focuses on problems that pertain to households both as consumers of goods and services and as sellers of economic resources. To this end, it includes a tour behind the scenes of the two sides of the product market. The tour behind the scene of the demand side includes a discussion of issues pertaining to household consumers' decision-making, rationalizing the inverse relationship between price and quantity demanded. The tour behind the supply side includes a discussion of issues pertaining to firms' decision-making. It focuses on the characteristics of production, costs, revenues, output, and price determination in the different market structures represented by perfect competition, monopoly, and imperfect competition. The tour ends with a discussion of the market for economic resources, especially labor.

To sum up, economists distinguish between two economic disciplines, macroeconomics and microeconomics. Macroeconomics deals with issues that pertain to the whole economy and microeconomics deals with issues that pertain to the economy taken in separate units. In microeconomics, economists focus on issues of resource allocation and organization. They look at the internal organization of firms and at the firm's environment, the industry and the market. Markets are classified into two major categories, product markets and resource markets. Product markets are further classified into perfect competition, monopoly, and imperfect competition. Resource markets are further classified into perfect competition, monopsony and oligopsony.

After the introduction into microeconomics, the next chapter moves on to the concept of consumer demand.

Real World Link 8: The Entrepreneurial Failure of Eastman Kodak

After 120 years of life, Eastman Kodak is about to become a distant memory like the images its innovative technology captured in photography. What caused the downfall and demise of this iconic company?

Entrepreneurial failure.

In every society, firms perform three functions: the social function, the managerial function, and the entrepreneurial function. The social function defines the very existence of the firm as a social institution: the serving of consumer and social needs; the provision of employment and income for labor; and the contribution of funds the support of the local and national community. The managerial function of the firm determines how economic resources should be allocated to alternative uses, and how different tasks are to be performed. The entrepreneurial function accommodates the discovery and exploitation of new business opportunities—the most important function, as it keeps the firm alive for decades, even centuries to come.

The three functions aren't independent from each other. The social function, for instance, imposes different constraints on the entrepreneurial and managerial functions, while the entrepreneurial and the managerial functions impose their own constraints on the social function. This means that a failure in any of the three functions undermines the other two functions, and if it goes unchecked, can end in the demise of the organization. That's exactly what happened in the case of Eastman Kodak.

In its early days, the company excelled in all three functions. In the social area, it generated thousands of jobs; and contributed resources to the national, state, and the local, Rochester, community. In the managerial area, it executed a shrewd marketing strategy by bundling nicely its cameras with the film processing photography technology, often giving cameras away to sell its film and processing chemicals, as Google (NASDAQ:GOOG), and Microsoft (NASDAQ:MSFT) have been doing these days. In the entrepreneurial area, it offered consumers innovative products that allowed them to capture everyday moments.

Over time, however, the company failed to come up with new versions of its products that will fend off imitators, as Apple (NASDAQ:AAPL) has been doing in recent years—Polaroid and Fuji's challenge is the case in point. The company further failed to leverage its core competences and capabilities in photography chemistry to expand into emerging industries, as other late 19th century American companies did. Corning Inc. (NYSE:GLW), for instance, survived and thrived by leveraging its core capabilities, the processing of glass substances, to develop a sting of blockbuster products, the glass for Edison's electric lamp, the traditional TV tubes, the heat-resistant glass for missiles and kitchen ware, the fiber-optic cables that power the Internet, and the glass for flat panel TVs. Procter & Gamble (NYSE:PG) has also survived and prospered by constantly replenishing and expanding its product portfolio to address emerging consumer needs.

The Bottom Line: Eastman Kodak's decline and fall is a failure of its leaders to develop the appropriate buffers to keep competition from imitating and replicating its strategy; and to match effectively corporate resources and capabilities with emerging market opportunities—an entrepreneurial failure that eventually undermined its other two functions, leading to its demise.

Source: *Forbes Magazine*

4.7 Review

1.   This chapter started with the distinction between macro- and micro-economics. Macroeconomics focuses on issues pertaining to the whole economy. Microeconomics focuses on issues pertaining to individual decision units of the economy (households and firms) and on the interaction between the two that takes place through markets.

2.   In order to abstract from the complexities of real world markets, economists have made up market structures, i.e., economic models. Depending on whether they pertain to commodities or to resources, market structures can be classified as commodity market structures and resource market structures.

3.   There are three types of commodity market structures: perfect competition, monopoly, and imperfect competition.

Perfect competition is a market of a large number of small sellers who sell identical products. Entry to and exit from the market is unrestricted, and consumers are perfectly informed about the product characteristics and prices across sellers. Perfect competition is beneficial both for consumers and for the society: while the former get the most out of their expenditures, the latter gets the most out of the available economic resources.

Monopoly is a market of one seller who sells a commodity without close substitutes. Entry to the market is restricted by legal, technical, or natural constraints. A monopoly imposes a burden on both consumers and society: while the former do not get the best value for their money, the latter does not get the most out of the available economic resources.

Imperfect competition is a market between the two extremes of monopoly and perfect competition. It includes two models, monopolistic competition and oligopoly.

Monopolistic competition is a market of many sellers who sell nonhomogeneous commodities. Entry to the market is restricted by legal constraints. Although not as bad as monopoly, monopolistic competition imposes a burden on both consumers and society: while the former do not get the best value for their money, the latter does not get the most out of the available economic resources. Oligopoly is a market of a few sellers who sell a homogeneous commodity or nonhomogeneous commodities. Entry to the market is restricted by legal, technical, and natural constraints. Although not as bad as monopoly, oligopoly imposes a burden on both consumers and society: while the former do not get the most out of economic resources, the latter does not get the most out of the available economic resources.

4.   There are three types of resource market structures: perfect competition, monopsony, and imperfect competition.

Perfect competition is a market of a large number of small buyers who buy identical resources. Entry to and exit from the market are unrestricted, and sellers are perfectly informed about the price of their services across buyers.

Monopsony is a resource market of one buyer, the case of a large company that is the main employer in a distant community, a company which has managed to get access to a raw material, etc.

Imperfect Competition includes a set of resource markets that fall between perfect competition and monopsony, displaying a mix of characteristics of the two models.

Review Questions

1. What are the problems with the separation of ownership and control in large enterprises?
2. What is perfect competition?
3. What is imperfect competition?
4. What is monopolistic competition?
5. What is oligopoly?
6. What is monopsony?
7. What is oligopsony?

Notes

1. The *New York Times*, Sunday, February 19, 1995.
2. See Michael Hammer and James Champy, *Reengineering the Corporation*, Harper Business, New York, 1993.

Homework 4

1. In what respects do markets differ from one another?

2. What is perfect competition in commodity markets?

3. What is monopolistic competition?

4. What is oligopoly?

5. What is monopoly?

6. What is perfect competition in resource markets?

7. What is oligopsony?

8. What is monopsony?

9. What is globalization?

10. Why is Japan's cost of living so high?

Chapter 5

CONSUMER THEORY, CONSUMER DEMAND, AND ELASTICITY

Preview

Chapter Three was an introduction to the concept of the product market. Chapter Four was a discussion of the different types of market structures. This chapter is a more detailed discussion of the demand side of the product market. Several questions are to be addressed: What are the logical explanations of the law of demand, i.e., why do consumers demand a lower quantity of a product as its price increases? How responsive are consumers to commodity price changes? Would price reductions lower or raise company revenues? How would changes in consumer income affect commodity demand? How would changes in the price of one commodity affect the demand for other commodities?

Introduction

In a market system, the consumer is the center of the economic universe, the beginning and ending of every economic activity, the ultimate boss of every capitalist enterprise. This is especially the case in a digital global market system where consumer-controlled media allow each consumer to have more choices as to where, when, and from whom to buy products. For instance, search engines like Google and MSN allow consumers to find almost instantly who sells what and at what prices. Technology from TiVo allows consumers to choose what shows to see without commercial interruptions, turning Prime Time into My Time.

Consumers can be further classified into two categories: rational and irrational (or emotional). Rational consumers decide with reason, they begin with the "Big Picture," the things that are important in their lives, setting needs ahead of desires. Before they pull out their wallet and head for the cash register, they always ask three simple questions: Is the product right? Is the price right? What is the opportunity cost of the money spent on this product?

Emotional consumers, on the other hand, see the "Big Picture" upside down, often placing desires ahead of needs. They become impulsive, rushing to buy a product without asking whether they really need it in the first place, the price is right, or it is the best choice for their money. They end up subscribing to magazines they never read; joining health clubs they rarely visit; and buying shoes and dresses they never wear, tools and accessories they never use, and toys children never touch. Though spending money on these sorts of things may be a waste for consumers, it is a bonanza for the marketers who push them.

In the pages that follow, we do assume that consumers are rational, that is, they decide by reason rather than emotion.

Understanding the importance of consumer demand, every day millions of businesses, small and large, domestic and foreign, compete for consumer dollars. Commercial after commercial and gimmick after gimmick is launched to persuade consumers what is good for them. While millions of dollars are spent on such campaigns, many more are spent on market surveys to reveal what consumers desire to buy and are willing to pay for. In a market economy where consumers are sovereign, studying consumer demand is the first step in succeeding in any kind of business.

Living in an affluent society like ours, consumers have many commodities to choose from, too many temptations to resist. Watching television, looking at consumer magazines, walking to shopping centers, consumers are fascinated by the variety of choices offered to them: nice houses, luxury cars, exotic cruises, VCRs, movie cameras, nice clothes, shoes, groceries. Perhaps consumers would like to grab all these things for themselves. Commodities are not offered for free, however. They must be purchased in the market. This means that commodity prices and income impose a constraint on what sort of things consumers can afford to buy. Compromises must be made and shopping lists must be tailored to both desires and possibilities. On what kinds of commodities do American consumers spend their dollars? What determines the decision to buy more of one commodity and less of another? What are the logical explanations of the law of demand, i.e., why do consumers demand a lower quantity of a product as its price increases? How responsive are consumers to a small change in commodity prices? Would a lower price decrease or increase a company's revenues? How would a change in consumers' income affect quantity demanded? How would the change in the price of a certain commodity affect the demand for other commodities?

This chapter addresses these questions in three sections. The first section is a review of the profile of the American consumer. The second section includes intuitive and technical explanations of the law of demand. The third section is a discussion of special topics of demand such as the price elasticity of demand, the income elasticity of demand, and the cross elasticity of demand.

5.1 The Spending Profile of the American Consumer

American society provides a variety of goods and services to consumers, but not for free. Consumers must pay the price. And as consumers' income is limited, choices must be made. Buying more apples may mean buying fewer oranges or strawberries. Some goods and services have priority over others. Medical attention and care, for instance, may have priority over entertainment, and food may have priority over traveling. As a result, some good and services absorb a larger portion of consumers' income than others. Shelter and food, for instance, absorb the largest portion of consumers' income, while life insurance, alcoholic beverages, and household operation absorb the smallest proportion (see Exhibit 5.1).

Exhibit 5.1

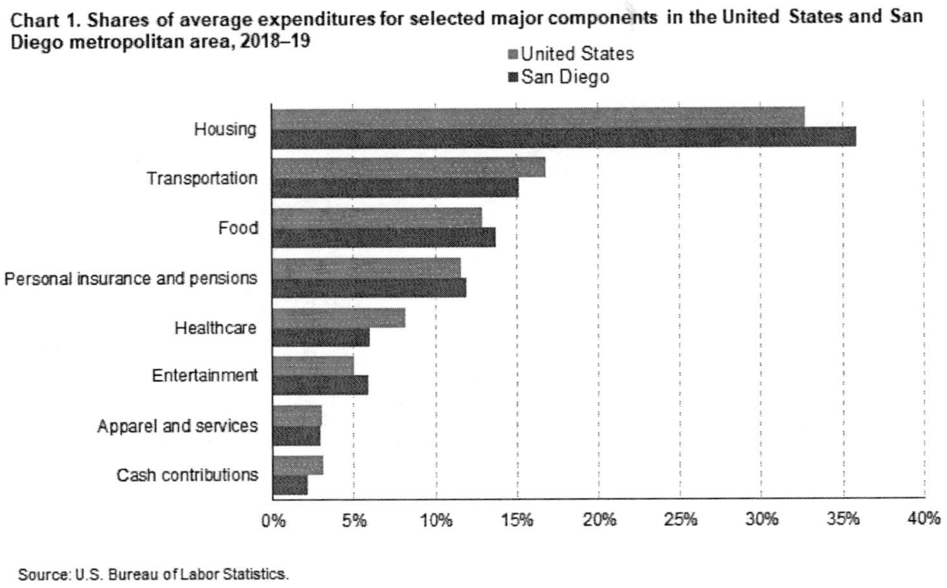
Chart 1. Shares of average expenditures for selected major components in the United States and San Diego metropolitan area, 2018–19
United States
San Diego
Housing
Transportation
Food
Personal insurance and pensions
Healthcare
Entertainment
Apparel and services
Cash contributions
0%
5%
10%
15%
20%
25%
30%
35%
40%
Source: U.S. Bureau of Labor Statistics.

Inflation-Adjusted Changes in Consumer Spending

One way to see how spending has changed over time is to look at spending on consumer goods and services adjusted by the changes in the prices of those items. Prices for most goods and services generally rise over time but there are some, computers for example, whose prices may actually fall. Consumers sometimes adjust their spending when the prices of some goods or services change relative to others. For example, a spike in gasoline prices may cause consumers to forgo long driving trips, or to purchase more fuel-efficient vehicles. Conversely, they may decide not to make such adjustments and pay higher prices, thereby increasing their nominal expenditures for gasoline.

The CPI is one measure of price changes that can be used to adjust nominal expenditures to estimate what are termed "real" expenditures on an item. If the percentage change in the price of an item over time matches the percentage change in expenditures for that item, then there is no change in real expenditures on that item. However, if the percentage price increase exceeds the percentage expenditure increase, then real spending on that item decreases. Conversely, if the percentage price increase is less than the increase in spending, then real spending increases.

Source: http://www.bls.gov/cex/ceturnsthirty.htm

5.2 Explanations of the Law of Demand

Recall from Chapter Three, the quantity of a commodity consumers are willing to buy depends on the commodity price. As the commodity price increases, the quantity demanded decreases. What are the scientific explanations of the law of demand? Why are consumers willing to buy a smaller amount of a commodity as its price increases? Two explanations are explored here, an intuitive and a technical one.

An Intuitive Explanation

You may recall that the law of demand is a hypothesis, valid only under a set of assumptions captured in the term "other things being equal." Namely, consumers' income remains unchanged, consumers' preferences and the prices of related commodities remain unchanged. With a fixed income and fixed prices for related commodities, a higher commodity price sets in motion two effects, the law of diminishing satisfaction, the income effect and the substitution effect, both already introduced in Chapter Three.

The Law of Diminishing Marginal Satisfaction

Consumers may have a need for a commodity. They may have an appetite for oranges. But that appetite diminishes as one consumes more and more oranges: the second orange may not be as satisfying as the first; and the third not as satisfying as the second; and so on. In fact, there will be a point where the consumer is fully content with oranges. Another orange will add no more satisfaction. If each additional orange is less satisfying, a consumer will not be willing to buy more oranges, unless the price declines.

Income Effect

To make things simple, you may think for a moment that consumers spend their entire income on one commodity, say oranges. As the price of oranges increases, consumers can no longer afford to buy as many pounds as before with the same income. A similar argument can be made in a more realistic situation where consumers spend their income on several commodities, in addition to oranges. Again, as the price of oranges increases, consumers' purchasing power decreases. Consumers must cut down on the quantity of oranges or on the quantity of some other commodities.

Substitution Effect

Suppose for a moment that consumers spend their income on oranges and apples, both selling at a dollar per pound. Now, assume that the price of oranges doubles. Responding to the higher orange prices, some consumers cut down on oranges and buy more apples. A similar argument can be made when consumers' income is spent on more than two commodities: as the price of a commodity increases consumers shift towards substituting other commodities for the higher priced one. The more substitutes available for a specific commodity, the less dependent on the commodity the consumer is, and the stronger the substitution effect.

Note: As the price of a commodity changes, the income and substitution effects are simultaneously set in motion, inducing consumers to demand a smaller amount of the commodity.

A Technical Explanation of Law of Demand: Consumer Preferences and Possibilities

To understand the concept of consumer demand, you may envision the following situation. Mr. Smith, the hero of our discussion in this chapter, is sitting at the kitchen table preparing his shopping list. As any other consumer, Mr. Smith has preferences and limitations. He may like, for instance, carrots with his dinner but not broccoli. He may love orange juice but hate apple juice. He may have donuts with tea for breakfast and tuna fish for lunch. He may drink a cup of hot milk at bedtime. He likes fashion clothes, furniture and oriental rugs for his home. He is also dreaming of a luxury car with a cellular phone. And a trip to Hawaii is in his dreams, too.

Not only these items make up Mr. Smith's shopping list. Broccoli and apple juice do not satisfy his tastes, and the luxury car with the cellular phone may not satisfy his budget and neither does the trip to Hawaii. Perhaps some other time, when the price of these items will be lower and his income higher. For an elaborate analysis of consumer preferences and possibilities, and the formal derivation of the consumer demand, economists have invented two theoretical concepts, the concept of the indifference map and the concept of the consumer budget. The indifference map and the consumer budget jointly determine what economists call consumer equilibrium: the choice that maximizes consumer satisfaction and is yet affordable.

Exhibit 5.2
Exhibits for Mr. Smith's Indifference Schedule, Indifference Curve, and Indifference Map

A. The Indifference Schedule

Commodity X Pounds of Apples	Commodity Y Pounds of Oranges
20	6
18	8
16	11
14	15
12	20
10	26

The two columns of this table give the various quantity combinations of apples and oranges consumed by Mr. Smith. The combinations are made up in such a way that each of them gives the same satisfaction.

Preferences and Possibilities

In an individualistic society, like America, preferences are an individual matter. Individuals themselves know what is best for them and they make their choices accordingly. In other countries, like the European Union and Japan in particular, individual preferences are constrained by social considerations. In making choices, individuals must consider how other people in their group, and how the rest of the society, will respond. In other words, in such societies, individual preferences are interdependent and that makes it difficult for economists to model consumer behavior. Although bearing these considerations in mind, to keep things simple we assume that individuals have their own preferences which are described by the indifference map; consumers also have their own incomes which, along with the commodity prices, determine the amount of commodities they can afford.

Preferences: The Indifference Map

Let us return to the familiar postulate of economic rationality: consumers are utilitarian agents in the sense that the pursuit of maximum satisfaction (utility) derived from various commodity combinations, is their sole motive. For the sake of simplicity, further assume that Mr. Smith can only choose between two commodities, apples and oranges, that are available for free. How does Mr. Smith rank the various combinations of the two commodities in terms of utility? Note that utility cannot be measured in pounds or kilograms. Nevertheless a new scale, called utils, could be invented for the purpose of our analysis. Applying this measure, Mr. Smith can classify commodities by levels of satisfaction. Some commodity combinations yield equal utils of satisfaction while some yield more than others. The set of all commodity combinations that yields equal utility define an *indifference* curve (see Exhibit 5.2B).

Exhibit 5.2
B. The Indifference Curve

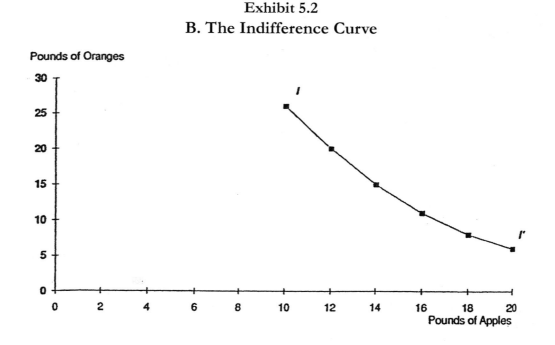

This curve is an "image" of the indifference schedule. The vertical axis denotes the pounds of oranges and the horizontal axis the pounds of apples. Each point on the curve represents a combination of apples and oranges from which Mr. Smith derives the same utility (satisfaction).

You may recall that in order for Mr. Smith to stay on the same indifference curve he must increase the consumption of the one commodity while reducing the consumption of the other commodity. What will happen if he consumes more of the one commodity without consuming less of the other commodity, or if he consumes more of both commodities? He will move to a new indifference curve, located to the right. The larger the quantity Mr. Smith consumes of both commodities, the more he will move to indifference curves located further to the right. This way, a whole array of indifference curves filling the positive quadrant can be constructed, in a parallel fashion, called an *indifference map* (see Exhibit 5.2C). Will Mr. Smith be happier as he climbs all the way up from one indifference curve to another? Yes, the more to the right he moves the higher the utility he derives since he consumes more of both goods (see Exhibit 5.2C).

To sum up, the indifference map is an abstraction describing a consumer's preferences; it is a consumer ranking of various combinations of commodities. There are combinations which he likes as much and combinations which he likes more than others. Moreover, being rational (preferring more to less) will induce him to move all the way up on the indifference map, until reaching the bliss point, i.e., a state of saturation, where he does not desire any more units of either of the two commodities. What is holding the consumer back from getting to the bliss point? The consumer budget constraint.

Exhibit 5.2
C. Mr. Smith's Indifference Map

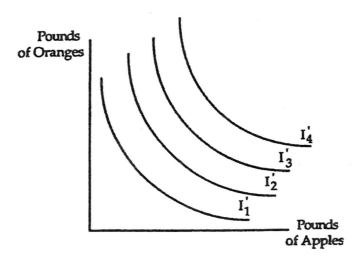

This figure is similar to 5.2B, but now more indifference curves are drawn. Indifference curves further to the right imply more consumption of *both* oranges and apples, and therefore a higher utility (satisfaction). Indifference curves further to the left imply less consumption of *both* oranges and apples, and therefore less utility.

Possibilities: The Consumer Budget Constraint

Let us now expand our initial model by assigning prices to the two commodities, $P_x = \$2$ for apples and $P_y = \$4$ for oranges. Assume that Mr. Smith's income of \$76 is all spent on the two commodities. What are Mr. Smith's consumption possibilities, i.e., what consumption combinations can he afford to put in his basket? Exhibit 5.3A gives an example of several such combinations. The numbers on the exhibit can be further used to draw a diagram (Exhibit 5.3B). This diagram shows what Mr. Smith can afford and what he cannot. He can afford all the commodity combinations on and inside the triangle, but nothing beyond it.

Exhibit 5.3
Exhibits for Mr. Smith's Consumption Possibilities and Budget Constraint

A. The Consumption Possibilities: Baskets Mr. Smith Can Afford with an Income of $76, and Commodity Prices of $P_x = \$2$ and $P_y = \$4$

Cost of Basket ($)	Commodity X (Pounds of Apples)	Commodity Y (Pounds of Oranges)
76	20	9
76	18	10
76	16	11
76	14	12
76	12	13
76	10	14

This exhibit gives an example of six different baskets Mr. Smith can afford with $76.

B. Mr. Smith's Budget Constraint for Apples and Oranges with an Income of $76, and Commodity Prices of $P_x = \$2$ and $P_y = \$4$

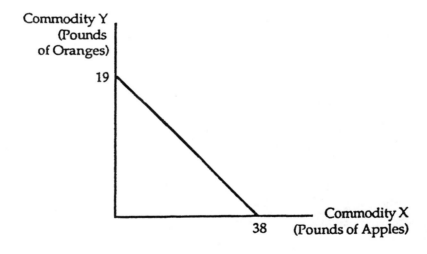

This exhibit is an image of the consumer's possibilities. The consumer can afford any commodity basket of $76 or less, i.e., any combination on or within the triangle, but nothing beyond.

Changes in the Relative Price: The Consumer Budget Rotates

How would Mr. Smith's consumption possibilities be affected by a change in the relative prices of the two commodities? How will Mr. Smith adjust his selection should the price of apples increase from $2 to $3, while the price of oranges remains at $4? Mr. Smith's consumption possibilities will be further restricted in a way that he cannot afford to buy as much as before. To understand this, take the extreme case that Mr.

Smith spends all of his income on apples. He can only buy 25.3 pounds of apples as compared to 38 pounds before (see Exhibit 5.4).

Exhibit 5.4
Mr. Smith's Consumption Possibilities with an Income of $76, and Commodity Prices of $P_x = \$3$ and $P_y = \$4$

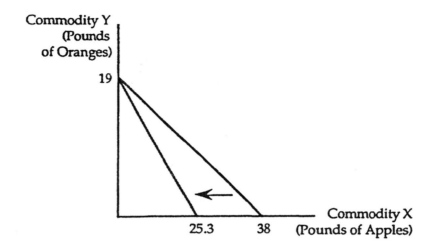

As the price of apples increases the consumer budget constraint rotates inwards, i.e. the consumers possibilities are further restricted.

Changes in Consumer's Income: The Consumer Budget Shifts

What happens to Mr. Smith's consumption possibilities should Mr. Smith's income increase, say from $76 to $82, while the prices of the two commodities remain at the original levels of $2 and $4? Certainly he can afford to buy more of each commodity, i.e., he can come up with a new list of affordable commodity baskets. To put it differently, as Mr. Smith's income increases, so do his consumption opportunities; the consumer budget shifts to the right (see Exhibit 5.5).

To sum up, the consumer's budget constraint is another abstraction describing a consumer's possibilities for given level of income and commodity prices. The indifference map is an abstraction, describing the consumer's preferences. Since consumer demand reflects the compromise of preferences and possibilities, the two must be put together.

Putting Preferences and Possibilities Together: The Consumer Equilibrium

Knowing Mr. Smith's preferences and possibilities as they are described in the indifference map and consumption possibilities budget, the following question can be raised: which is the best choice for Mr. Smith, i.e., the choice that balances desires and possibilities? The combination of 16 pounds of apples and 11 pounds of oranges (see Exhibits 5.4 and 5.6B).

Exhibit 5.5
Mr. Smith's Consumption Possibilities
with $82 as Compared to $76

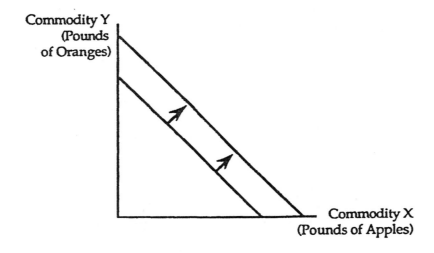

As Mr. Smith's income increases from $76 to $82, his consumption opportunities expand, i.e., the consumer budget shifts to the right.

Exhibit 5.6
A. The Consumer Equilibrium: Putting the Indifference Map (Preferences) and the Consumer Budget (Possibilities) Together

Preferences		Possibilities	
Pounds of Apples	Pounds of Oranges	Pounds of Apples	Pounds of Oranges
20	6	20	9
18	8	18	10
16	11	16	11
14	15	14	12
12	20	12	13
10	26	10	14

This exhibit contrasts Mr. Smith's preference and possibility combinations. Only one combination matches Mr. Smith's preferences and possibilities and that is 16 pounds of apples and 11 pounds of oranges. In other words, given the prices of the two commodities and given Mr. Smith's income the best he can do is to stay with the combination of 16 pounds of apples and 11 pounds of oranges. With this combination, the consumer is at equilibrium in the sense that any other combination would be either unattainable or inferior in satisfaction.

Exhibit 5.6
B. The Consumer Equilibrium:
Putting Preferences and Possibilities Together

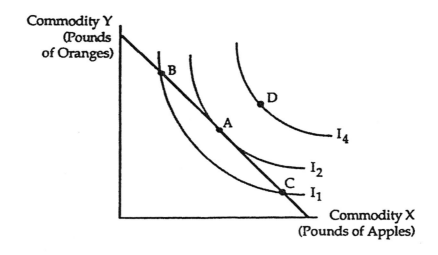

This exhibit describes consumer equilibrium. It brings together consumer preferences and possibilities. The selection which balances consumer preferences and possibilities (consumer equilibrium) is point A. Any other choice is either non-affordable (choices outside the triangle) or will yield the consumer lower satisfaction.

Consumer Equilibrium and Commodity Rationing: The Case of Gasoline

While the prevailing norm in a market system is that consumers know what is best for them and should be left alone in the pursuit of consumption, government interference may not always be ruled out. During wars or periods of severe shortage of a necessity, governments may ration a commodity, i.e., dictate or paternalize consumption. The case of gasoline shortage in the middle seventies is one of the most recent episodes of commodity rationing. How does rationing affect consumers?

The answer to this question depends on whether rationing is binding or not. Consumers who would ordinarily buy a large quantity of the rationed commodity are obviously made worse off. Consumers who buy a quantity equal to or smaller than amount allowed under rationing will remain unaffected. Take the case of gasoline rationing for instance. A rationed quantity of ten gallons a week will make consumers who plan to buy more than ten gallons worse off (see Exhibit 5.6C), while consumers who were planning to buy ten gallons or less will be unaffected.

Exhibit 5.6
C. Gasoline Can Reduce a Consumer's Satisfaction

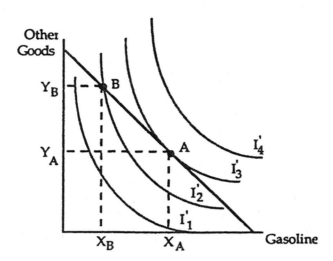

Where X_A: Quantity before rationing, X_B: Quantity after rationing

This exhibit portrays the impact of gasoline rationing on consumer equilibrium. With the assumption that the rationed quantity is set below the consumer equilibrium quantity, the consumer moves from point A to point B, a point that satisfies both the consumer budget and the rationing constraints. As B is on a lower indifference curve, the consumer is made worse off (moving to a lower indifference curve).

The Derivation of the Individual Demand

How can these two devices be used to explain the question raised at the beginning of the chapter, i.e., the inverse relationship between price and quantity demanded? To put it differently, what will happen to Mr. Smith's equilibrium as the price of apples increases from $2 to $3? He will consume fewer pounds of apples. This is demonstrated in Exhibit 5.7. The upper part is a replication of Mr. Smith's equilibrium as demonstrated in the previous exhibit, but the price of apples has increased. This has caused a twist of the budget line to the left in which Mr. Smith cannot afford as much as before of the two commodities (recall Exhibit 5.3). Mr. Smith has now moved from the initial equilibrium point A to a new equilibrium point F to the left of A, consuming fewer apples and more oranges. This means that there is an inverse relationship between the price of apples and the quantity demanded of apples. This is explicitly demonstrated in the lower part of Exhibit 5.7, which gives the price of apples on the vertical axis and the quantity of apples on the horizontal axis.

Exhibit 5.7
The Derivation of the Individual Demand for a Product

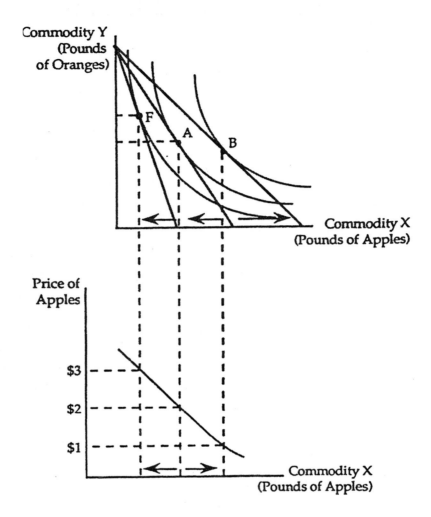

The upper panel of this exhibit replicates the consumer equilibrium as was discussed earlier, but now the price of apples has increased from $2 to $3 and the consumer budget has twisted inwards. The lower panel demonstrates explicitly the relationship between the price and quantity of apples demanded by the consumer.

From the Individual to the Market Demand

You may recall that the demand derived thus far refers only to one individual out of many in the market. What about the market demand? Assuming that consumers' preferences are independent of one another, the market demand is the horizontal summation of all individual demands. Exhibit 5.8 demonstrates this exercise. The first chart represents Mr. Smith's demand curve, the second Mr. Brown's, and the third the market demand (the combined demand for both consumers). Note that the market demand is the summation of the corresponding individual quantities at each single price.

Exhibit 5.8
The Market Demand: The Horizontal Summation
of All the Individual Demand Curves

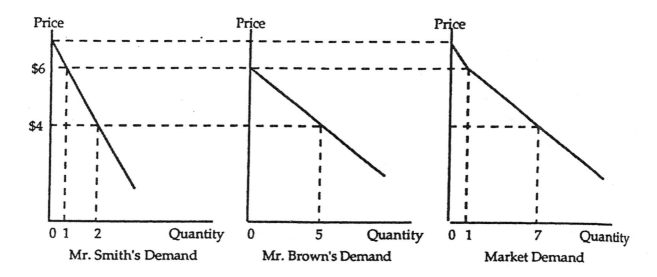

The first and the second panels of this exhibit give Mr. Smith's and Mr. Brown's demand curves while the third gives the market demand (the horizontal summation is the total of the two individual curves). Note that horizontal summation is the total of each consumer's demands at a given price. For example, let us say that at a price of $4 Mr. Smith demands 2 pounds of apples and Mr. Brown 5 pounds, so the horizontal sum of these two quantities will be 7 pounds (see third panel).

5.3 Special Topics: Elasticity of Demand

How do consumers respond to a small change in the price of a commodity? Do they cut the quantity demanded considerably or not at all? What factors determine such a response? Does a price reduction increase or decrease the total revenues of a firm? Does an increase in consumers' income increase or decrease the quantity demanded of a commodity? Does an increase in the price of a commodity result in a higher demand for the commodity's substitutes or complements? To answer these questions economists have come up with concepts such as the price elasticity of demand, the income elasticity of demand, and the cross elasticity of demand.

Price Elasticity of Demand

Definition: The price elasticity of demand for a product is a measure of the consumers' responsiveness to a given price change, i.e., a measure of how consumers adjust quantity demanded in response to a price change.

Calculation: The price elasticity of demand is the ratio of the percentage change in the quantity of the commodity demanded to the percentage change in the price i.e.,

$$e_P = \frac{\%\text{ change in } Q}{\%\text{ change in } P}$$

where Q is the quantity demanded and P is the commodity price.

An alternative price elasticity formula is,

$$e_p = \frac{\Delta Q/\overline{Q}}{\Delta P/\overline{P}}$$

where $\overline{Q}$ is the average of the old and new quantities demanded and $\overline{P}$ is the average of the old and new commodity prices.

Note that the elasticity of demand is a pure number, i.e., free of the units that the price and quantity are expressed in. As calculated, it is always a negative number because the two variables, price and quantity, move in opposite directions. However to facilitate a better comparison between two elasticity numbers, elasticity can be expressed in absolute value, i.e., without the negative sign.

Example: Take for example the demand schedule for a commodity, say apples, given below.

P (cents)	Q (pounds)
100	20
120	19
140	17

How do consumers respond to each price change, i.e., what is the elasticity of demand for each pair of price and quantity? Note that for the first two pairs the quantity demanded decreases by 1 pound, with a midpoint (average) of 19.5, as the price increases by 20 dollars, with a midpoint of 110. Thus, for the first two pairs: $| e_p | = 0.28$, while for the second two pairs $| e_p | = 0.72$. Thus, in the first case an increase in the price by 10 percent results in a 2.8 percent decline in the quantity demanded. Subsequently, a 10 percent increase in price results in a 7.2 percent decline in the quantity demanded. Note, again, that the elasticity of demand is a pure number, that is to say independent of the units of measurement.

Interpretation. Price elasticity of demand is the number that the percent change in price is multiplied by in order to find the percent change in the quantity demanded. The more elastic the demand, the more responsive consumers will be to a price change. For example, an elasticity of two means that a 10 percent reduction in the price of a commodity will result in a 20 percent increase in the quantity demanded.

Size of the Elasticity of Demand

As was mentioned earlier, according to the law of demand, the price elasticity of demand is always a negative number. However, for comparison purposes, economists take the absolute value of the elasticity (the calculated number without the sign), distinguishing among three sizes of elasticity.

(i) $| e_p | > 1$ (elastic demand)

(ii) $| e_p | = 1$ (unitary demand)

(iii) $| e_p | < 1$ (inelastic demand)

Note: The price elasticity of demand is not the same as the slope of the demand curve at a given point but it does depend on this slope. To demonstrate this the elasticity formula can be rewritten in a different fashion:

$$e_p = (dQ/dP)*(P/Q)$$

This formula consists of two parts: dQ/dP, and P/Q.

The first part gives the inverse of the slope of the demand curve (in absolute terms) while the second gives the precise point on the demand curve. This suggests that the larger the slope the smaller the elasticity of demand. This is depicted in Exhibit 5.9A. Also, given the slope of the demand curve, the size of elasticity increases from the left to the right of the curve (see Exhibit 5.9B). To put it another way, the price elasticity of demand becomes smaller from a point on the left to points on the right. This is because as consumers get larger, quantities of the commodity approach the saturation point and become less responsive.

Exhibit 5.9
A. The Slope of the Demand Curve
and the Value of the Elasticity of Demand

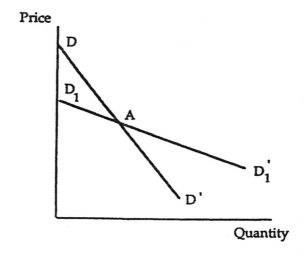

As it can be seen from this exhibit, the steeper the demand curve the smaller the elasticity of demand is. Thus $e_d < e_{d'}$.

B. The Value of Elasticity Along a Demand Curve

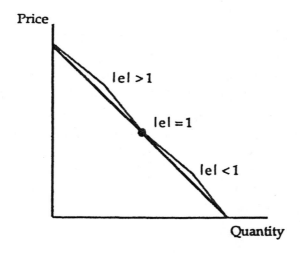

As can be seen from this exhibit, the elasticity of demand is equal to one at the midpoint point of the demand curve, greater than one to the left, and lower than one to the right.

Factors Which Influence the Size of the Elasticity of Demand

As you may expect, demand elasticity may vary from commodity to commodity and from consumer to consumer. Essential commodities such as milk, coffee, and grocery items may have a low elasticity. And the same may be true for commodities consumers have become addicted to such as tobacco. Nonessential items such as cellular phones, VCRs and speed boats may have a high elasticity. But let us discuss each factor separately.

The absolute size of the price of the commodity. Not all commodities sell for the same price. Some items are selling only for a few cents or dollars, while others sell for hundreds or even thousands of dollars. Chewing gum, milk, and coffee fall into the first category, while high-ticket items such as cars, furniture, and cellular phones fall into the second category. To have a substantial effect on the consumer, the price change must be a significant percentage of the absolute (initial) price. For example, would a $1 change in price have the same effect when the commodity sells at ten dollars as when it sells for ten thousand dollars? The effect will definitely be larger in the first case.

Consumer addiction. Addiction ties consumers to a particular commodity. This means that price changes have little or no effect on the quantity demanded. Could someone quit smoking because the price of cigarettes increased by 10 percent? Even 15 percent? Most likely not. Addiction may overshadow the effect of the higher price on the consumer's income. They may cut back on other items but not on cigarettes. By contrast, consumers are very responsive to things they are not addicted to. For example, a 10 percent increase in the price of apples may induce many consumers to stop eating apples.

Seasonality. Consumers desire for a commodity may not be the same at all times. It may change with seasons. For instance, are you as fond of ice cream in the winter as in the summer? Would you give up a cone of ice cream in the summer when the temperature is hitting a hundred just because the price has increased by a few cents? The season adds another dimension to the desire for this commodity. The same may be true for other seasonal commodities such as strawberries, blueberries, and so on. Consumers are less responsive to a price change during one season than another.

The time reference period: short-run versus long-run elasticities. Time is crucial in measuring the consumer's response to a change in the price of a commodity. The longer the time the consumers have to respond to a given price change, the higher the e_p. Take again the example of gasoline. Faced with a sudden increase in the price, consumers find themselves unable to cut down demand in the short-run. However, in the long run consumers can find alternative ways to conserve gasoline, such as using car pools, moving closer to their work place or buying a smaller car, thereby reducing the quantity of gasoline demanded.

Advertising. Advertising can reach consumers in various ways. First, it informs them of the existence of a product. Second, it informs them about any price changes. Third, it may influence consumer preferences and tie consumers to the product. By reaching consumers, advertising can impact the speed and the size of consumer response to a given price change. Furniture sale advertising, for instance, can bring consumers into a furniture room faster than otherwise; and the already elastic demand for furniture becomes even more elastic. And cigarette advertising can remind consumers of their addiction; and the already inelastic demand for cigarettes becomes even more inelastic.

Empirical Estimates of the Elasticity of Demand

As was discussed earlier, price elasticity is a very useful concept for business and government policy. It can be used to predict how revenues will be affected by a change in commodity prices. Estimating price elasticities is not an easy task, however. One must have a good background in statistical techniques. In the mean time, elasticity estimates can be obtained from existing publications (see Exhibit 5.10).

The Relationship between Elasticity, Total Revenues, and Price Changes

After we have become familiar with the concept, the meaning, and the estimates of price elasticity, we come to the discussion of the relationship between elasticity and total revenues.

Exhibit 5.10
Empirical Estimates of the Price Elasticity
for Selected Commodities (British Post-War Data)

Item	Price Elasticity
Food	0.04
Clothing	1.51
Housing	0.79
Fuel	1.37
Drink and Tobacco	1.22
Transportation and Communication	1.73
Other Goods	1.15
Other Services	1.28

Note: Food and housing have a price elasticity of less than one and so are price inelastic, while all the other items have an elasticity greater than one and so are price elastic. Source: Excerpted from "An Almost Ideal Demand System" by Angus Deaton and John Muellbauer (1980), *American Economic Review*, Vol. 70, No. 3, p. 320.

Assume for the time being that the objective of a firm is to maximize revenues. What is the appropriate pricing policy? Should the firm increase, decrease, or keep the price of the commodity the same? As was mentioned earlier, the price elasticity of demand is a very useful concept in business decisions. It can serve as a decision-making aid in the effort to maximize a firm's revenue. Exhibit 5.11, below, gives the relationship between the size of the elasticity, the pricing policy, and the change in total revenues.

Exhibit 5.11
Elasticity, Pricing Policy, and Changes
in the Total Revenues of a Firm

Price Change	Size of Price Elasticity		
	$\lvert e_p \rvert > 1$	$\lvert e_p \rvert = 1$	$\lvert e_p \rvert < 1$
Price Increases	TR Decreases	No Change in TR	TR Increases
Price Decreases	TR Increases	No Change in TR	TR Decreases

As can be inferred from this exhibit, a decrease in the commodity price will increase the total revenues in cases where the price elasticity of the commodity is more than one, while an increase in the price will have the same result when the price elasticity is less than one (see Exhibit 5.12).

Exhibit 5.12
The Value of Elasticity and Total Revenues

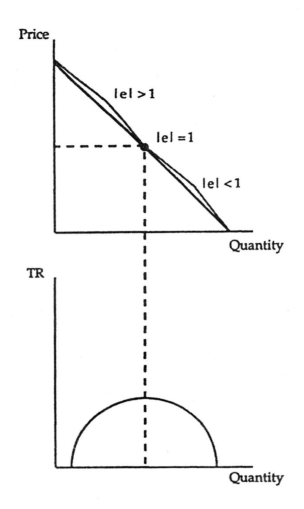

As long as the elasticity of demand is greater than 1 (upper panel), any price decrease will result in higher revenues. As the elasticity of demand becomes equal to 1, total revenues level off, while as the elasticity of demand becomes less than 1, TR starts to decline.

The following numerical example elaborates on the previous exhibit.

P	Q	$\lvert e_p \rvert$	TR = PQ
10	20	—	200
8	30	1.8	240
9	28	0.6	252

In this example, for the first pair the elasticity of demand is greater than 1, and thus a reduction in price results in greater revenues, while for the second pair the elasticity of demand is less than 1, and thus an increase in price results in greater revenues, as was suggested in the exhibit.

So far, we have discussed how consumers respond to changes in commodity prices. Price is not the only variable that determines consumer demand, however. Other factors play an important role, especially income. How do changes in income affect commodity demand? To answer this question, economists have invented another concept of income elasticity.

Income Elasticity of Demand

Definition: Income elasticity is a measure of consumers' responsiveness to a given income change. It is measured as the ratio of the percent change in the quantity demanded to the percent change in income, i.e.,

$$e_i = \frac{\%\ \text{change in Q}}{\%\ \text{change in I}}$$

where Q stands for quantity demanded and I stands for income.

An alternative version of this formula is,

$$ei = \frac{\Delta Q / \overline{Q}}{\Delta I / \overline{I}}$$

where ΔQ stands for the change in quantity demanded, $\overline{Q}$ stands for average quantity demanded, ΔI stands for a change in income, and $\overline{I}$ stands for the average income.

Income elasticity is used to classify commodities into two categories, normal and inferior.

Normal and Inferior Commodities

Normal are commodities that have an income elasticity greater than 1. (Recalling the income elasticity formula, this means that an income increase, say 10 percent, stimulates an increase in the quantity demanded of the commodity of more than 10 percent). Normal commodities are usually commodities which consumers do not buy every day but rather once in a while, spending a relatively large proportion of income (high-ticket items). Household appliances, furniture, automobiles, cellular phones, health food products, physical services are all normal commodities.

Inferior are commodities that have an income elasticity less than 1. As income increases the demand for an inferior commodity also increases but at a smaller proportion. Inferior commodities are those which are usually purchased by low-income classes. Used cars, black-and-white television sets and no frill items are all inferior commodities.

Neutral are commodities that have an income elasticity equal to 1. The demand for neutral commodities changes at the same pace with income. If income increases by 10 percent, the demand for a neutral commodity increases exactly by the same amount.

In short, normal commodities are those with an income elasticity greater than 1; inferior commodities are those with an income elasticity less than 1; and inferior commodities are those of an income elasticity less than 1; and neutral commodities are those of an income elasticity equal to 1 (see Exhibit 5.13A).

The demand for normal goods moves at a higher pace than income; the demand for inferior goods moves at a lower pace than income; the demand for neutral commodities moves at the same pace as income.

Empirical Estimates of Income Elasticity

Along with price elasticity, income elasticity is not just a concept for the exercise of the mind but rather something which can be estimated empirically. The exhibit below gives such estimates for a group of commodities consumed in Great Britain in the post-war period (Exhibit 5.13).

In formulating their shopping plans for buying a certain amount of a given commodity, consumers respond not just to income changes, but also respond to a change in the price of related commodities.

Exhibit 5.13

Empirical Estimates of the Income Elasticity of Demand for Selected Commodities (British Post-War Data)

Item	Income Elasticity
Food	0.21
Clothing	2.00
Housing	0.30
Fuel	1.67
Drink and Tobacco	1.22
Transportation and Communication	1.23
Other Goods	1.21
Other Services	1.40

Note: Food and housing have an income elasticity of less than 1 and therefore can be classified as inferior, while all other items can be classified as normal. Source: Excerpted from "An Almost Ideal Demand System" by Angus Deaton and John Muellbauer (1980), *American Economic Review*, Vol. 70, No. 3, p. 320.

Cross Price Elasticity of Demand

Definition: Cross price elasticity is a measure of consumers' responsiveness in demanding a commodity in response to a given change in the price of another commodity. Formally,

$$e_{xy} = \frac{\%\text{ change in the Quantity Demanded of Commodity X}}{\%\text{ Change in the Price of Commodity Y}}$$

Cross elasticity is useful in classifying commodities in three categories, complements, substitutes, and unrelated.

Complements and Substitute Commodities

Complements are commodities with a negative cross elasticity. This means as the price of the one commodity increases the quantity of the other commodity decreases (see Exhibit 5.14 for coffee and sugar). More simply, complements are commodities jointly satisfying a consumer need. Eggs and bacon, peanut butter and jelly, coffee and sugar, a computer terminal and a keyboard are good examples of complementary commodities.

Substitutes are commodities with a positive cross elasticity. This means that as the price of the one commodity increases the quantity of the substitute commodity increases to fill demand (see Exhibit 5.14 for apples and oranges, below). In common sense, substitutes are commodities which can be used instead of one another in satisfying consumer needs. Donuts and croissants, coffee and tea, pens and pencils, apples and oranges are some good examples of substitute commodities.

Unrelated are commodities of a zero cross elasticity. For example, groceries and computers. An increase in the price of computers will have no effect on the quantity of groceries demanded.

Note: When commodities are considered from the point of a consumer budget, there is no such thing as unrelated commodities. As consumers spend more on one commodity, they must spend less on another.

Exhibit 5.14
Complements and Substitute Commodities

Complements		Substitutes	
Coffee	Sugar	Apples	Oranges
P↑	P: Same	P↑	P: Same
Q↓	Q↓	Q↓	Q↑

where P stands for price, and Q stands for quantity

Note: As the price of coffee increases while the price of sugar remains the same, consumers demand a smaller quantity of both coffee and sugar. Also, as the price of apples increases while the price of oranges remains the same, the quantity demanded of oranges increases.

To sum up, this chapter was a discussion of consumer theory. The first section was a discussion of the profile of the American consumer. The second section was a discussion of consumer choices and consumer opportunities and the way they jointly determine the consumption combinations demanded. The relationship between price and quantity demanded was also discussed and explanations of the law of demand were provided. The third section was a discussion of special topics of demand such as price elasticity, income elasticity and cross elasticity.

While studying consumer demand is the first step before a firm commits resources in the production of a commodity, producing it efficiently is the second. This is the topic of the next chapter.

5.4 Review

1. The consumer demand is negatively sloped because of the income and the substitution effects. The *income effect* refers to the fact that as price increases consumers cannot afford as much as before. They must reduce their consumption. The *substitution effect* refers to the fact that as the price of a commodity increases, substitute commodities become relatively less expensive and therefore more price appealing to consumers, which induces some of them to buy more of the substitutes.

2. An *indifference map* is an analytical tool economists have invented to describe consumers' preferences. Across the indifference map, there are consumption combinations which give the consumer equal satisfaction, consumption combinations which give the consumer more satisfaction, and consumption combinations which give the consumer less satisfaction. Since satisfaction increases as one moves to indifference curves further to the right, the consumer's objective is to climb as high as possible on the indifference map.

3. The *consumer budget* is another analytical tool economists use to describe consumer possibilities, i.e., commodity combinations which the consumer can afford given the commodity prices and the consumer's income. The consumer can afford any commodity combination on or within the budget line but nothing beyond it. An increase in the consumer's income expands consumption possibilities (the whole budget line shifts out to the right). Similarly a reduction in the price of one of the commodities twists the budget line outwards.

4. The indifference map and the consumer budget jointly determine the *consumer's equilibrium*, i.e., the commodity combination which gives the maximum satisfaction to the consumer and is yet affordable. To put it differently, the equilibrium combination balances consumers' desires and possibilities.

5. The concept of consumer equilibrium can be used to derive formally the inverse relationship between price and quantity demanded. As the price of one commodity, say apples, increases, the consumer budget twists inwards, and the consumer moves to a new equilibrium combination to the left of the old one, buying less of apples and more of oranges. This inverse relationship between the price of apples and the quantity demanded gives the individual demand curve.

6. The *market demand* curve for a product is the horizontal summation of all individual demand curves within a certain geographical region.

7. The *price elasticity* of demand is a measurement of the consumers' responsiveness to a given price change. For some commodities a small increase in price is sufficient to induce a large number of consumers to buy less of or to give up the idea of buying the commodity altogether (elastic demand). For other commodities even a large increase in price has only a small effect on the quantity demanded (inelastic demand).

8. The size of the price elasticity of demand is closely related to the revenues of a firm. A price elasticity of greater than 1 implies that a price reduction increases revenues. Conversely, a price increase lowers revenues. Similarly, a price inelastic demand implies that an increase in price will result in higher revenues.

9. *Income Elasticity of Demand* is a measurement of consumers' responsiveness to a given change in income. The concept of income elasticity is used to classify commodities into *normal* and *inferior*. Normal commodities are those of an income elasticity of more than 1. Inferior commodities are those of an income elasticity of less than one.

10. *Cross Elasticity of Demand* measures the impact of a change in price of commodity Y on the quantity demanded of commodity X. Based on the size of cross elasticity, commodities can be classified into three categories, substitutes, complements and unrelated: commodities with a positive cross-elasticity, called *substitutes*; commodities with a negative cross-elasticity, called *complements*; commodities with a zero cross elasticity, called *unrelated*.

Review Questions

1. On which items do American consumers spend most of their income?
2. What is an intuitive explanation of the law of demand?
3. What is the indifference map?
4. What is the consumer budget?
5. What is consumer equilibrium?
6. How do we derive the individual demand?
7. How do we derive the market demand?
8. What is price elasticity?
9. What does elastic demand mean?
10. What does inelastic demand mean?
11. Which factors determine the size of price elasticity?
12. How does price elasticity relate to company revenues?
13. What is income elasticity?
14. What are normal commodities?
15. What are inferior commodities?
16. What is cross elasticity?
17. What are complement commodities?

Real World Link 9: The Price of Roses on Valentine's Day

Key Concepts:

Increase in Demand: A shift of the whole market demand curve to the right caused by an increase in consumers' income, preference, or number of consumers in the market.

Increase in Quantity Supplied: An upward movement along the same supply curve caused by an increase in the price of the commodity.

Elasticity of Demand: A measure of consumers' response to a given price change. The larger the elasticity for a commodity, the more responsive the consumer will be.

Do you think that expressing your love is cheap? Try to buy roses on Valentine's Day for your loved ones. The price of roses on that day shoots up faster than the space shuttle. You may have to pay two or three times as much as you have to pay on a regular day. Why?

As with any other commodity, the price of roses is determined by demand and supply. Any change in the demand for and/or the supply of roses for a particular time of the year will affect the price of roses. There are two factors influencing the demand for roses on Valentine's Day. First, the demand for roses increases (shifts to the right) that day because more people want to buy roses. Second, people are very strict with their preference for roses, i.e., they would not take any substitute for roses. Daisies won't do. Orchids won't, either. In technical terms, this means a lower elasticity of demand for roses, i.e., the demand for roses "twists" to the right.

There is no good reason to believe that the supply curve of roses will increase on Valentine's Day. However, as the demand for roses increases and its elasticity becomes lower, suppliers will supply a larger quantity of roses in the market (a move along the same supply curve). As a result of the responses of both consumers and suppliers, the market price of roses shoots higher on Valentine's Day (see Exhibit 5.15).

Exhibit 5.15
The Price of Roses on Valentine's Day

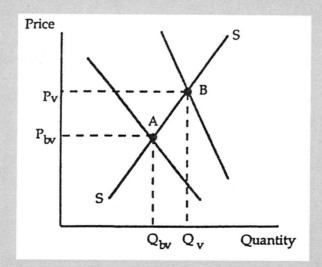

As a result of the responses to both consumers and suppliers, the market price of roses shoots higher on Valentine's Day.

Discussion Question

Why does the elasticity of demand for roses become lower on Valentine's Day? Does the supply curve for roses shift to the right on Valentine's Day?

Suggested Essay

What will happen to the price of marijuana if it becomes legal?

Real World Link 10: Linde: A Good Investment for an Inflationary Environment

Investors looking for opportunities to invest in assets that provide some protection for their money against inflation should take a close look at Linde PLC, in my opinion.

The global industrial gas giant has little competition in products with inelastic demand, which means that Linde has a great deal of pricing power in both good times and bad times and can offset rising costs on the supply chain.

"LIN was able to realize meaningful price gains even in the down volume Covid-period last year," says Barclays Equity Research. "Now that volumes are coming back, the sequential data shows an uptick in pricing. The outlier is APAC, where price increases have been +1% for four quarters in a row even as volume has grown 7% and 10% over the last two quarters. We believe Linde can increase the rate of price increases per quarter as the year progresses more than offset cost inflation and pushing margins even higher."

Price hikes, in turn, help generate a good stream of earnings and free cash flow to reward its stockholders with dividend hikes and share repurchases.

On May 6, Linde reported the 9th consecutive quarter of what it calls "beat and raised," beating consensus earnings per share estimates by $0.24 and raising full-year guidance by $0.50.

Societe General is also bullish on Linde. They point to soaring margins and cash flow as primary reasons. Q1 adjusted Ebit grew 25% year-over-year to $1.688 billion and adjusted EPS rose 32% to $2.49. Q1 operating cash flow grew 57% to $2.109 billion, with free cash flow up 148% to $1.347 billion, representing 18.6% of sales. The ratio of operating cash flow to Ebitda was 87% vs. a five-year average in the mid-60s.

Solid free cash flow has allowed the company to raise its dividend every year since 2018, when it merged with Praxair, Inc. This strong dividend will likely be able to "protect" shareholder income from inflation by offering cash returns that will hopefully not be surpassed by inflation numbers.

Then there's also Linde's $5 billion share repurchase program announced on Jan. 25, providing even more downward protection if higher inflation pushes the value of the company's shares lower.

The only problem for me is that it seems Wall Street has already priced in Linde's prospects. At $301, its shares trade well above the GF Value of $216.61. Thus, if I were a new investor, I might wait for a better entry point, though I am comfortable holding the shares I do own.

Source: *Gurufocus*

Real World Link 11: Is Amazon Making a Big Strategic Mistake?

Of all big strategic mistakes leaders of fast-growing corporations make, one stands out: Taking the customer for granted. Blinded by growth, these leaders assume that their products and services are unique and indispensable, so customers will always be there to buy them at any price.

This mind-set may have worked in the old days when corporations and managers were at the center of the economic universe. But it doesn't apply in today's world, where customers occupy that position.

Aside from a few exceptions, products are no longer either unique nor indispensable. Customers will search elsewhere for value, when corporations fail to meet their expectations or become greedy.

Amazon.com may be making this strategic mistake.

For years, the company has been building warehouses and distribution centers, and expanding its subscription customer base by keeping the price for its product and services low. That's how it amassed close to $75 billion in revenues at razor thin margins (see table).

Amazon.com versus Wal-Mart Stores

Company	Amazon.com	Wal-Mart Stores
Forward PE	83	13.54
Profit Margin	0.37%	3.62%
Operating Margin	1.00%	5.93%
Return on Assets (ttm)	1.28%	8.47%
Total Debt/Equity	62.96	77.27
Revenue (ttm)	74.45B	474.88B

Wall Street, fixated on Amazon's fast growth and sizable sales, has taken notice—with the stock trading at a forward PE of 83, six times higher than that of Wal-Mart.

What about the razor thin margins?

No problem, say Wall Street analysts. The assumption here is that Amazon can raise margins at any time—by raising prices.

But a recent survey of Amazon's prime customers showed a big decline in membership would occur, should Amazon raise the price of its service.

This means that Amazon.com runs the risk of facing the opposite problem from that which eToys had, back in the late 1990s—building too much capacity.

One year, shortly before Christmas, eToys set up a web page, selling toys. But the company didn't have warehouses to stack inventory and fill orders. It had to rely on third party suppliers, who didn't have enough inventories either.

That was certainly a recipe for disaster, as eToys failed to fill orders before Christmas arrived. The following year, eToys built warehouses and stacked up the toys, but Santa Claus didn't bring sufficient orders to keep eToys in business.

By contrast, Amazon.com followed a different strategy. First, it built the warehouses—it stacked the books, and filled the orders. Second, it launched a shrewd strategy of promotions (discounts and free shipping) that allowed the company to attain economies of scale. Third, it branched out to all sorts of merchandise, to attain economies of scope—sometimes by signing up on-line affiliates. Fourth, it expanded into the content development business, by partnering with first time and recently with experienced authors.

Fifth, it jumped into the electronic device market, which provided a vehicle to sell electronic content and other online merchandise.

In a sense, Amazon.com has been applying a number of strategies regular companies have deployed for years, including Standard Oil, the famous monopoly of the 1880s. Amazon.com has been expanding both horizontally and vertically, raising barriers that keep competition off its turf, as other successful web-based companies have been doing, including Microsoft, Google, and Oracle.

But with customers resisting a price hike, Amazon may find itself with too much capacity in the face of slowing demand, extinguishing already thin profit margins.

Source: *Forbes Magazine*

Homework 5

1. Define and explain the concept of Indifference Map.

2. Define and explain the concept of Consumer Budget Constraint.

3. Define and explain the concept of Consumer Equilibrium.

4. How does Rationing affect consumer welfare?

5. What is Price Elasticity?

6. What determines the size of Price Elasticity?

7. What is Income Elasticity? How is it used?

8. What is Cross Price Elasticity? How is it used?

Chapter 6

PRODUCTION AND COSTS

Preview

Chapter Five took a closer look at the demand side of the product market. This chapter takes a closer look at production and costs. The first part of the chapter is a discussion of the characteristics of production; the chapter begins with the discussion of the importance of productivity for competition; it continues with the definition of production and the discussion of certain characteristics of production, both in the short run and long. The second part is a discussion of the characteristics of production costs; the distinction between explicit and implicit costs; and the distinction between short-term and long-term costs.

Introduction

In 1965, Zenith, a pioneer in color TV technology, failed to expand production in line with the explosive demand for color TVs. As a result, Zenith and the United States gave away the color TV market for good. In 1985, Apple Computer failed to integrate computer design and manufacturing. As a result, Apple Computer lost business to competition and its stock tumbled. In the first quarter of 1990, Xicor, a small semiconductor company in California, failed to keep up with demand for computer chips because of production problems. Xicor's performance tumbled, from a significant profit a year earlier to a significant loss. By contrast to Zenith, Apple Computer and Xicor, Compaq, Intel, and Southwest Airlines have managed to introduce a variety of new products at low cost, and so keep up with consumer demand. Reflecting their successful strategies, the stock price of all three companies has taken off, rewarding their stockholders.

What is productivity? How is it measured? What is production? What is cost? These are some of the questions we address in this chapter.

The remainder of the chapter is in six parts. The first part discusses the problems associated with the definition and the measurement of productivity. The second and third parts are a discussion of the characteristics of short-run production. The third part is a discussion of long-run production. The fifth part is a discussion of production costs. The chapter ends with a review.

6.1 Productivity: Problems of Definition and Measurement

Though a popular concept, productivity is hard to define and measure. In theory, productivity is a measure of how efficiently economic resources are allocated. In practice, productivity is a ratio of output divided by different inputs (resources): output/labor, capital/labor, land/labor, and output divided by a weighted average of all resources. This way, one can calculate the output per worker per hour, day, month, and year; the output per unit of capital or land. Calculating productivity can be a rather complex task, especially when a company produces hundreds, even thousands of commodities and employs a variety of nonhomogeneous inputs. To overcome these problems, one must be imaginative and creative. To measure productivity in the airline industry, for instance, one can look at employees per aircraft, passengers per employee, and cost per available seat mile. Based on these definitions, in 1993, Southwest (LUV) was the most efficient company (see Exhibits 6.1A and 6.1B); and has delivered a great deal of value to its stockholders (see Exhibit 6.1C).

Exhibit 6.1
A. Airline Productivity: Cost Per Available Seat Mile

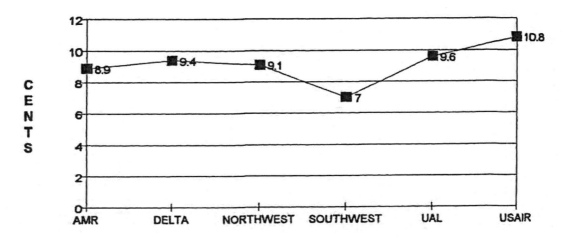

Source: Adapted from *Fortune*, May 8, 1994.

B. Airline Productivity: Passenger Per Employee

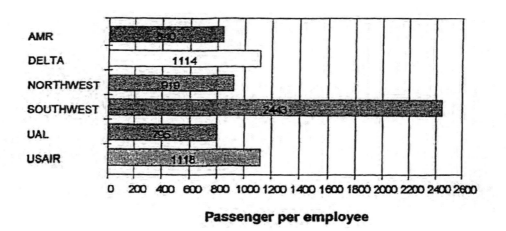

Source: Adapted from *Fortune*, May 8, 1994.

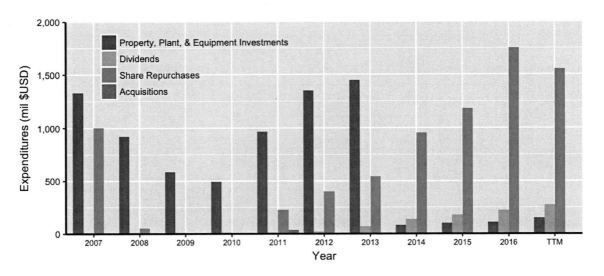

Exhibit 6.C
How LUV Creates Value for Shareholders

Source: Seekingalpha.com

6.2 Production: General Considerations

As we have stated several times so far, commodities do not exist for free, hanging from the trees of a paradise land. They are produced with the use of economic resources (inputs). In modern societies the production of commodities is organized by firms, i.e., decision entities that pull economic resources (inputs) together and turn them into commodities (output). IBM brings together engineers and other workers who, with the use of the assembly lines and the appropriate materials, produce computers. A farming company, employing labor and using other inputs such as sheds, tractors and land, produces wheat. What is the relationship between production and economic resources? How does production vary when some of the resources vary as compared to when all resources vary?

Definition. Production is a technical and social process that transforms economic resources (inputs) into means that satisfy human needs, i.e., goods and services (outputs). To simplify matters, economists assume away the former aspect of production and take it just as a technical relationship between economic resources and output. Formally,

$$q = F (K, L, E, O)$$

where q stands for production or output,

    K stands for capital input

    L stands for labor input,

    E stands for land input, and

    O stands for other resources.

For example, in the case of IBM, output would consist of the number of computers of a particular model the company produces during a specified period; capital input would consist of the assembly lines as well as any other machine or equipment used during the production; labor input would consist of the number of man-hours employed.

Production and costs can be analyzed from two perspectives, the short run and the long run (see Exhibit 6.2). In short run, some economic resources remain fixed throughout different production levels, while other resources are variable, i.e., they change along with output. In the long run, all economic resources are variable. To comprehend this distinction, you may think of the production process of a bakery. Which resources are fixed and which resources are variable in the short run? Obviously, the physical capital, that is, the flour mixing machines, the ovens, the cooling and packaging machines, etc., do not change along with output, they are all part of fixed resources. By contrast, the amount of flour used, the energy consumed, and the number of hours employed, all are variable factors. Production cannot expand indefinitely with just one input, however. Ultimately, production can expand only through the expansion of all inputs, something that is feasible only in the long run.

Exhibit 6.2
Short Run versus Long Run Production

	Period	
Inputs	Short Run	Long Run
Labor	Variable	Variable
Capital	Fixed	Variable
Technology	Fixed	Variable
Land	Fixed	Variable

In the short run, all economic resources but labor are fixed. In the long run all resources are variable.

Note: The time length is not so relevant in drawing the line between short run and long run. What is rather more relevant is whether the firm is in a position to vary all or some of the employed resources along with output.

6.3 Production in the Short Run: Total, Average, and Marginal Products

As we have already stated, in the short run some inputs remain fixed while others vary along with output. Conventionally, economists assume that capital is the fixed input and labor is the variable one. This allows for a further simplification of the production function, which can be rewritten as follows:

$$q = F (L)$$

In general, production is in a direct relationship with the size of the labor input. The more labor the firm employs the larger the output. However, the labor input-output relationship is not a straight line; i.e., equal changes in labor input do not always result in equal changes in output. To comprehend the features of production, economists use the concepts of Total Output, Average Output, and Marginal Output.

Total Product, Average Product, and Marginal Product

Total product of labor (TPL) is the maximum output that can be attained through different labor input levels. To understand how total output varies along with labor input, we return to our earlier example of the bakery and discuss with numbers how the output of bread varies along with labor input (see Exhibit 6.3). As can be seen from that exhibit, at low levels of labor input the production of bread increases fast; then, as labor input continues to increase, production increases at a slow pace, and ultimately, at higher and higher labor input levels, production may even decline. Why? To answer this question, we must first discuss the concepts of average and marginal products.

Average product of labor (APL) or average productivity is the output per labor input unit (see Exhibits 6.3A and 6.4); the ratio of total output to the labor input:

APL = Total output (q)/ Labor input (L)

Marginal product of labor (MPL) or marginal productivity is the contribution of each additional labor unit to the total output (see Exhibits 6.3A and 6.4); the ratio of the change in total output to the change in the labor input:

MPL = Change in total output/change in the labor input

Exhibit 6.3
Short-Run Bread Production
A. Short-Run Bread Production Schedule

Labor Input	Total Product	Average Product	Marginal Product
1	4	4.00	—
2	12	6.00	8
3	22	7.33	10
4	31	7.75	9
5	38	7.60	7
6	43	7.17	5
7	46	6.57	3
8	43	5.37	−3

The total production schedule is a numeric presentation of the relationship between labor input and total output. At low levels of labor input, the production of bread increases at a fast pace; then, as labor input continues to increase, production increases at a slower pace, and, ultimately, at higher labor input levels, production may even decline. For example, as the labor input increases from one unit to two, output increases from four to twelve. Then as labor input increases from two units to three, production increases from twelve units to twenty two, etc.

B. The Short-Run Bread Production Curve

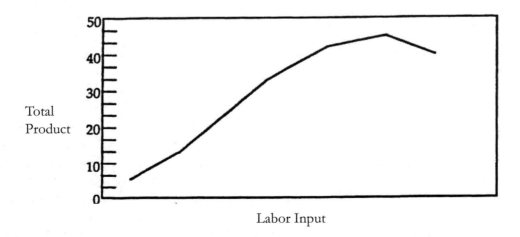

The total production curve is a graphic presentation of the relationship between labor input and output. It describes in another way the relationship between labor input and total output. At low levels of labor input, production increases fast, gradually slowing down and even declining at higher levels of labor input.

Exhibit 6.4
Average and Marginal Productivity

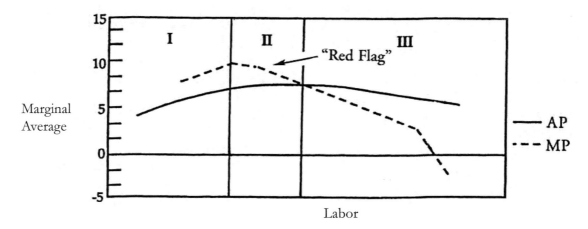

The average productivity curve demonstrates how the per unit output varies along with labor input. The marginal productivity curve demonstrates how the marginal product varies along with labor input. Both curves increase at the beginning and then, after they attain a maximum, decline.

The Three Stages of Production

A close look at the production curve reveals that production follows three stages: the first stage when production rises very fast with labor; the second stage when production begins to slow down; and the third stage when production slow down accelerates. These three stages can be better identified if one looks at the graphs of average and marginal productivity. In the first stage, both marginal and average productivity rise. In the second stage, marginal productivity begins to decline, but average productivity continues rising. In the third stage, both marginal and average productivity decline.

The Most Important Limit of Short-Term Production: The Law of Diminishing Marginal Productivity

Output cannot be increased forever with the same capital and land. It runs into limitations reflected in lower marginal productivity. Additional workers are less and less productive. This remark which dates back to the writings of Robert Malthus suggests that without capital and land expansion productivity will drop and costs will rise. But let us see the law of diminishing returns.

The Law of Diminishing Marginal Productivity

The Law of Diminishing Marginal Productivity states that in any production process there is an employment level beyond which successive units of labor added to the fixed factors of production contribute less and less to the total output. This law, dating back to the times of classical economists, has important implications for the limitations of increasing production through the increase of one factor alone. Pointing to this law, Malthus, a pessimist classical economist, came to the conclusion that, one day, the world would come to starvation. As the population in his times grew faster than in our day and agriculture was backward, he claimed that, as a result of the law of diminishing returns, successive additions of labor to the existing land would contribute less and less to agricultural production. As a result, food production would increase at a slower pace than the population, resulting in lower per capita production and ultimately in starvation. But what is the reasoning behind this law? Let us return to our earlier example of bread production and see what happened to total output as more and more laborers are added to the existing machines. In the beginning, when there are a few workers and many machines, it is plausible that successive workers contribute more and more to the total output. However, as more and more workers are added to the machines, the working place becomes crowded, too many workers try to work with too few machines; it is more difficult for workers to coordinate their efforts. When one worker cuts in front of another, the production slows down. In an extreme case of overcrowding total production may even decline.

Note: First, the law of diminishing returns is not a law within the strict definition of the concept, but rather a common facet of most production processes. Second, the labor input level beyond which the law applies may vary from one production process to another. Third, the law applies only in the short run, when some factors of production remain fixed, and not in the long run, when all factors vary, and this is why Malthus' predictions have not, generally, been fulfilled. With an expansion in the fixed factors of production, the marginal and the average products increase (see Exhibit 6.5). Because of mechanization and the extensive use of fertilizers, many advanced developed countries, including the U.S., can produce more than they need to feed their people employing less than 5 percent of their labor force. Nevertheless, there are still countries today that, due to ecological, environmental, and social constraints, have failed to modernize their agriculture, and their people are sentenced to starvation.

Experiencing Diminishing Returns: The Case of XYZ Depository Company

XYZ Depository Company is in the business of accepting stock and bond certificates for safe keeping. Instead of keeping security certificates at home, investors can deposit the certificates with company XYZ until they decide to sell them. In other words, company XYZ operates like a bank. Instead of accepting cash funds for deposit, it accepts securities.

As stock certificates must be counted, validated, stored, and retrieved, XYZ's business is labor intensive. The rapid growth of financial transactions in the 1970s and the 1980s brought an explosion in XYZ's business. As more stocks and bonds were traded, more certificates had to be counted, validated, stored, and retrieved. How did the company handle the new business? In the beginning, the company hired more workers. In fact, the number of employees of the company increased from 350 in 1975 to 3,274 in 1990. But as more and more employees made use of the same facilities, production become overcrowded, "bursting," to use the term of an executive. How did the company solve the problem? By expanding office and storage facilities and by implementing a new technique called Account Analysis.

The Importance of Productivity for a Company's Performance

As stated earlier, productivity is an important measure of efficiency at the company, industry, and economy level. In general, efficiency translates to lower costs, higher sales, and higher profits. For practical purposes, companies with productivity above the industry average can be considered as efficient, and so are economies with productivity level above the international productivity average. Conversely, companies and economies with productivity below the corresponding industry and international productivity averages are considered as inefficient. Take for instance the steel industry. National Steel and LTV are both inefficient. In 1988 they had lowest productivity levels in the steel industry (see Exhibit 6.6). Employment of labor beyond limitations, low investment in physical capital, outdated technology, and bad management are some of the factors that explain such low productivity levels.

Exhibit 6.5
An Expansion in the Fixed Factors Increases
Marginal and Average Productivity

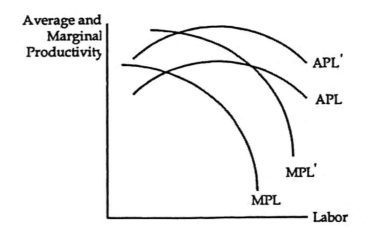

An increase in the fixed factors shifts the average and marginal productivity curves to the right. With more fixed costs per worker, each worker is more productive.

Exhibit 6.6
National Steel's Productivity Is Lower than Its Competitors

Productivity in the most efficient hot-rolled, flat-rolled steel plant of each producer:

Company	Plant	Hours of Labor per Ton of Steel Produced
USX	Gary Works	3.1
Inland Steel	Chicago	3.2
Bethlehem Steel	Burns Harbor	3.3
LTV Steel	Indiana Harbor	3.5
National Steel	Great Lakes	3.6

Source: Adapted from the WEFA Group, as published in the *New York Times*, January 1, 1989.

To sum up, output expansion through a greater use of labor runs into limitations: additional workers contribute less and less to the total output. Only expansion of all economic resources can overcome this limitation, a strategy feasible only in the long term.

6.4 Production in Long Run: Returns to Scale

The law of diminishing returns, which we have just discussed, refers to the relationship between changes in one input (labor) and changes in total output. Another interesting production feature that economists investigate is the ratio between changes in output and a proportional change in all inputs, called returns to scale.

There are three types of returns to scale, increasing returns to scale, constant returns to scale, and decreasing returns to scale.

Increasing Returns to Scale. A production process exhibits increasing returns to scale if a doubling of all inputs results in more than doubling of output (see Exhibit 6.7).

Constant Returns to Scale. A production process exhibits constant returns to scale if a doubling of all inputs results in a doubling of output.

Decreasing Returns to Scale. A production process exhibits decreasing returns to scale if a doubling of all inputs results in less than doubling of output (see Exhibit 6.8).

Note: The concept of returns to scale applies when all inputs are changed by the same proportion; i.e., if we double or triple labor we must also double capital, land, etc. In other words, returns to scale follow the relationship between the firm size and costs.

Exhibit 6.7
Retailing Displays Increasing Returns
to Scale: The Bigger the Better

Company	Revenues	Employees	Three-Year Average ROE	Three-Year Average Sales Growth
Wal-Mart	$15.9 billion	183,000	26.9%	35.6%
Jamesway	$701 million	9,400	11.3%	13.8%

Source: Standard and Poor's data as published in *Business Week*, March 27, 1989.

Note: Sales growth may have to do with other factors such as marketing strategy, location, etc. Statistics should, therefore, be interpreted with caution.

Exhibit 6.8
Steel Industry Displays Decreasing Returns
to Scale: Bigger Is Not Better

Company	Revenues	Employees	Three-Year Average ROE	Three-Year Average Sales Growth
LTV	$7.6 billion	48,200	–11.6%	–1.2%
Birmingham	$701 million	1,830	18.3%	55.8%

Source: Standard and Poor's data as published in *Business Week*, March 27, 1989.

How to Achieve Economies of Scale:
Technological Innovations, and Mergers and Acquisitions

Economies of scales are gains in cost efficiency associated with a large output size, and a mass-market, where the additional output can be sold. A mass-market comes with a lower unit cost and price—the lower the price, the larger the size of the market; and the larger the size of the market, the greater the production scale and the competitive edge. In the late 19th century steel industry, Andrew Carnegie could improve efficiency by mass-producing steel, and this translated into lower production cost and lower steel prices. In the early 20th century automobile industry, Henry Ford improved efficiency by mass-producing his T-model car in assembly lines. In the late 20th century retail industry, Sam Walton could improve efficiency with large retail outlets and volume sales, which again translated to lower costs and lower prices for consumers. Mass production of the T-model, for instance, allowed Ford to cut car prices from $850 in 1908 to $360 by 1916. Mass production of kerosene allowed Standard Oil Corporation to cut kerosese production costs from 2.5 cents in 1879 to 0.4 cents by 1885. Mass production allowed German chemical producers BASF, Bayer, and Hoechst to cut the price of Alizarin from DM200 per kilogram in 1878 to DM9 by 1886, underselling foreign competitors.

But how can companies achieve large scale production? What does it take? Sometimes, it takes technological innovations that replace the existing production process with a radically different, more efficient one. Andrew Carnegie's Bessmer mill did exactly that. It produced larger quantities of steel with fewer resources. Other times, it takes mergers with, or acquisitions of, competitors and the elimination of duplicate divisions and departments, producing a larger output with fewer resources. In the late 19th century oil industry, John D. Rockefeller expanded the scale of his company's operations by acquiring competitors or driving them out of business. In the first quarter of the 20th century, William C. Durrant merged twenty-five smaller automobile companies, including Buick, with Oldsmobile and Cadillac to create a larger General Motors. In the 1980s and the 1990s, banks expanded the scale of their operations by merging with other banks and financial service companies. Chemical merged with Chase and J. P. Morgan, and Citibank with Travelers. The merger between Chase and Chemical bank in the mid-nineties is a case in point. By merging divisions and eliminating duplication, the two companies eliminated 12,500 jobs. In the early 2000s, computer hardware makers used mergers and acquisitions to expand the scale of their operations while eliminating product duplication at the same time. The merger of Compaq with Hewlett-Packard allowed the two companies to eliminate a number of product duplications including the elimination of HP Jornada and Omnibook, and Compaq's Itanium-based servers. This, in turn, allowed the new company to save $0.9 billion in sales costs, $1.6 billion in operating expenses, and $0.5 billion in R&D costs.

6.5 Production and Costs

As we have seen, production depends on the use of economic resources, i.e.. labor, capital, land, etc. Economic resources may be *internal*, company owned, or *external*, purchased in the market. For any level of output the firm must commit its own resources and, in addition, pay a sum of money for resources purchased from third parties, i.e., wages for labor, interest payments for borrowed capital, rent for buildings, etc. Thus, production is inevitably linked to costs. Needless to say, precise knowledge of production costs is very important for evaluating a firm's efficiency and market performance. How do firms measure costs? What items should be included as costs? Depending on whether one talks to accountants or to economists, there are different answers to these questions. As bookkeepers are responsible for reporting to tax authorities, accountants are usually interested in cost of external resources that can be easily identified and recorded. *Accounting costs* include payments the firm makes to third parties for the purchase of economic resources. Wages, payments for energy and raw materials, interest payments, etc., are examples of accounting costs. As economists are interested in the scarcity of resources, they consider the opportunity cost of all resources: *economic costs* include the opportunity cost of all resources, external and internal. Imputed rent, imputed interest, and imputed salaries are examples of "payments" for internal resources that economists add to accounting costs. In other words, economic costs are more broad than accounting costs; they include both payments to third parties and "payments" for company-owned resources.

As we discussed in the first chapter, opportunity cost is the cost associated with choice. Committing economic resources to a particular production process takes them away from the next best alternative. When a farming company decides to grow wheat on a particular piece of land, it forgoes the next best alternative, which, for example, could be growing rice. To elaborate on the conceptual difference between accounting and economic approaches to costs, we distinguish between explicit and implicit costs:

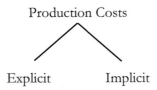

Explicit Costs

Explicit costs are the same as accounting costs. They include payments for the use of external resources, i.e., resources that are owned by third parties. Wages, interest payments, payments for raw and energy materials are all examples of explicit costs.

Implicit Costs

Implicit costs are imputed payments for the use of internal resources, i.e., resources that are owned by the firm. Implicit costs are not part of accounting costs but they are part of economic costs. "Payments" for raw materials, buildings, labor, etc. provided by the owners of the company are all part of implicit costs. An important item that is considered as part of implicit costs is normal profit.

Normal Profit—Opportunity Cost of Capital

Normal profit refers to the minimum return required to commit capital to a particular type of business. By definition, this minimum return is the capital return on the best forgone alternative, i.e., the opportunity cost of capital. To understand this rather tricky concept, let us assume that an entrepreneur has a given amount of capital that can be committed to any of the three business alternatives:

Alternatives	Return (%)
A: Open a Restaurant	15
B: Open a Flower Shop	10
C: Open a Money Market Account	8

Given this schedule, it does not take much to realize that the best alternative for the entrepreneur's capital is alternative A. Now let us assume that the return on alternative A drops down to 12 percent. Would the entrepreneur still stay with alternative A? Obviously, he is still better off than alternatives B and C. However, if the return on A continues dropping and reaches a level below 10 percent he is better with alternative B. Thus, the opportunity cost of his capital while in alternative A is 10 percent, i.e. the return he could gain in the next best alternative. Similarly, the opportunity cost while in alternative B is 8 percent

Note: Paradoxical as it may sound, normal profit is part of business costs. It is a reward for the entrepreneur's capital committed in advance to production of a particular commodity. To understand this distinction between explicit and implicit costs, let us take a look at a company that manufactures tables. In producing a given volume of tables, which costs are explicit and which are implicit? Following our earlier distinction, explicit costs include money the firm must pay for the use of resources owned by third parties. Rent (if the company does not own the required building facilities), salaries, raw materials, etc. Implicit costs include imputed salaries, i.e. salaries that should be paid to the entrepreneur in case he offers his labor services at a particular work post as a manager, as a consultant, etc. Implicit costs also include normal profits, i.e. the minimum amount of return required to commit capital in a particular business.

In summary, costs can be classified as accounting costs and economic costs. Accounting costs include just explicit costs, while economic costs include both explicit and implicit costs. *Note:* Since normal profit is part of economic costs but not of accounting costs, the former will always be larger than the latter (see Exhibit 6.9).

Economic versus Accounting Profit

Corresponding to the distinction between accounting costs and economic costs, there is a distinction between economic profits and accounting profits. The former is the difference between total revenues and economic costs, while the latter is the difference between total revenues and accounting costs. Two things follow from this distinction. First, economic profit is always smaller than accounting profit. Second, in economics, zero profit does not necessarily imply that the firm breaks even. The firm still makes a normal profit. To understand the distinction between explicit and implicit costs as well as that between economic and accounting profits, we look at the accounting books of the case of a hypothetical restaurant (see Exhibit 6.9).

Exhibit 6.9
Explicit and Implicit Costs and Profits

Mr. Smith's and Mr. Brown's Pancake Breakfast Place Statement
of Economic Performance for Oct. 1987

Total Revenues		$80,000
Less Explicit Costs		$72,000
(Materials, Energy, Salaries to Employees, etc.)		
Accounting Profit		$8,000
Implicit Costs		
Imputed Salaries	$3,000	
Imputed Rent	$2,000	
Normal Profit	$200	$5,200
Economic Profit		$2,800

As can be inferred from this exhibit, because of the implicit costs, economic profits are below accounting profits.

In conclusion, high accounting profits does not necessarily mean high economic profits. There may even be cases of firms which own a lot of economic resources and show high accounting profits. If the objective of the company is to maximize returns on all economic resources, the firm may be better off closing down and renting their own resources to third parties.

Bearing these comments in mind, from now on whenever we talk about costs in economics we will be referring to economic costs, i.e., the sum of explicit and implicit costs. But let us look at some other important cost classifications.

Short-Run versus Long-Run Costs

Corresponding to the distinction between short-run and long-run productions, costs can be distinguished as short-run and long-run:

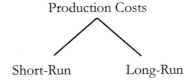

Short-Run Costs

In discussing short-run costs, economists distinguish among total, average, and marginal costs:

Total Cost (TC): The dollar value of all economic resources required to produce successive quantities of a commodity (see Exhibits 6.10A and 6.10B).

Total cost includes fixed costs and variable costs.

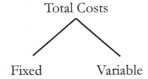

Fixed Costs (FC): Costs that do not change along with output (see Exhibits 6.10A and 6.10C). Rent, insurance on buildings, interest payments, salaries of top management are examples of fixed costs.

Variable Costs (VC): Costs that do change along with output (see Exhibits 6.10A and 6.10D). Wages, payments for energy and raw materials, insurance on merchandise are examples of variable costs.

Returning to our example of the factory that makes tables, which costs are fixed, and which are variable?

Fixed costs would include:

*   Rent, insurance on buildings
*   Interest payments on borrowed capital
*   Fire Insurance

Variable costs would include:

*   Salary payments
*   Energy, e.g., utilities
*   Spending on raw materials
*   Insurance on merchandise
*   Insurance on employees

To understand the special features of short-run costs, we must further distinguish between average costs and marginal cost.

Average total cost is the cost per unit of output (see Exhibits 6.10 and 6.12). Formally, it can be defined as the ratio of the total cost to the total output:

$$ATC = TC/Q$$

Corresponding to the distinction between fixed and variable costs, there is the distinction between average fixed cost and average variable cost.

Average total fixed cost (AFTC) is the fixed cost per unit of output (see Exhibit 6.10). Formally, average total fixed cost can be defined as the ratio of total fixed cost to total output:

$$ATFC = TFC/Q$$

Average total variable cost is the variable cost per unit of output (see Exhibits 6.10 and 6.11). Formally, it can be defined as the ratio of the total variable cost to the total output:

$$ATVC = TVC/Q$$

Marginal cost is the contribution of each additional output unit to the total cost (see Exhibits 6.10 and 6.12). Formally, it can be defined as the ratio of the change in total cost to the change in the total output:

$$MC = \text{Change in total cost}/\text{Change in total output}$$

Exhibit 6.10
A. Short-Run Cost Schedules

The Short-Run Total Average and Marginal Cost Curves

Output (q)	Total Fixed Cost (TFC)	Total Variable Cost (TVC)	Total Cost (TC)	Average Fixed Cost (AFC)	Average Variable Cost (AVC)	Average Total Cost (ATC)	Marginal Cost (MC)
0	$200	—	$200	—	—	—	—
1	200	$170	370	$200.00	$170.00	$370.00	$170
2	200	320	520	100.00	160.00	260.00	150
3	200	450	650	66.00	150.00	216.00	130
4	200	560	760	50.00	140.00	190.00	110
5	200	690	890	40.00	138.00	178.00	130
6	200	840	1040	33.33	140.00	173.33	150
7	200	1010	1210	28.57	144.28	174.28	170
8	200	1220	1420	25.00	152.50	177.50	210
9	200	1480	1680	22.22	164.44	186.66	260
10	200	1740	1940	20.00	174.00	194.00	350

The cost schedules are numerical presentations of the relationship between output and costs. For example, the total cost schedule (columns one and four) displays the relationship between output and total cost. In general, as total output increases total cost increases too. For example, as output increases from one unit to two, total cost increases from $370 to $520, and so on.

B. The Short-Run Total Cost Curve

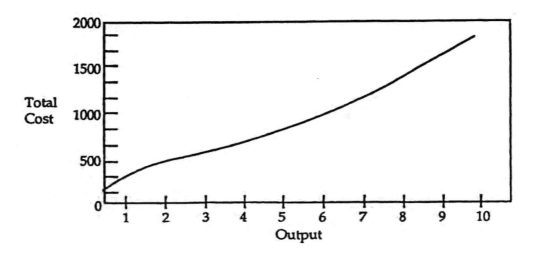

The total cost curve is a graphic representation of the relationship between output and total cost. In general, as the output increases, total cost increases too. For example, as the output increases from one unit to two, total cost increases from $370 to $520.

C. Total Fixed Cost

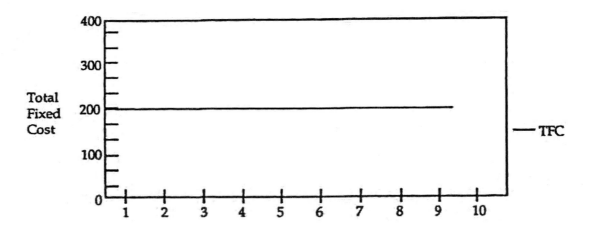

The total fixed cost is a straight line parallel to the horizontal axis. It shows that fixed costs remain at $200 at any output level.

D. Total Variable Cost

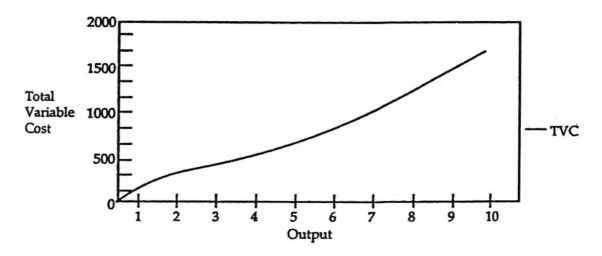

In general, total variable cost increases with output. As output increases from one unit to two, variable cost increases from $170 to $320, etc.

Exhibit 6.11
Average Total and Average Variable Costs

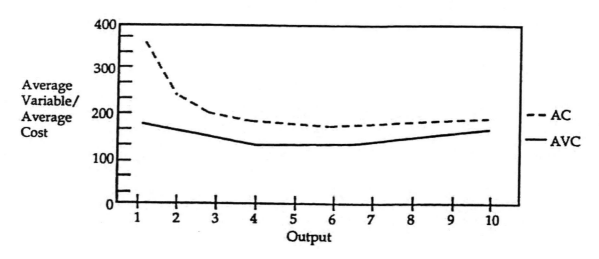

Both average total and average variable costs decrease to begin with; after attaining a minimum, they start to increase.

Exhibit 6.12
Average Total and Marginal Costs

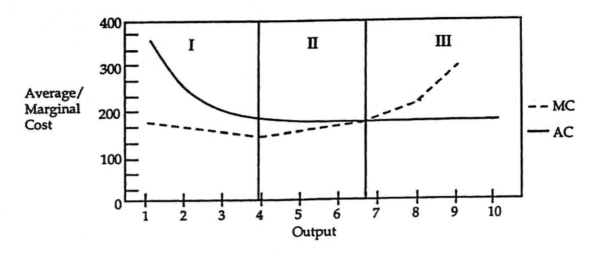

Both average total and marginal costs decrease first, and then, after attaining a minimum, they start to increase. Note, however, that marginal and average costs intersect at the point where the latter is at a minimum. You should further notice that corresponding to the three production stages, average and marginal cost undergo three stages. In the first stage, both average and marginal cost decline. In the second stage, marginal cost begins to rise, but average cost continues to decline. In the third stage, they both rise.

Exhibit 6.13
The Relationship Between Marginal Cost
and Marginal Product

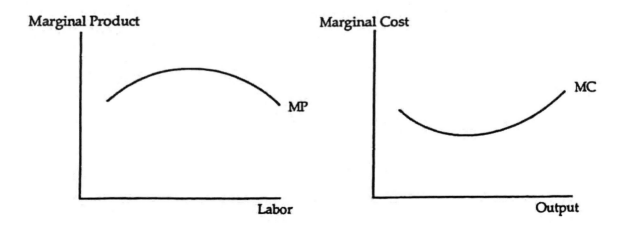

Marginal product and marginal cost move in opposite directions. As marginal product increases, marginal cost decreases, and vice versa. In this way, marginal product and cost serve as signals as to what is going to happen to the average product and the average cost.

The Relationship between Marginal Cost and Marginal Product

Since costs are associated with production, there is a correspondence between the characteristics of production and those of costs. Here we point to the relation between marginal product and marginal cost. As you may recall, marginal product increases to begin with and then, after attaining a maximum, declines. This shape of marginal product is responsible for the shape of marginal cost. As marginal product increases, production increases at a fast rate, and therefore marginal cost decreases. Subsequently, as the marginal product declines, the marginal cost increases (see Exhibit 6.13).

After we have reviewed the characteristics of short-term costs, i.e. costs that assume that some economic resources are fixed, we move on to the discussion of long-term costs, i.e., costs that assume that all resources are variable.

Long-Run Costs

All cost curves we have drawn thus far refer to short-run costs, i.e., costs during a period when at least some inputs remain fixed. A similar set of curves could be drawn for the long run, i.e., during a period that all inputs are variable. Here, we focus only on the long-run average and marginal costs that are most relevant in the firm's profit maximization decisions.

The Long-Run Average Cost Curve

The shape of the long-run average cost curve depends on two factors, (i) the kind of resource market the firm is faced with, (ii) the kind of returns to scale that the production process exhibits. Assuming that the firm is faced with competitive resource markets, and therefore with a fixed price of resources, we can distinguish among three shapes of long-run average cost that correspond to increasing, constant, and decreasing returns to scale.

Increasing Long-Run Cost. Under decreasing returns to scale, average long-run cost increases along with output: a larger output is associated with a higher cost (see Exhibit 6.14).

Constant Long-Run Cost. Under constant returns to scale, average long-run cost is independent of the size of output: cost remains the same throughout different levels of output (see Exhibit 6.14).

Decreasing Long-Run Cost. Under increasing returns of scale, average long-run cost decreases along with output: a larger output is associated with a lower cost (see Exhibit 6.14).

Which of the three cases represents the real world? In general, economists agree that at early stages of expansions a firm experiences economies of scale and costs, therefore, decline, but as expansion continues there is a turning point beyond which the firm experiences decreasing returns to scale and therefore cost increases (see Exhibit 6.14).

Note: The long-run average cost curve is the envelope of all short-run cost curves, something that reflects the fact that in the long run the firm has more choices to attain cost levels below the short-run ones.

Exhibit 6.14
Long-Run Average Costs under Different Assumptions about Returns to Scale

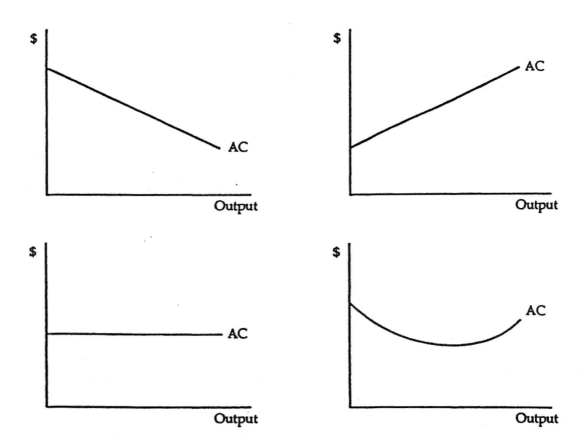

Long-run cost can take any one of the above shapes. In the first, upper left case, reflecting increasing returns to scale, long-run costs are decreasing. In the second, upper right case, long-run costs are increasing, reflecting decreasing returns to scale. In the third, lower left case, long-run costs are decreasing at first and then, after attaining a minimum, start to increase, reflecting a compromise among increasing, constant, and decreasing returns.

Exhibit 6.15
Long-Run Marginal Cost

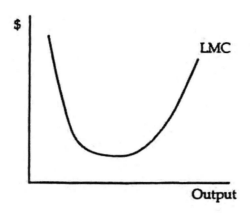

The long-run marginal cost gives the cost of producing an additional output unit, when all inputs are variable.

The Long-Run Marginal Cost

As with long-run average cost, long-run marginal cost also depends on the assumptions one makes about the resource markets the firm is faced with, as well as about the type of returns-to-scale that characterize production. In general economists draw the marginal cost curve as it appears in the Exhibit 6.15.

To wrap up the discussion, in this chapter we reviewed the characteristics of production and costs. After we made a distinction between short-term and long-term production, we discussed the concepts that describe short-term production, average and marginal productivity, and the concepts that describe long-term production. Then we defined the concept of costs and emphasized the difference in the way accountants and economists look at costs. Corresponding to the distinction between short term and long term production, we distinguished between short-term and long-term costs.

After we have become familiar with the general characteristics of production and costs, we next turn to the discussion of output and price determination in the market of perfect competition.

Trading Places: Why Outsourcing May Destroy Your Business

As last quarter profit reports continue to pour in, an interesting trend emerges in the high tech industries and most notably in the handset phone segment: Long time American and European leaders like Motorola and Nokia are trailing in sales growth behind their Asian counterparts like Samsung Electronics. What makes this "changing places" trend interesting is that many of these Asian companies have been contract manufacturers of their American and European counterparts. First, they performed assembly operation for them. Then they performed component manufacturing. And eventually they performed everything, from product development, to manufacturing, and after sale services. In short, by outsourcing every piece of their business, American and European companies gave business away to the formidable competitors they created. Is this a good strategy? Hardly.

Economists are almost unanimous: Outsourcing is a good business strategy. It improves efficiency, cuts costs, speeds up product development, and allows companies to focus on their "core competencies." And for the most part, they are right. Outsourcing has helped American companies deal with the destructive forces of globalization; that is, the intensification of competition and the price and profit erosion associated with it. For some companies, outsourcing has made the difference between staying in business and going out of business. But, as with every other business strategy, outsourcing has its own limitations and "unintended consequences" that if not addressed, can turn it into a bad business strategy.

Outsourcing is easy to be replicated by the competition; it leads to fragmentation and disintegration of the product supply chain, inviting new competitors into the industry. It also nurtures corporate complacency; and it undermines a company's relations with its labor, customers, and the domestic and local community.

Outsourcing is easy to be replicated, and therefore, it is not a source of sustainable competitive advantage. Outsourcing provides certain competitive advantages to early movers—that is, to companies that adapt it first, but it isn't proprietary. It cannot be patented, preventing others from adapting it. For example, if outsourcing hardware manufacturing provides IBM a cost advantage, it also does for its competitors, such as HP, Dell Computers, and Sun Microsystems that will follow suit. If outsourcing call centers cut costs for American Express, it also does for its credit card competitors. This means that outsourcing works only as long as some industry members have yet to adapt it. Once this happens, outsourcing is no longer a source of competitive advantage.

Outsourcing leads to the fragmentation and disintegration of the product supply chain, inviting new competitors into the industry, and undermining pricing power and profitability. Outsourcing of manufacturing, for instance, is feasible only if it can be separated from other supply chain activities: product development, branding, marketing, distribution, and after sales services. The same is true when it comes to outsourcing marketing or distribution and so on. This means that as more and more activities are outsourced, the supply chain turns from a single integrated process performed within the boundaries of traditional corporations to a fragmented and disintegrated process, a collection of separate and disjointed activities, performed across several independent subcontractors. And although such a fragmentation and disintegration of the value chain offers corporations a number of well publicized advantages, it has an unintended consequence: it makes entry of new competitors to the industry easier, intensifying competition, shortening product cycles, and squeezing return on invested capital.

To understand how this works, let us imagine a perfectly fragmented and disintegrated TV supply chain: every activity from the new TV concept development, to design, manufacturing, marketing, and so on can be performed by independent subcontractors. This means that any company that has no capabilities in making and selling TVs can enter the TV industry, as long as it comes up with the sufficient capital to pay the subcontractors handling the different value chain activities. The problem, though, is that once the product hits the market, nothing prevents another company from doing exactly the same thing, and then another, and another, until the TV industry becomes crowded with companies pitting against each other in a cut throat competition that eliminates industry profitability. What seemed to be a good strategy for each company in the beginning turned into a bad strategy for everyone at the end. By carrying outsourcing to the extreme, industry members open the door widely to competition, reversing whatever outsourcing's early positive effects, and then some.

But what if outsourcing isn't carried that far? What if companies outsource only their "non-core activities," and retain their "core activities"—the things they can do best inhouse? Certainly this strategy cuts costs and improves product quality, but it has another unintended consequence: it nurtures corporate complacency. By focusing on things that they can do best, company managers become complacent with their achievements, they think that what is a best product for their customers today will be the best product tomorrow. Corporate complacency, in turn, leads into corporate blindness, the failure of management to see that their markets reach saturation or are undermined by alternative products.

Outsourcing's unintended consequences for companies and industries that adopt it are not confined to the intensification of competition and corporate complacency. They extend to the relations of these companies with one of their partners—labor. If each and every activity of the product supply chain is gradually farmed out, what binds labor with management and stockholders? If company engineers and marketers who develop new product ideas can sense that their jobs will eventually be farmed out, why should they be loyal to the company? Wouldn't it be better to part from the company and pursue their own product supply chain by farming out the development, the manufacturing and so on, to outsourcing companies themselves?

Outsourcing's unintended consequences extend to company relations with another partner—the customer. If each and every activity is outsourced, customers may feel betrayed. If I hire Sears or Home Depot to make certain improvements in my house because they have a reputation for reliable services, I would feel betrayed if I get services from strangers hired by the said companies, especially if they perform a sloppy job. And I would feel even more betrayed if I end up discussing my medical or financial records with some stranger in an overseas call center.

Outsourcing undermines relations with a third company partner—the domestic and local community. By shifting production and jobs overseas, outsourcing has a devastating impact on both levels that often unleash tidal ideological and political waves that may reverse all the gains from outsourcing, and then some. Let's not forget that people who live in these communities are not just workers, they are customers and citizens, too. As customers, they may end up boycotting the products of corporations shifting production from one location to another, just for the sake of profits. As citizens, people may end up supporting legislation that increases the cost of doing business in their community.

In short, what seems to be trendy in business strategy isn't always a good strategy. If carried to the extreme, outsourcing turns corporations into opportunistic institutions, without a vision in a collision course with its most valuable partners, labor, customers, and the community. True, in a competitive world, it is hard to swim like a salmon against the current. Yet the salmon that swim hard always make it to their destination.

Real World Link 12: Cisco Is Getting Bigger, but Is It Getting Better?

With the acquisition of NDS Group, Cisco is getting bigger, expanding the scale and scope of its operations, but is it getting better in competing effectively against its peers? Is it getting better for its stockholders?

If history offers any clues, the answer is no. Over the last 15 years, Cisco has been on an acquisition spree, buying-up scores of companies every year, but has yet to come up with blockbuster products to beat competition, open up new markets, and enhance shareholder value. The company has been losing market share to Juniper Networks (NYSE:JNPR) and Alcatel-Lucent; and its stock still trades close to 70 percent below its all time high in 2001.

The trouble with an aggressive acquisition strategy is that it is usually costly and unsustainable, especially when applied to the high-tech industry that competes on breakthrough innovation. It is costly because would-be acquirers end up buying companies that either fail to produce any marketable products, or are behind the curve compared to early-movers. It is unsustainable because it often ends up fueling bidding wars, as the owners of these smaller companies demand higher and higher premium to compensate them for the risks they assume. Cisco ended up paying top prices for Net Speed and Growth Networks acquired at the peak of the high-tech bubble. Acquisitions further ended up being dilutive to existing stockholders when paid with the issuing of new stock. That's how Cisco ended up with 5.4 billion shares—though the most recent acquisition was paid with the company's overseas cash.

Cisco isn't the only high-tech company that pursued an aggressive acquisition strategy; Hewlett-Packard (NYSE:HPQ) is another, sharing a similar fate. In 2001, HP purchased Compaq Computer to compete effectively against Dell Computer. In April 2010, HP purchased the near-bankrupt Palm to compete against Apple that enjoyed the first-mover advantage in this market. Recently, HP acquired enterprise software maker, pitting the company against three early market movers, Salesforce.com, Oracle, and IBM.

Cisco's and HP's strategy is radically different than that of other technology companies that have resisted the temptation of going on acquisitions sprees. Corning Inc., Apple, and Google, for instance, have been coming up with one innovative product line after the other, rather than buying-up start-ups.

The Bottom Line: acquisitions have helped Cisco expand the scale and scope of its operation, but have yet to turn the company into a better competitor that enhances shareholder value.

Source: *Forbes Magazine*

6.6 Review

This chapter was an introduction to the characteristics of production and costs.

1. *Production* is both a technical and a social relationship that describes the transformation of economic resources (inputs) into output(s).

2. Economists discuss production from two perspectives: the *short run*, a time period during which some inputs remain fixed while others vary along with output, and the *long run*, a time period during which all factors vary along with output.

3. Conventionally, it is assumed that labor is the only variable input in the short run, while all other inputs are fixed.

4. To study the complexities of short-run production economists distinguish among the total product, average product, and marginal product of labor:

Total product of labor is the maximum output that can be produced by successive levels of labor input.

Average product of labor is the output per unit of labor input.

Marginal product of labor is to the contribution of each additional unit of labor input to the total production. The marginal product follows a particular pattern that is called the law of diminishing returns.

5. The law of diminishing returns states that, in general, as successive units of the variable input are added to the fixed inputs, there is a point beyond which the marginal productivity of the variable input diminishes.

6. The production of goods and services is associated with costs. Depending on the purpose of the discussion, there are several types of costs. One important contrast is that of explicit and implicit costs:

Explicit cost is the sum of money a firm pays for the use of resources that are owned by third parties. Since accountants are concerned only with explicit costs, such costs are also called accounting costs.

Implicit cost is the opportunity cost of the resources that are owned by the firm. An important item that is part of implicit costs is normal profit.

Normal Profit is the minimum return required to commit capital in a certain line of business.

Since economists are concerned with both explicit and implicit costs, the sum of the two costs is called economic cost.

Corresponding to the distinction between implicit and explicit costs, there is a distinction between *economic* and *accounting profits*. While the former refers to the difference between total receipts and both implicit and explicit costs, the latter refers to the difference between total receipts and explicit costs alone.

7. Another distinction among costs is that between short-run and long-run.

In analyzing short-run costs economists distinguish between fixed and variable costs.

Fixed costs are those cost items that do not change with the output level.

Variable costs are those cost items that do change along with output level.

In addition, economists distinguish between average and marginal costs.

Average cost is the cost per unit of output.

Marginal cost is to the contribution of each additional output unit to total cost.

In discussing long-run costs economists introduce the concept of returns to scale. There are three types of returns to scale, constant returns to scale, increasing returns to scale, and decreasing returns to scale.

Constant returns to scale: A production process exhibits constant returns to scale if a doubling of all inputs results in a doubling of output.

Increasing returns to scale: A production process exhibits increasing returns to scale if a doubling of all inputs results in more than doubling of output.

Decreasing returns to scale: A production process exhibits decreasing returns to scale if a doubling of all inputs results in less than doubling of output.

8. Returns to scale is one of the factors that determine the shape of the long-run cost curve. In general, economists draw the long-run supply curve as U-shaped, something that reflects increasing returns at low output levels, constant returns at high output levels, and decreasing returns at very high output levels. The long-run average cost curve is the envelope of all short-run cost curves, something that reflects the fact that a firm has more choices in the long run in determining the lowest cost output level.

9. The long-run marginal cost curve is derived in a similar fashion and gives the total cost contribution of each additional unit of output when all inputs are variable.

Review Questions

1. What is the basis for distinguishing between short-run and long-run analysis?

2. What is the reasoning behind the law of diminishing returns?

3. Why has Malthus' theory on overpopulation and starvation not come true in many countries?

4. What is returns to scale? Give some examples.

5. What is the difference between economic and accounting costs?

6. What is normal profit?

7. A family in Bethpage, Long Island, owns and operates a restaurant. Make up a list of explicit and implicit costs.

8. John and Bill established a computer consulting company in 1980. They each contributed $100,000 dollars in the initial capitalization. In 1990, John wants to leave the company. What will be his fair share of the company? How would you calculate it?

Homework 6

1. What is the relation between productivity and competitiveness?

2. What is the difference between short-term and long-term production?

3. What is the law of diminishing marginal productivity? What are the factors behind it?

4. What are returns to scale?

     Increasing returns

     Constant returns

     Decreasing returns

5. What are the differences between implicit and explicit costs?

6. What is average cost?

7. What is marginal cost?

8. What is the relationship between marginal cost and marginal product?

9. What is the relationship between returns to scale and long-term average cost?

Chapter 7

PRICE AND OUTPUT DETERMINATION: PERFECT COMPETITION

Preview

The last chapter was a discussion of the characteristics of production and costs. This chapter shifts the discussion to issues of output and price determination in a perfectly competitive market: what determines the price at which a firm sells output? What determines the quantity which a firm is willing to sell in the market? Under what conditions does a firm close down altogether? What determines the shape of the firm and market supply curves? Under what conditions do firms enter and exit an industry?

Introduction

Pricing and output decisions may sound trivial, but they are not. A too-high price may drive the firm out of the market, especially if the firm sells exactly the same product as the competition; a too-low price may be matched by the competition and result in lower revenues and profits. Likewise, a too-low output may not be sufficient to cover the costs of the company; a too-high output might have the same effect, costs may run ahead of revenues. How does the firm find the right price and output for its products? Does it make a difference between short-term and long-term? As the rules of the game change from market structure to market structure, these questions can be addressed separately for each market structure.

Addressing these questions for the market of perfect competition, our discussion in this chapter starts with the objectives of a competitive firm and continues with the concept of revenues that are employed, along with the concept of costs to determine the output decision of the firm. In turn, and after we have established a decision rule, we deal with the question of shut-down point and the shape of the firm and industry supply curves as well as with the questions of entry and exit that determine the long run output level.

7.1 The Competitive Market and the Competitive Firm

As we discussed in Chapter Four, perfect competition is a market structure that assumes a large number of small firms selling identical products. Entry into the market is open to new sellers without any barriers such as licenses and patents. Entry is also open to consumers who are assumed to be perfectly informed about product quality and product price.

The strict assumptions of this model ensure that the price is the only vehicle of competition among sellers. Price is determined by the market, i.e., by demand and supply, and each firm is a *price-taker*; the firm must go along with the competition. Reflecting the firm's inability to influence the commodity price, the demand for the firm's product is a horizontal line at the price set by the market (see Exhibit 7.1).

A Competitive Market: The Fulton Fish Market in New York City

Established in 1821 in the South Street Seaport in New York City, the Fulton Fish Market is a historical example of a competitive market that "supplied the common people with the necessities of life at reasonable price."

In an area covering six city blocks around the crossing of South Street and Fulton on the East River, a large number of small wholesalers lined up everyday to sell fish. Buyers could walk up and down the streets, from one seller to another searching for the best bargain. And as a certain type of fish may not vary substantially from seller to seller, the focus of bargaining was on price.

Entry and exit to the market was relatively easy. A small counter and a money advance for merchandise were the only things required to become a seller in this market. And sellers that felt they were not doing enough of business, making enough of a profit, could simply move to a new location or, for that matter at the end of the day having sold all of the fish, they could move out of the fish business all together.

Exhibit 7.1
The Competitive Firm and the Competitive Industry

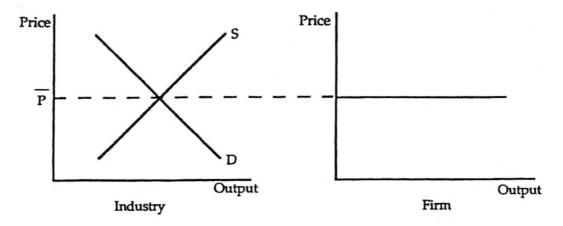

Price in a competitive industry is determined by the market, i.e., by the market demand and the market supply. Each firm has no choice but to go along with that price. The firm's demand is given as a horizontal line at the market price.

7.2 The Firm in a Competitive Market: Objectives and Choices

As discussed in Chapter Four, firms have several objectives: maintaining and expanding market shares, establishing a public image, maximizing profits, etc. Conventional models of firm behavior assume that it is the last objective, i.e., profit maximization, that is of primary concern to the owners of the firm and that all other objectives are secondary to it. Taking this objective for granted, how can the firm pursue this objective? To answer this question economists establish the rules that will guide the firm to the attainment of maximum profit.

Profit is defined as the difference between total revenues and total costs. Formally,

$$\text{Total Profit} = \text{TR–TC}$$

where TR stands for total revenue and TC stands for total cost.

As we can see from the profit formula, profits depend on price and output. However, one of the characteristics of perfect competition is that the firm is a *price-taker*, i.e., it has no power to influence the commodity price. It can only offer successive quantities of the commodity at that price (see Exhibit 7.1). Therefore, setting the appropriate quantity is the only option available to the firm. What is the output that maximizes profits? Before we attempt to answer this question, we must discuss, in addition to production and costs, the firm's revenues.

7.3 The Firm in a Perfectly Competitive Market: Revenues

Which factors determine a company's revenues? The commodity price and the output that the firm sells to the market. As the commodity price is set by the market, a competitive firm can raise revenues only by selling a larger quantity of the product. Conventionally, economists distinguish among three types of revenues, total revenue (TR), average revenue (AR), and marginal revenue (MR).

Total Revenue is the dollar value of all output the firm sells in the market (see exhibits 7.2A and 7.2B). Formally, total revenue can be defined as the product of the commodity price and the output sold in the market:

TR = pq

where p stands for price, and q stands for output.

Average Revenue is the revenue per unit of output (see Exhibits 7.2A and 7.2C). Formally, average revenue can be defined as the ratio of total revenues to the total output:

AR = Total Revenue/Output

Marginal Revenue is the contribution of each additional output to the total revenues (see exhibits 7.2A and 7.2C). Formally, it can be defined as the ratio of the change in total revenues to the change in the total output:

MR = Change in Total Revenue/Change in Total Output

Note: Because the price of the commodity is set by the market and remains the same for each additional unit sold, marginal and average revenues are equal to each other and equal to the commodity price.

Exhibit 7.2
A. Total, Average, and Marginal Revenue Schedules

Output	Price	Total Revenue	Average Revenue	Marginal Revenue
0	$211	0	—	—
1	211	$211	$211	$211
2	211	422	211	211
3	211	633	211	211
4	211	844	211	211
5	211	1055	211	211
6	211	1266	211	211
7	211	1477	211	211
8	211	1688	211	211
9	211	1899	211	211
10	211	2110	211	211

Since commodity price is set by the market, all output units are sold at the same price. Thus, the price schedule is exactly the same as the marginal and average revenue schedules. Any time the firm sells a unit of output, total revenues increase at the rate of $211 per unit.

B. Total Revenue Line

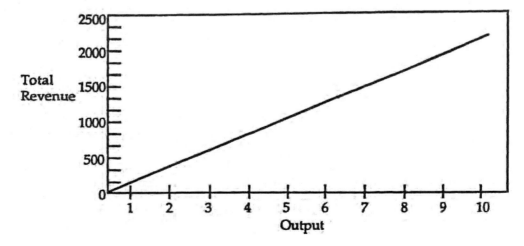

Output and total revenues are directly related. With a fixed price, higher sales bring higher revenues.

C. Average and Marginal Revenues

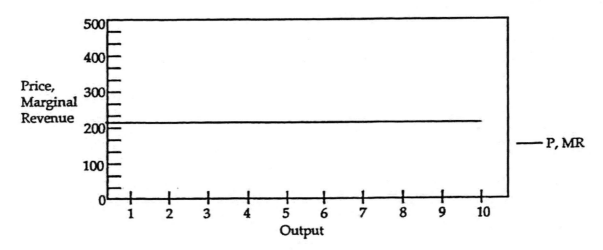

Because the commodity price is set by the market, both marginal revenue and average revenue are also fixed at that price.

Now, since we are familiar with both sides of business operations, i.e., costs and revenues, we can resume the search for a decision rule, i.e., the choice of the output that maximizes total profits.

7.4 The Short-Run Output Decisions

One way to find out which output maximizes a firm's profit is to examine profits step by step, i.e., unit by unit. To do this, the contribution of each additional unit of output to total revenues and total costs must be compared; marginal revenue must be compared to marginal cost. As long as marginal revenue exceeds marginal cost, a larger output raises profit. You may recall that the price of the commodity and the marginal revenue are predetermined for the competitive firm, marginal cost first declines and then rises (see Exhibit 7.3). Therefore, as the marginal cost declines at first and stays below the marginal revenue, each additional unit adds to total revenues more than it adds to total costs, and therefore profit increases. This continues up to the point where marginal cost cuts through the marginal revenue (see point A on the exhibit). Production beyond that point adds to total cost more that it adds to total revenues so total profit declines. Therefore the point where marginal cost is equal to marginal revenue is the cutting point (the break-even point for the last unit). Production up to that point adds to profits while production beyond that point subtracts from it. Thus setting marginal cost equal to marginal revenue is the decision rule that we have been searching for. It is the rule that, if followed, results in the maximum profit. Specifically,

Profit Maximization Rule

To maximize profits, perfectly competitive firms must set marginal cost equal to marginal revenue. Moreover, since in perfect competition marginal revenue is equal to price, profit is maximized at the output level where marginal cost is equal to price.

Profit maximization rule: MC=MR=P

Note: at the cutting point, marginal cost must be increasing and ATC < P (see Exhibit 7.3).

Exhibit 7.3
Short-Run Profit Maximization Output

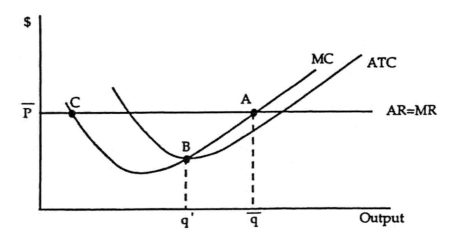

As a general rule, a competitive firm maximizes profits at the output level where marginal cost is equal to marginal revenue provided that marginal cost is increasing. This rule is satisfied at point A.

Question: Why is the firm better off at point A instead of point B? As you may notice, at point B the difference between price and average cost is at a maximum, which means that by producing q units the firm maximizes profit per unit. However, the firm's objective is not to maximize profit per unit but total profit. By producing beyond q and up to q, the firm continues to increase total profit (marginal cost is below marginal revenue throughout this region). Therefore the firm is better off at point A than at point B.

Now, after we have conceptually derived the profit maximization rule, we apply the rule in a numerical presentation of the profit maximization of our hypothetical firm. As we discussed earlier, what one needs to determine the profit maximization output is the marginal cost and marginal revenue. This is given in exhibit 7.4, along with the columns of total revenue, total cost, average cost, and total profit.

Following our previous reasoning, we look at how much each additional unit contributes to total costs and to total revenues; i.e., we compare the marginal cost and marginal revenue curves. At very low levels of output, marginal cost is above marginal revenues, and therefore the firm is losing money. However, if you keep looking down the columns, the marginal revenue soon exceeds the marginal cost, and therefore profit increases for each successive output unit. This holds true until the output reaches the level of eight units (see Exhibits 7.4 and 7.5). At that level, marginal cost is equal to marginal revenue and to the commodity price, and profit is at maximum. Any production beyond that level reduces profit.

Exhibit 7.4
Profit Maximization of a Hypothetical
Competitive Firm: Cost and Revenue Schedules

Output (q)	Average Total Cost (ATC)	Marginal Cost (MC)	Marginal Revenue (MR)	Total Revenue (TR)	Total Cost (TC)	Total Profit (TP)
0	—	—	—	0	$200	−$200
1	$370.00	$170	$211	$211	370	−159
2	260.00	150	211	422	520	−98
3	216.00	130	211	633	650	−17
4	190.00	110	211	844	760	84
5	178.00	130	211	1055	890	165
6	173.33	150	211	1266	1040	226
7	174.28	170	211	1477	1210	267
8	177.50	210	211	1688	1420	268
9	186.66	260	211	1899	1680	219
10	194.00	350	211	2110	1940	170

This table puts together the cost schedules of the firm we discussed in the previous chapter and the revenue schedules. Following our decision rule, we identify the output level that sets marginal cost equal to marginal revenue, and that is 8 units. Total profit at that output level is at maximum, $268.

Exhibit 7.5
Profit Maximization of a Hypothetical
Competitive Firm: Cost and Revenue Curves

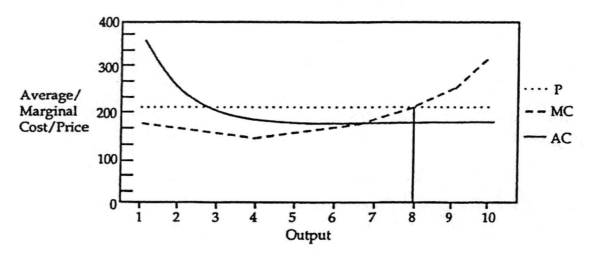

This exhibit puts together the cost curves of the firm we discussed in the previous chapter and the revenue curves. Following the profit maximization rule, we identify the output level that sets marginal cost equal to marginal revenue, and that is 8 units. Total profit at that output level is at maximum, $268.

Having established the profit maximization rule, the next question is what determines market shares? Are shares equal across all companies or do they differ from company to company?

The Question of Market Shares

Market shares in perfect competition depend on the assumption one makes regarding production and costs across firms. Conventionally economists assume that all firms have identical production and cost functions. In that case, the marginal cost curves are the same and the market shares equal across companies. Thus, if we assume that a competitive industry consists of one thousand firms and produces eight thousand units, each firm produces eight units.

Losses, Profits, the Firm, and the Industry Supply Curves

Losses and the Shut-Down Point

Setting marginal cost equal to marginal revenue does not guarantee profits. The firm must be efficient, i.e., at the equilibrium output, average cost must be below the market price. But even so, changes in consumer demand may drive the price below average total cost, and turn profits into losses (see Exhibit 7.6). What happens then? Should the firm close down right away? Not always. It depends on whether the price is below the average *variable* cost. Specifically:

If P > AVC The firm should stay in business.

P = AVC Shut down point.[*]

P < AVC The firm should drop out.

Losing money or not, a firm cannot close down overnight. Shutting down operations may not terminate losses. Fixed costs must still be covered in the interim period. In other words, closing down may mean zero variable cost but not zero fixed cost. The firm will continue to pay rent until liquidation. Losses may, therefore, be smaller if the firm stays in business. Specifically, if the product price is below the average total cost but still above the average variable cost, the firm is better off staying in business for a while. If the price drops below the average variable cost, however, the firm is better off shutting down right away. Why? As long as the price is above the average variable cost, the firm by staying in business covers the variable cost as well as part of the fixed cost. As soon as the price drops below the average variable cost the firm makes losses in addition to fixed cost. Therefore, when price is equal to average variable cost, the firm is at the shut-down point. It follows that setting marginal cost equal to marginal revenue does not always imply profit. There is an additional condition to be taken into consideration: the marginal revenue or price must be above the average variable cost.

The Short-Run Firm and Industry Supply Curves

In discussing the profit maximization rule of the competitive firm, it is assumed that the commodity price is set by the market and is taken as fixed by the firm (recall Exhibit 7.1). Now it can be further assumed that, due to an increase in the market demand for the commodity, price increases. How would that influence the firm's output decision? Since price in perfect competition is always equal to price given the marginal cost curve, successive production units that were not profitable before now become so. Thus as the price increases, the firm moves along the marginal cost curve offering a larger quantity in the market (see Exhibit 7.7). This positive association between the commodity price and the quantity the firm is willing to sell in the market is nothing else than the firm's *supply curve*.

Note: The firm's supply curve is the same as the marginal cost curve but only the part above the shut down point, i.e., the part above the average variable cost.

---

[*]   Shut down price in this case means that the firm is indifferent between staying in business or dropping out. Either decision will have no impact on the company's performance.

After we have identified the competitive firm's supply curve, we can advance to the market supply curve, summing the individual supply curves horizontally. The market supply curve indicates what all firms are willing to sell in the market at different prices (see Exhibit 7.8).

Note: The market supply curve may be something more or something less than the horizontal sum of the individual firm supply curves. As many firms change output the marginal cost of each may change. In that case the slope of the market supply curve may be different from that of the individual firms.

Exhibit 7.6
The Shut Down Point

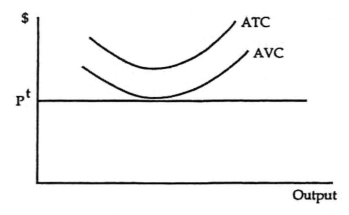

As the product price declines, the firm's profits are wiped away. Ultimately, as profits drop below ATC the firm makes losses. However, as long as price is above average variable cost the firm is better off staying in business, while as the price drops below that level the firm is better off closing down altogether. Therefore, the point where price is equal to average variable cost is the shut down point.

Exhibit 7.7
The Firm Short-Run Supply Curve

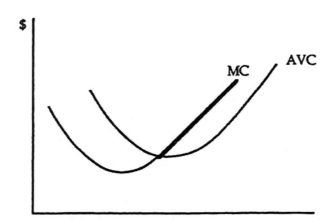

Provided that the firm is above the shut down point, as the market price increases, the competitive firm moves along the marginal cost curve supplying a larger quantity to the market. The part of the marginal cost curve that is lying above the average variable cost is the same as the firm's supply curve.

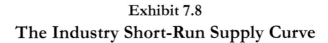

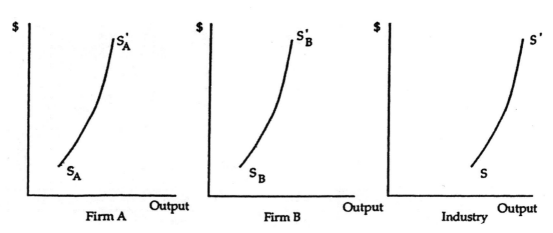

Assuming that the production of one firm is not interfering with the production of other firms, the industry supply curve is the horizontal summation of all individual supply curves.

The Slope of the Firm and Industry Supply Curves

As you can see from Exhibits 7.7 and 7.8, the firm and the industry supply curves are positively sloped. This means that firms are willing to supply larger quantities only at higher prices. Why? Because marginal cost is rising, i.e., because of the law of diminishing returns.

As you may recall from Chapter Six, in the short term a firm can come up with a larger output only by employing more units of the variable factor, that is, labor. However, as more and more units of labor are added to the existing capital, marginal productivity declines. As marginal productivity declines marginal cost is rising (remember the firm's supply curve is the same as the part of the marginal cost that lies above the average variable cost). As marginal cost rises, the supply of additional units of output is profitable only at a higher price.

The Elasticity of the Market Supply

How do firms respond to a small change in the price of a commodity? Do they change quantity supplied considerably or not at all? To answer this question, economists have come up with a concept similar to that of the price elasticity of demand we discussed in Chapter Five, the price elasticity of supply.

Definition. The price elasticity of supply for a product is a measure of the firm's responsiveness to a given price change, i.e., a measure of how firms adjust quantity supplied in response to a price change.

Calculation. The price elasticity of supply for a commodity is calculated as the ratio of the percentage change in the quantity supplied of the commodity over the percentage change in the price, i.e.,

$$e_p = \frac{\% \text{ change in Q}}{\% \text{ change in P}}$$

where Q is the quantity supplied and P is the commodity price.

An alternative price elasticity formula is,

$$e_p = \frac{\Delta Q / \overline{Q}}{\Delta P / \overline{P}}$$

where $\overline{Q}$ is the average of the old and new quantities and $\overline{P}$ is the average of the old and new prices.

Note: The elasticity of supply is a pure number, i.e., a number free of the units the price and quantity is expressed in. It is always a positive number because the two variables, price and quantity supplied, move in the same direction.

Economists distinguish among three kinds of elasticity of supply:

e > 1 elastic supply

e = 1 unitary supply

e < 1 inelastic supply

In plain words, elastic supply means that a 10 percent increase in price results in a more than 10 percent increase in the quantity firms supply to the market. Unitary supply means that a 10 percent increase in the commodity price results in a 10 percent increase in the quantity firms supply to the market. Inelastic supply means that a 10 percent increase in price results in a less than 10 percent increase in the quantity firms supply to the market.

To sum up, in short run a competitive firm makes production decisions by setting marginal cost equal to price. Assuming that this rule applies at a point where marginal cost is rising and assuming that the market price is above the average total cost, the firm's production choice is consistent with profit maximization. In making production decisions in short run the competitive firm is under certain limitations that may not apply in long run.

7.5 The Long-Run Output Decisions

How do the firm's output decisions vary in the long run? Recall that in the long run two things change. First, the firm has more production choices. All factors of production may vary, including physical capital. The firm can replace old machines with new ones, install new assembly lines, buy office equipment, expand in size. Thus it is the long-run average and marginal cost curves rather than the short-run curves that are relevant in the firm's decision making. Second, entry and exit to the market causes shifts in the supply side of the market driving prices up and down accordingly. How does the firm maximize profits? What is the rule that must be followed?

The Long-Run Profit Maximization Rule

To understand a firm's decision to stay in or exit a competitive industry, we must recall the concept of normal profit, i.e., the opportunity cost of the capital committed in the industry at question. As long as profits are above normal profit, the existing firms stay in the market and are joined by new ones. As new firms enter the market, however, the commodity price drops and so do profits. If profits drop below normal profit, entry will be halted and even reversed; some firms will not find the industry attractive any more and exit in order to join other industries where profits are above normal. Exit from the industry, however, reduces supply, the commodity price rises, and profits return to normal, and if too many firms exit the market, profits may rise above normal levels, again. In other words, entry and exit to the market tend to equate profits to the normal profit. It is only when the marginal firm earns just a normal profit that entry and exit stops, and that holds true at the point where the price line is tangent to the long-run average cost (see exhibit 7.9). Formally,

$$LMC = LAC = p$$

Therefore, while in the short run profits of a competitive firm may differ from normal profit, in the long run, due to entry into and exit from the industry, they will tend to equal it (see Exhibit 7.10).

Exhibit 7.9
Entry and Exit and Profit Maximization in the Long Run

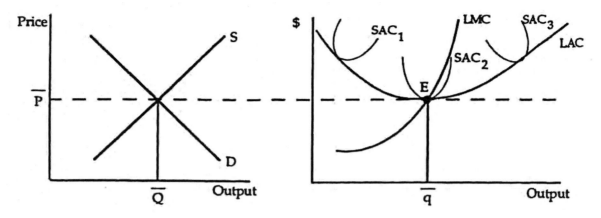

Entry into and exit from the market dictate that output is set at the level where price is equal to the long run average and marginal cost, provided that the former is at a minimum. This will be true when output level q corresponds to point E.

Exhibit 7.10
Entry and Exit and Profits

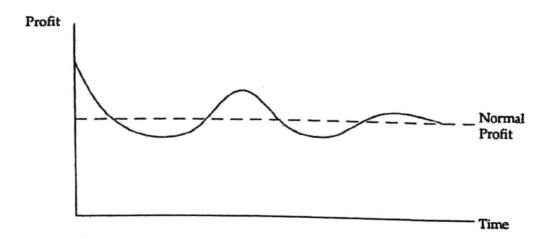

Short run profits of a competitive firm may be above or below normal profits. However, long run profits, due to free entry and exit, will tend to normal profit.

Perfect Competition and Globalization

The elimination of entry barriers and the intensification of competition has brought global industries close to the ideal of perfect competition, which has three important applications for corporate pricing and profitability. First, an unstable and unpredictable product demand, which makes company revenues erratic and unpredictable. Second, the "invisible hand" of the markets sets commodity prices; that is, firms have no pricing power, they are price-takers. Third, global industries are under the constant influx and outflux of competitors that create profit and price gyrations. Profitable industries attract entry of new competitors and that drives prices and profits lower, and in some cases, turning profits into losses. Conversely, unprofitable industries prompt the exit of inefficient firms and that drives prices and profits higher. This process perpetuates itself until profits converge to the economy average.

The influx and outflux of competitors is often exacerbated in the face of demand fluctuations. A precipitous decline in demand, for instance, could accelerate price and profit declines and speed up the exit of inefficient companies from the industry. The personal computer industry is a case in point. In 2001, personal computer prices in the U.S. dropped by 28 percent and new motor vehicle prices dropped by 0.5 percent. One of the companies that pulled out of this industry is Arrow Electronics: [Our] "strategy requires us to participate in those markets where our ability to provide products and value-added services differentiates us and generates acceptable financial returns. During 2002, we examined our role in the commodity computer products business and came to the conclusion that, in this market, customers require fewer value-added solutions and base their decisions primarily on price."[1] A number of other companies, including Gateway, suffered heavy losses. The fiber optic industry is another case in point. In the late 1990s when demand was high and profit margins hefty, a number of European and Asian competitors entered the industry. Combined with market saturation, the entry of new competitors was followed by a crash in fiber optic gear prices and a squeeze in profit margins. This in turn causes an outflux of firms from the industry. According to *Telegeography Inc.* statistics, annual fiber optic prices of 150 megabyte-per-second-data in New York declined from around $1.16 million to below $100,000. By the early 2000s, a number of competitors, including Japanese giant Fujitsu exited the fiber optic market. The electronics industry is a third case in point. Sony's success with a number of electronic gadgets in the early 1990s, for instance, attracted the entry of Korean and Chinese manufacturers in the industry, driving prices lower and dragging down Sony's profits. For the period 1992–2003, Sony's operating profit margins fluctuated between 5 percent and 15 percent. Applied Materials profits fluctuated between 12 percent and 33 percent, and Teradyne's profits between 12 percent and 28 percent.

Conversely, an outflux of companies improves profit margins. In the aftermath of the dot.com crash, a number of surviving companies turned profitable. In the travel industry, Expedia has turned profitable. In computer direct sales, Dell turned profitable. In the financial service industry, mortgage banks and mortgage brokers like Lending Tree have turned profitable. In retailing, Amazon.com, Yahoo, and e-Bay also turned profitable.

1 Arrow Electronics Inc., *2002 Annual Report*, Melville, NY, 2003, p. 2.

7.6 Practical Usefulness of the Competitive Model

After going through all the mechanics of the perfectly competitive model, students often wonder whether the model is something more than an academic exercise, i.e., whether it is of any practical importance for real world decision making. As the assumptions of the model are very strict, it is very hard to find a real world market that comes close to the requirements of the model. And even if we could design such a market, it may not stay the same for long. Sooner or later it may turn into another form, imperfect competition, or monopoly. However, there are situations where small firms have almost no power to influence the commodity price. In these cases, the competitive model suggests that in real world markets of many small firms that sell similar commodities, the firm should not play around with price, but rather should take it for granted and supply as much as possible at that price.

In addition to limited direct applications, because the perfectly competitive model implies efficient allocation of resources, it is often used as a benchmark against which real-world markets are judged. The more a real world market diverges from the requirements of perfect competition, the more inefficiently resources are allocated.

To sum up, in perfect competition firms have no power over price. They must accept the price determined by the market. They do have the power, however, to choose the level of output that maximizes profit. In short term, provided that average total cost is below the market price and that marginal cost is rising, short-term profits are maximized at the output level that sets marginal cost equal to price.

As not all firms are as efficient, average total cost may not always be below the market price. In that case the firm makes losses. And if the market price is even below the average variable cost, the firm must close down right away.

In perfect competition, the part of the marginal cost curve that lies above the average variable cost constitutes the supply curve of the competitive firm. The horizontal summation of all individual supply curves is the industry supply curve.

Alike with market demand, economists estimate the elasticity of supply, a measure of how responsive firms are to a given price change. If a 10 percent increase in price results in a more than 10 percent increase in quantity supplied, supply is elastic. Conversely, if a 10 percent increase in price results in a less than 10 percent increase in quantity supplied, supply is inelastic.

As firms are faced with different constraints and opportunities in the long term, output decisions may vary in the long run. First, entry and exit to the market changes the number of firms in the market and the market prices. Second, as firms can choose among alternative technologies, average total cost changes. Such provisions dictate a different profit maximization rule than that in the short term. Output is set at the point where average total cost is equal to price; the firm makes just normal profit.

As you may recall from the beginning of the chapter, output and price decisions may vary from market to market. In the next chapter, we discuss output and price decisions for the case of monopoly.

7.7 Review

1. This chapter is a discussion of price and output determination in a competitive market. Given the strict assumptions that define a perfectly competitive market, prices are determined by demand and supply and are taken as fixed by each individual firm which in turn will search for the output level that maximizes profits.

2. Total profits are defined as the difference between total revenues and total costs. Total revenue refers to the dollar value of a given volume of sales. In discussing revenues, economists introduce the concepts of average revenue and marginal revenue. Average revenue refers to the revenue per unit of sales. Marginal revenue refers to the contribution of each additional unit of sales to total revenues.

3. Putting together costs and revenues we derive the short-run profit maximization rule for the competitive firm. To maximize profit, the firm must set marginal cost equal to marginal revenue and price.

4. A competitive firm does not always make profits. If the commodity price drops below average total cost the firm loses money, and at a price below the average variable cost it closes down altogether.

5. Conversely, as the commodity price exceeds the average variable cost, the firm supplies larger quantities to the market. Thus, the part of the marginal cost curve that is above the average variable cost constitutes the supply curve of the competitive firm. Summing the individual supply curves horizontally we get the market supply curve.

6. The elasticity of supply is a measure of a firm's responsiveness to a given price change. There are three kinds of elasticity of supply:

      e > 1 elastic supply

      e = 1 unitary supply

      e < 1 inelastic supply

7. In the long run, entry into and exit from a competitive industry sets a commodity price equal to the long-run average cost of each firm; economic profit becomes equal to normal profit, i.e., the opportunity cost of capital committed by a firm to this kind of industry.

8. Although there are very few real world markets that comply with the strict requirements of perfect competition, the model is very useful as a benchmark for evaluating real world markets.

Review Questions

1. What does it mean that a firm is a "price-taker"?
2. How does a competitive firm make output decisions in short run?
3. Does a competitive firm make profits in short run?
4. Under what conditions might a firm close down in short run?
5. How does a firm make output decisions in long run?
6. How do economists derive the firm and the industry supply curves? Why are both curves positively sloped?
7. What will be the effect of a sales tax imposed on just one competitive industry?
8. In a competitive industry, are there any recipes for making more money than others?

Homework 7

1. How are prices set in perfect competition?

2. What does it mean that a competitive firm is a price-taker?

3. What is the main business objective of a perfectly competitive firm?

4. What is the short-term profit maximization rule of a competitive firm?

5. What is the shut-down rule of a perfectly competitive firm?

6. What is the supply curve of a perfectly competitive firm?

7. How is the supply curve of a competitive industry derived?

8. What is the long-term profit maximization rule?

9. Why does a competitive firm make only normal profits in the long term?

10. What is the relationship between perfect competition and globalization?

Chapter 8

OUTPUT AND PRICE DETERMINATION: MONOPOLY

Preview

The previous chapter was a discussion of output and price determination in an extreme market structure, perfect competition. This chapter continues the discussion of output and price determination in another extreme market structure, monopoly. The discussion starts with the definition of monopoly, continues with monopoly revenues and profit maximization, issues of resource allocation, regulation, deregulation, and ends with the discussion of a popular monopoly pricing practice, price discrimination.

Introduction

Monopolies have a distinct place in economic history. In mercantile Europe, monopolies like the East India Corporation controlled the flow of raw materials from the colonies to Europe. In late 19th century America, monopolies like U.S. Steel, Alcoa, and Standard Oil controlled the emerging raw and energy material sectors of the economy until they were ruled illegal and dissolved by subsequent regulation.

Today, in all industrialized countries monopolies are still under attack by economists, politicians, sociologists, and the general public. And many countries have legislation that declares monopolies illegal (see Exhibit 8.1). In particular, in the U.S., anti-monopoly legislation is one hundred years old. Throughout this period many companies with a most recent example of AT&T were regulated one way or another. Why are economists against monopolies? How does regulation work? What about deregulation? To answer these questions, we must first address the issues of price and output determination in a monopoly market and compare this process with that of perfect competition.

As we saw in the previous chapter, a competitive firm is a price-taker, i.e., has no power over price. It can only choose the quantity that maximizes profit. Things are quite different in the case of monopoly, however. Being the only firm in the market, the monopolist can set the commodity price, i.e., can be a price-maker. Output and price decisions are, therefore, different in the case of monopoly.

This chapter is in seven sections. The first section provides the definition of monopoly. The second section discusses monopoly revenues and the market demand. The third section discusses the profit maximization rule. The fourth section addresses the issue of resource allocation. The fifth and the sixth sections deal with issues of regulation and deregulation. The last section addresses monopolistic pricing strategies such as price discrimination.

Exhibit 8.1
Comparison of Japanese and U.S. Antitrust Systems

	U.S.	Japan
Applicable Statutes	Sherman Act Clayton Act Federal Trade Commission Act	Antimonopoly Act
Enforcement Bodies	Justice Department Antitrust Division (549 employees + FBI) Federal Trade Commission (980 employees)	Fair Trade Commission (461 employees)
Penalties	Restraining Orders Criminal Penalties (malicious price-fixing) Treble Damage Awards	Restraining Orders Fines (price cartels) Criminal Penalties Actual Damage Awards

Standard Oil: The Making and the Breaking of a Monopoly

The time, January 10, 1870. The place, Ohio. Taking advantage of an oil glut, Rockefeller and Flagler established Standard Oil Company, a major player in the oil industry. Buying up competitors or driving them out of business, and expanding control into the oil transportation industry, Standard Oil managed to have virtual control of American oil. By 1879, Standard Oil was refining close to 90 percent of American oil, and owned tank car fleets, ship fleets, and warehouses. Four years later, Standard Oil formed its first "trust" that allowed the company to consolidate its operations, raising productivity and cutting cost. By 1885, Standard Oil cut down the number of refineries from 53 to 32. In fact, two-fifths of the world petroleum output was refined in three Standard Oil refineries; refining costs dropped from 1.5 cents to 0.5 cents per barrel. With such good control over the market, Standard Oil's lower production cost wasn't passed on to consumers, but to stockholders.

Standard Oil's greed and tactics raised an upheaval throughout the U.S. that invited a close scrutiny by the Federal government. In 1906, the Theodore Roosevelt Administration, in a lawsuit filed in the Federal Court in St. Louis, charged Standard Oil with "conspiracy to restrain trade," under the Sherman Act. Five years later, Standard Oil was found guilty as charged and broken into several units: Standard Oil of New Jersey (today's Exxon), Standard Oil of New York (Mobil), Standard Oil of California (Chevron), Standard Oil of Ohio (today's American arm of BP), Standard Oil of Indiana (Amoco), Continental Oil (Conoco), and Atlantic Richfield (ARCO).

8.1 What Is Monopoly?

Monopoly stands on the other side of the market spectrum from perfect competition. As was discussed in Chapter Four, monopoly is a market of one seller or a group of sellers controlling an entire market. Market control is attained through entry restrictions. Possession of know-how, possession of a license, possession of a unique raw material, unique access to a distribution system, and economies of scale are examples of such restrictions. Because of market control, a monopolist can influence the commodity price; such influence is reflected in the monopolist's demand and revenue curves (see section below).

While theoretically, the definition of monopoly is quite clear, identifying real world monopolies is a difficult task. Most commodities have close or distant substitutes, and, therefore, it is hard to argue that a market is controlled by just one seller. Moreover, it is hard to prove that sellers in a market have "fixed the price" or "conspired" to keep potential competitors off the market. And to complicate matters even more, what may appear as a monopoly in a community, may not be so at the state or national level.

Near Monopolies: Then and Now

100 Years Ago		
Steel 67%	**Refined Oil 87%**	**Sugar 98%**
US Steel Corporation	Standard Oil	American Sugar Refining Co.
Today		
Health Insurance 80%	**Beef 85%**	**Beer 70%**
Blue Cross Blue Shield	Tyson Foods National Beef	AB InBev
United Health	JBS USA	Molson Coors
Anthem	Cargill	
Aetna		
Cigna		

Examples of Today's Near Monopolies

Amazon	Google	Facebook

Cable TV—A Natural Monopoly?

Do you think that the cable TV industry is a natural monopoly and should be regulated? Federal regulators do not seem to have a clear answer to this question. Prior to 1984, federal regulators thought that the industry was indeed a natural monopoly and they regulated it. In 1984, they changed their minds, however, and they deregulated it. In 1993, they changed their minds and re-regulated it. In 1995, they attempted to deregulate it again! What is the case here? Is the cable TV industry a natural monopoly? Are consumers better under regulation or deregulation?

From a theoretical perspective, the cable TV industry has many of the characteristics of a natural monopoly market. Entry to the cable TV industry requires a large amount of fixed capital outlays in building a cable infrastructure, i.e., wiring neighborhoods, broadcasting facilities, etc. Large fixed costs create economies of scale: the larger the number of cable TV-customers the lower the cost per average or additional viewer; i.e., both average and marginal costs are declining. Cable TV service is a natural monopoly. Services can be provided at a lower cost through one company rather than many. Take the case of the town of Islip in Suffolk County, Long Island. The town originally granted permission to three companies to wire neighborhoods. Soon after, one of the three companies dropped out and the other two joined efforts in wiring neighborhoods. In order to ensure that cost savings associated with economies of scale are passed on to consumers, many states have regulated the cable TV industry. But what is the evidence from the last twenty years of regulation and deregulation? Prices during the regulation periods were rising but slowly. Prices during the deregulation periods declined slightly in the beginning but took off later.

Exhibit 8.2

The Monopolist's Demand versus the Competitive Firm's Demand

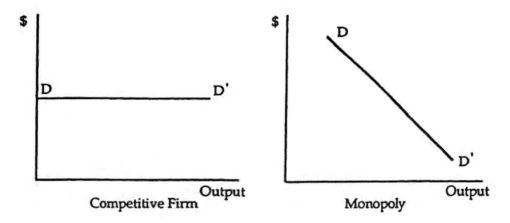

Unlike a competitive firm, which is a price-taker and faced with a horizontal demand, a monopolist is a price-maker and faced with a negatively sloped demand.

8.2 Monopoly Demand and Revenues

Monopoly Demand

As a result of market control and unlike the perfect competitive firm, which is a price-taker, a monopolist is a *price-maker*, i.e., can influence the commodity price. Monopolist's power is limited, however, by two factors: (i) consumers' income is limited, and if price is set too high, too few consumers will be in a position to afford the commodity, (ii) consumers can turn to commodity substitutes. Because of these limitations, the monopolist does not control both price and output independently. An attempt to increase price results in lower quantity (see Exhibit 8.2).

After we have explained the monopolist's demand, we can now examine the monopolist's revenues. As in the case of perfect competition, we can distinguish among three concepts of revenues, total, average, and marginal.

Total Revenue

As in the case of perfect competition, a firm's total revenue is the product of price and quantity. Formally:

$$\text{Total Revenue} = (\text{Price}) \times (\text{Quantity})$$

While the definition of total revenue is straightforward, the relationship between quantity (sales) and total revenue is far from clear. As a monopolist is faced with a negatively sloped demand, larger sales can only come at lower prices. The issue, therefore, of the relationship between total revenues and sales depends on the elasticity of demand. An elastic demand implies rising total revenues. A unitary demand implies flat total revenues, and an inelastic demand implies declining revenues. As the demand for a product is elastic at low output levels and inelastic at high output levels, one would expect total revenue to increase at low output levels and decrease at high ones (see Exhibits 8.3, 8.4, and 8.5).

Note: As lower prices bring lower revenues when demand is inelastic, the monopolist will never produce at the inelastic part of the demand curve.

Exhibit 8.3
Monopoly Revenues and Costs

Output	Price	Total Revenue	Marginal Revenue	Marginal Cost	Average Total Cost
1	$900	$900	$900	$170	$370.00
2	825	1650	750	150	260.00
3	750	2250	600	130	216.00
4	675	2700	450	110	190.00
5	600	3000	300	130	178.00
6	525	3150	150	150	173.33
7	450	3150	0	170	174.28
8	375	3000	−150	210	177.50
9	300	2700	−300	260	186.66
10	225	2250	−450	350	194.00

This table is a numerical demonstration of a monopolist's costs and revenues. The first four columns of the table provide the monopolist's price, total cost, and the marginal revenue. The last three columns give the monopolist's marginal, average, and total costs, which are the same as those of perfect competition (see chapter six).

Exhibit 8.4
Monopoly Revenues

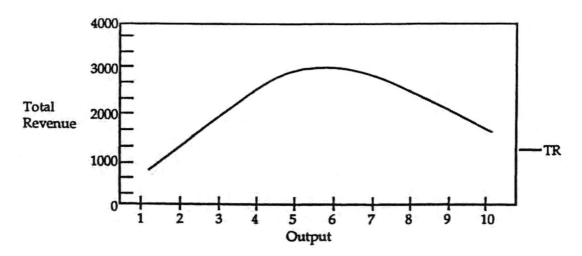

Monopoly total revenues rise at the beginning, and then, after they attain a maximum, they decline.

Exhibit 8.5
Size of Elasticity and Total Revenues

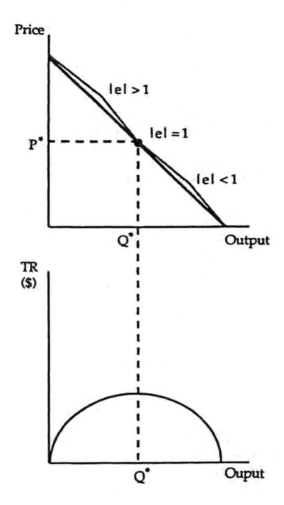

This exhibit connects the size of the demand elasticity with total revenues. With a demand elasticity greater than one (upper panel), lower prices raise total revenues (lower panel). With an elasticity equal to one, total revenues level off, while with an elasticity less than one, total revenue starts to decline. These remarks suggest that a monopolist's price will always be greater than P* and the quantity smaller than Q*.

Average Revenue

Average Revenue. Average revenue is revenue per unit sold in the market. Formally:

Average Revenue = Total Revenue/Total Quantity

Note: As total revenue is equal to price times quantity, average revenue is equal to price. Formally:

Average Revenue = (Price)×(Quantity)/Quantity = Price

This means that average revenue is the same as the price line, i.e., the demand curve for the commodity (see Exhibits 8.3 and 8.6).

Marginal Revenue

Marginal revenue is the contribution of an additional unit of sales to total revenue (see Exhibits 8.3 and 8.6). Formally:

Marginal Revenue = Change in Total Revenue/Change in Quantity

Note: Because of a negatively sloped demand curve, the monopolist can sell additional output units only at lower price; marginal revenue is negatively sloped too and lies below the demand curve (see Exhibit 8.6).

Exhibit 8.6
Monopoly Demand and Marginal Revenues

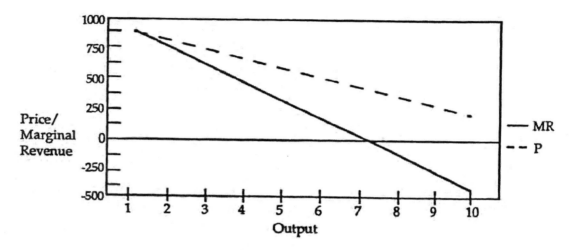

Based on the date of Exhibit 8.3, this exhibit provides the monopoly demand and revenues. Both lines are negatively sloped, with marginal revenue below the demand line.

Exhibit 8.7
Monopoly Price and Output Determination

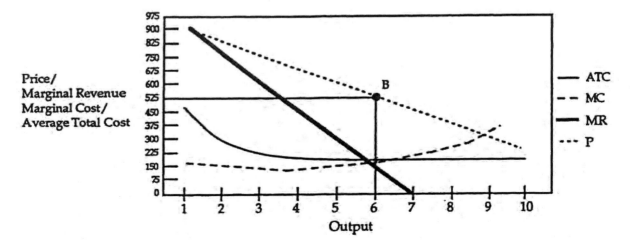

A monopoly maximizes profits at the point where marginal cost is equal to marginal revenue. By contrast to the case of the perfectly competitive firm, price is above marginal cost.

8.3 Profit Maximization: Output and Price

Assuming that the monopolist buys resources in a competitive market, cost curves look like the ones we discussed in Chapter Six. Putting costs together with the monopolist's revenues, we can turn to the questions: What is the output level that maximizes the monopolist's profits? What is the price? In answering these questions, we follow the same reasoning as that in the case of the perfectly competitive firm: for each output level, we must compare the marginal cost to the marginal revenue. As long as the marginal revenue exceeds marginal cost, successive output units add to total profits. Conversely, as soon as the marginal cost exceeds the marginal revenue, successive output units subtract from profits. Thus, the decision rule for profit maximization is:

$$MC = MR$$

You should notice that unlike in perfect competition where marginal cost is equal to price in monopoly, price is above marginal cost (see Exhibit 8.6B).

8.4 Monopoly and Resource Allocation

In any developed economy, a monopoly's image is not popular. Economists, sociologists, politicians, and consumers are all after monopolies. They all want to see them regulated by government. Why?

Compared to perfect competition, monopoly is an inefficient market. Monopolies produce at output levels below that of competitive firms at higher prices (see Exhibit 8.8A). As a result, too little of resources are allocated to commodities produced in monopoly industries compared to commodities produced in competitive industries. To put it differently, monopolies do not serve consumers' needs as well as competitive firms. There is what economists call *dead weight loss* or *welfare loss* expressed in the size of triangle EFG. Not only are consumers not best served by monopolies, but they are exploited: welfare is transferred from consumers to monopolies. This is represented by $P_m P_c EL$.

Note: A comparison between perfect competition and monopoly is valid only under the assumption that the marginal cost curve is identical to that of the perfectly competitive firm.

Exhibit 8.8
A. Monopoly versus Competitive Pricing

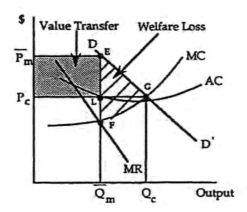

Under the competitive rule, the monopolist's profit is maximized at a larger output and a lower price (compare P_m and P_c with Q_m and Q_c). Actually, the difference between price P_c and P_m shows the premium consumers pay to monopoly. Such pricing shifts income from consumers to the monopoly (box $P_m P_c EL$).

LILCO (now PSEG): A Regulated Natural Monopoly*

The Long Island Lighting Company (LILCO) is a good example of a regulated natural monopoly. Formed in 1910, it was initially the sole supplier of electricity to the areas of Amityville, Northport, Brookhaven, Islip, Babylon, and Huntington in Suffolk County, and Oyster Bay and Hemstead in Nassau County, and ultimately in almost every town of Long Island (Rockville Center, Freeport and Greenport are the only towns that do not buy electricity from LILCO). Being a monopoly, LILCO prices are set by the Public Service Commission of New York State.

LILCO's formation marked the shift from individual production to county and ultimately to island-wide production. Indeed, LILCO's formation followed a period of competition of many small electric companies that supplied power separately in Long Island communities, Port Jefferson, Sag Harbor, Roselyn, Patchoque, etc. As Long Island began to grow, these smaller companies were unable to keep up with the increase in demand for electricity. Installing poles, the cost of them, power lines, transformers, pruning of trees, larger electric generators required massive fixed capital investment that only a large company could assume.

---

* LILCO is now part of National Grid.

8.5 Monopoly Regulation

Acknowledging the effects of monopoly on output, prices, and income distribution, many economists, including the classical economist Adam Smith, were very critical of monopolies, advocating government policies that would restrict monopoly power and protect consumers. Faced with several monopoly situations, the U.S. government introduced antimonopoly legislation as early as the end of the nineteenth century. Specifically, the Sherman Act was introduced in 1890 declaring illegal every contract, trust, or conspiracy which restrained interstate trade, foreign trade, or commerce. The Act refers not just to cartels and trusts, but also to any agreements to fix prices or market shares. The Sherman Act was further complemented and expanded with subsequent acts such as the Clayton Act and the Federal Trade Commission Act (1914), the Webb-Pomerene Export Act (1918), the Wheeler-Lea Act (1938), and the Celler-Kefauver Antimerger Act (1950). Several companies have been regulated up to now. Companies and industries regulated by early legislation include the Aluminum Company of America (ALCOA), U.S. Steel, and other industries including meat packing, sugar, railroad, tobacco, and coal. Industries regulated by subsequent legislation include transportation (trucking industry), public utilities (natural gas and electricity), communications (telephone, radio, and television), i.e., industries that are natural monopolies.

Exhibit 8.8
B. Regulating a Natural Monopoly

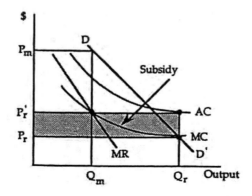

This exhibit points to the problems associated with marginal cost-pricing regulation of a natural monopoly. As the market size may be too small compared to the firm's capacity, price is below average cost. The firm must be subsidized.

Regulation Policies

Theoretically speaking, the adverse effects of monopoly power can be corrected in two ways. First, they can be corrected through marginal cost pricing, i.e., forcing monopolies to produce at the point where marginal cost is equal to price (compare P_m with P_c and Q_m with Q_c of the Exhibit 8.8). In doing so, monopolist price drops, output increases, and income shifts back to consumers. Second, the adverse effects of the monopoly can be corrected by stimulating competition by breaking down monopolies into smaller companies. Nevertheless, there are problems with both policies that make them not applicable in the real world. Marginal cost pricing requires a precise knowledge of the monopolist's marginal cost and marginal revenue curves, a piece of information that may not be available to regulating authorities. But even if such information is available, if price is below the average total cost, as is the case in natural monopolies, the firm may not survive without government subsidies (see Exhibit 8.8B). Breaking down a monopoly into smaller firms may be impractical because the cost advantage associated with economies of scale will be lost and small firms may end up with losses. Because of these difficulties, practical policies may differ from theoretical solutions. They often include cost mark up or capital mark up pricing (a profit margin expressed as a percentage of average total cost or as a percentage of the invested capital). But even this policy is not without caveats. Regulated monopolies may invest too much on capital and too little on labor, i.e., the capital-labor combination may not be optimal.

8.6 Monopoly Deregulation

Despite its positive effects on consumers, monopoly regulation and the bureaucratic networks associated with it have often deteriorated the situation that they were designed to correct: monopoly power has been strengthened. As expected, regulation has come under heavy criticism, and deregulation legislation has already been introduced in industries such as communications, airlines, and the trucking industry. The main avenue of implementing deregulation is the breaking-up of the monopoly and the encouragement of new entrants to the industry. The rationale behind this move is that as more firms enter the industry, competition lowers price and raises output and consumption.

Has deregulation born fruits? Have prices come down in deregulated industries? It is hard to say. In the airline industry, for example, prices have come down, but this has happened in a period of lower energy prices (see case study below). In the communication industry, long distance rates have dropped by about 20 percent, while local rates have increased by about 34 percent. In the New York State milk industry, prices dropped by 17 percent (see case study below). It is hard, therefore, to say whether such price declines have to do with deregulation or with lower energy prices. Moreover, even if deregulation benefits consumers in the short run, these benefits may be eroded in the long run through bankruptcies of small firms and mergers that strengthen monopoly power.

Deregulation at Work: Two Case Studies

Case 1: Airline Deregulation: Has It Worked?

The airline industry is, perhaps, the only industry that was regulated at infancy, since the origin of aviation in the U.S. Aviation regulation dates back to 1926, to the Air Commerce Act that established the government rules in promoting commerce and safety. In 1938, aviation regulation was strengthened with the Civil Aeronautics Act that placed aviation under the same regulatory agency as any other form of transportation. Air travel safety, fares, routes, and entry to the aviation market were all under the auspices of the Department of Transportation.

After four decades of regulation, Congress passed the 1978 Airline Deregulation Act which allowed air-carriers to set prices and choose flying routes; it further encouraged entry of new carriers to the industry. Have consumers benefited from airline deregulation? To answer this question, one must address several other questions. Have more companies entered the industry? Have airfares declined? Has air traffic expanded? Are airlines serving more routes? Is air traveling safer? The answers to these questions depend on the time horizon of investigation.

Seven years later, in 1984, Donald Engen stated:

> Increased competition has generally kept average fares lower and made them more cost based than they would have been under regulation . . . in addition, service is more widely available nationwide and more

convenient, while profits have varied widely among airlines. These changes result in the industry operating more efficiently and offering more price/quality options than it did under regulation.

Vital Speeches, p. 335.

Indeed, by 1985 there were 106 carriers compared to 39 prior to 1978; with the total number of available seats rising by more than 50 percent. Airfares have declined substantially. From about $4.80 per traveled mile in 1975 to $3.20 in 1987 (figures in constant 1967 dollars). The percent of passengers using discount fares increased from 36.9 percent in 1977 to 91.3 percent in 1987. And the number of passengers increased from 222.3 million in 1976 to 450 million in 1987. Lower fares and more traveling have added to passengers' welfare. According to economists Morrison and Winston, deregulation added $5.7 billion to travelers' welfare. In the meantime, the number of fatalities per billion of passenger miles dropped from an average of 1.19 in the period 1972–1979 to an average of 0.48 in 1979–1986. The number of near mishaps increased, however, from 231 in 1972 to 840 in 1986 in almost direct proportion to total passenger miles flown.

While the short-term effects of airline deregulation appear positive, the long-term effects cannot be taken for granted. In a market where economies of scale play a major role for competitiveness and profitability, smaller carriers are doomed to be either driven out of the market or acquired by larger carriers. The example of Peoples Express, Allegheny Air, Air Florida, and Frontier Air that went bankrupt and Eastern and Republic Airlines that were acquired by Texas Air and Pan Am, respectively, are only a few good examples of the re-emerging market concentration. And as the market moves back to a few carriers the benefits of deregulation may not be sustained. Fares may rise and the number of flights may be reduced. Following the acquisition of Republic Airlines by Northwest Airlines, for instance, the number of flights from the Twin Cities dropped by 15 percent and fares rose. And so did flights and fares from Denver Airport following the bankruptcy of Frontier Air. In fact, by 1994, close to 60 percent of all airline traveling was done on the three largest companies.

Case 2: New York Milk Industry Deregulation: Has It Worked?

The early thirties were a bad time for New York milk suppliers. Cut-throat competition and bankruptcy threatened the supply of this essential commodity. In 1937, the state introduced legislation that required milk producers to obtain a license before they entered the market of a particular county. Such legislation did two things. First, it kept out-of-state suppliers out of the New York State market. Second, it established local monopolies.

On August 5, 1987, new state governor Mario Cuomo signed a bill that ended the fifty-year-old regulation of the milk industry. Soon after the signing of the bill, milk consumers felt the benefits of deregulation. Entry of out-of-state suppliers drove milk prices down by an average of 17 percent. In Manhattan, milk prices dropped from $2.40 a gallon to $2.01. On Long Island, milk prices dropped from $2.29 to $1.99.

While the short-term benefits of the New York milk industry deregulation cannot be undermined, as in the case of airlines, one must keep an eye on long-term effects. Increased competition is expected to fuel bankruptcies of small suppliers and mergers of small suppliers with bigger ones. With market concentration, the milk industry could evolve to an oligopoly with severe consequences for consumers.

8.7 Monopoly Pricing Strategies: Price Discrimination

While many countries have ruled pure monopolies illegal, firms with substantial market power can apply monopoly practices. They can exert their power in the market to raise price and restrict quantity. A broadly known practice is price discrimination.

Definition. Price discrimination is the charging of a different price to different consumers for the same product or similar products produced at the same cost. Airlines, for instance, have one price for business travelers and another for non-business travelers. And they offer student and senior citizen discounts. Movie theaters give discounts during off-peak times; and telephone companies charge different rates at different times of the day. What are the conditions for price discrimination? What are the pricing rules?

Conditions for Price Discrimination

The effective application of price discrimination must meet two conditions. First, the seller must be in a position to screen out different types of consumers, i.e., consumers with different demand elasticities. This policy could be implemented by classifying consumers by age, sex, income, professional status, etc. Second, the seller must find ways to separate one group from another, i.e., if a discount is offered to senior citizens, the seller must find ways to keep nonsenior citizens from taking advantage of this discount. Coupons that are published in newspapers and magazines read by the target consumer group are a frequently deployed instrument of market segmentation.

Pricing Rule

Companies applying price discrimination charge prices according to the elasticity of demand by different consumer groups. Consumers with an inelastic demand are charged a high price and consumers with an elastic demand are charged a low price (see table below).

Group	Elasticity	Price Charged
Group 1	Low	High
Group 2	High	Low

Exhibit 8.9
Price Discrimination and Profit Maximization

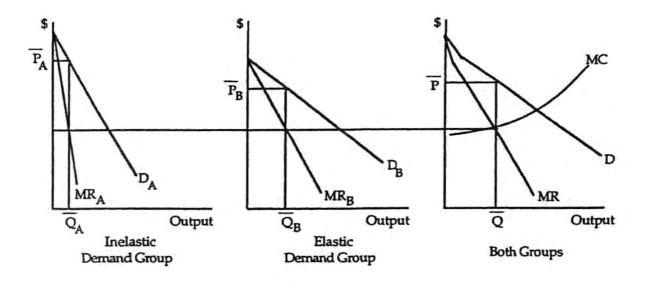

As a pricing strategy, price discrimination makes sense only if total revenues under price discrimination exceed those under a uniform price strategy. Charging consumers with an inelastic demand a high price and consumers with an elastic demand a low price is consistent with the price discrimination strategy (see Exhibit 8.9).

To sum up, a monopoly is a market controlled by one seller or a group of sellers. Having market control, the monopolist can exert power over consumers. Monopoly power is reflected in either price control or sales control. Compared to perfect competition, monopolies charge too high a price (a price above marginal cost) and sell too small a quantity. This means that monopolies are inefficient, i.e., misallocate resources. To correct monopoly inefficiencies, many countries have adopted regulation, i.e., governmental authorities set prices for monopolies. While the motivation for regulating monopolies is clear, regulation has often reinforced a situation that it was designed to correct. As a result, many governments around the world have lifted regulation.

While monopoly and perfect competition are two extreme market situations, there are other markets falling in between that economists call imperfect competition, which we will discuss in the next chapter.

8.8 Review

1. *Monopoly* is a market of one seller with a good control over market entry and selling a product without close substitutes.

2. Unlike the competitive firm which takes the commodity price as given and is faced with a horizontal demand curve, a monopolist has the power to influence the commodity price and is faced with a negatively sloped demand curve. Because of this demand curve, total and marginal revenues differ from those of the perfectly competitive firm. Total revenues depend on the elasticity of demand. Revenues rise along with lower prices at low levels of output and while the elasticity of demand is greater than one. Revenues drop with lower prices at higher output levels and while the elasticity of demand is less than one. Because the monopolist can sell larger quantities at lower prices, marginal revenue is declining and lies below the demand curve.

3. A monopolist maximizes profits at the point where marginal cost is equal to marginal revenue. However, unlike the situation with perfect competition, price is no longer equal to marginal cost: the monopolist charges a price above marginal cost.

4. As a result of such pricing, monopolies charge consumers too high a price (compared to that of the perfectly competitive firm), restricting output at the same time; i.e., they allocate resources inefficiently.

5. In order to protect consumers and society from monopolies, governments all over the world have instituted policies to regulate monopolies. Several regulatory acts are in force, and many industries have been regulated including ALCOA, U.S. Steel, transportation, and communications.

6. Despite some success, regulation often turns in support of what it is supposed to abolish: monopoly power. This has set the process for a reversal: deregulation, i.e., the lifting of regulation restrictions. Many industries have been deregulated by now, including the telecommunication, airline, interstate trucking, and the New York State milk industries.

7. Although monopolies are illegal, firms with substantial market power often apply *price discrimination*, a policy that charges different consumers different prices.

Review Questions

1. What is monopoly?
2. What are the sources of monopoly power?
3. What are the limits of monopoly power?
4. Does a monopolist control both price and quantity?
5. How does a monopolist maximize profits?
6. How does a monopolist's profit maximization rule compare with that of a competitive firm?
7. What is wrong with monopolies?
8. What are the principles of regulation, and what are the problems?
9. What are the principles of deregulation, and what are the problems?
10. What is the relationship between total revenues and the size of demand elasticity?
11. What is the relationship between marginal revenues and the size of demand elasticity?

Homework 8

1. What is a monopoly?

2. What are the sources of monopoly power?

3. What are the limitations of monopoly power?

4. How does price elasticity relate to MR and TR of a monopolist?

5. How does price elasticity affect the pricing power of a monopoly?

6. What is the monopoly profit maximization rule?

7. Does a monopolist always make profits?

8. Why should monopolies be regulated?

9. What are the problems of regulating monopolies?

10. What is price discrimination? What are the conditions for successfully implementing it?

Chapter 9

OUTPUT AND PRICE DETERMINATION: IMPERFECT COMPETITION

Preview

Perfect competition and monopoly are two extreme market structures that serve more as benchmarks than as illustrations of real-world markets, most of which fail to comply with the strict requirements of either model; they rather exhibit characteristics that place them in between the two models, in what economists call imperfect competition. Two types of market structures discussed in this chapter are included in imperfect competition—monopolistic competition and oligopoly.

Introduction

You do not have to be an economist to realize that markets in the United States do not comply with the strict requirements of either perfect competition or monopoly models. In some U.S. markets, power is concentrated in a few large sellers of homogeneous or differentiated commodities; entry to the market is restricted by technological, financial or marketing constraints; and consumers must spend time or even money searching for the right product at the right price. The cereal market, for instance, includes a few large sellers of nonhomogeneous products and so does the computer hardware industry. Entry to either market is difficult but not impossible. And information about product quality and prices across sellers may be costly to obtain. Consumers of cereal may have to be nutrition specialists to compare one box of cereal with another. And buyers of computers may need to take a course in computer literacy before they shop around for the right computer. In other U.S. markets, power is scattered over many firms of nonhomogeneous commodities. Entry is restricted, and product and price information are imperfect. The market for legal services, for instance, includes a large number of firms and so does the market for dental services. Entry to either market requires the appropriate academic and professional credentials. And consumers must search around for the right attorney and the right dentist. Otherwise they may end up in pain.

Obviously, none of these examples fall under either monopoly or perfect competition. They rather fall in between, in what economists call imperfect competition (see Chapter Four). In particular, the cereal and computer markets fall under oligopoly, and the markets for legal and dental services fall under monopolistic competition. How do firms maximize profits in monopolistic competition and oligopoly? What about resource allocation? Do they allocate resources efficiently or inefficiently?

Addressing these questions, the chapter is in three sections. The first discusses market concentration at the aggregate and industry levels, the second discusses the model of monopolistic competition, and the third discusses the model of oligopoly.

9.1 Market Concentration in the U.S. Economy

Talking about real-world markets is not as easy as talking about market models. Many real-world markets may fall on the borderline of two models and, therefore, choosing the appropriate model may be a difficult issue. The fast food industry, for instance, includes six or seven major chain restaurants and thousands of individual restaurants. Where should this market be classified? To simplify matters, economists have developed market concentration indicators, i.e., ratios that give the percentage of market controlled by the top three, ten, one hundred, or two hundred firms in the market. The larger the concentration rates, the more market power is concentrated in a few sellers (Exhibit 9.1).

Exhibit 9.1
What's Market Concentration

- Market concentration is the percent of sales controlled by the top firms in an industry.

- It's used to draw the line between Monopolistic Competition and Oligopoly.

- The higher the concentration, the closer the market is to oligopoly model.

- The lower the concentration, the closer the market is to monopolistic competition model.

Sectoral Measures of Market Concentration

While at the aggregate level economists focus on the market share of the top hundred or two hundred firms, at the sectoral level, the focus is on the market share of the top one, two, three, or ten corporations.

Case 1: The Wireless Telecom Market—High Concentration

The wireless telecom market is a highly concentrated market, and therefore, is an oligopoly. In the cell tower services, three companies control 80% of the market, while in the wireless carrier service market four companies (soon to be three after the merger of Sprint and T-Mobile) control 100% of the market (see Exhibit).

Exhibit 9.2
A. Market Shares in the Wireless Tower and Carrier Market

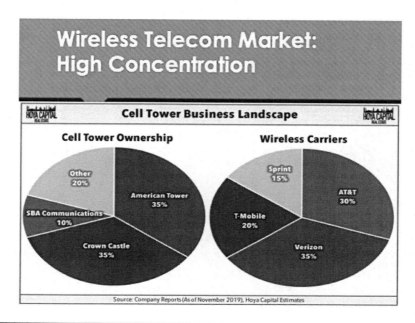

Case 2: The Market for Mobile and Smart Phones: Then and Now

The market for mobile phones is also a highly concentrated market, and therefore, is an oligopoly. At the end of 2000, six companies controlled almost two-thirds of the market (see Exhibits 9.2 and 9.3). Nokia had the largest market share, followed by Motorola and Ericsson. As was the case with the supercomputer market, the complexity of the mobile phones and the high technological and investment requirements restrict the entry of new competitors. In 2019, Samsung, Apple, and three Chinese smartphone makers controlled closed to 65% of the market.

Exhibit 9.2
B. The Market for Mobile Phones in 2000

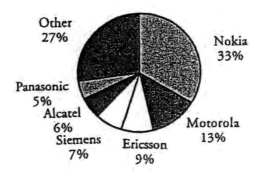

Source: Data compiled from corporate reports.

Exhibit 9.3
Market Shares in the Smartphone Industry in 2019

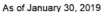

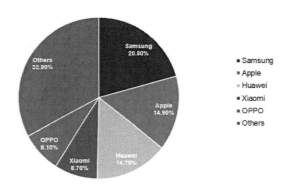

Source: IDC Quarterly Mobile Phone Tracker, January 30, 2019. The companies shown herein are used solely for illustrative purposes; any investment may or may not be currently held by any portfolio advised by Franklin Templeton Investments.

Case 3: The Fast Food Market

The fast food market is a low concentrated market, and therefore, is monopolistic competition market. In China, six franchises control roughly 10 percent of the market (see Exhibit 9.4). Entry to this market is restricted, but nowhere nearly as restricted as in the coffee, computer, and automobile markets. And while the large number of sellers may lead one to think of perfect competition, product differentiation, an essential characteristic of this industry, should discourage such a thought.

Exhibit 9.4
The Chinese Fast Food Market

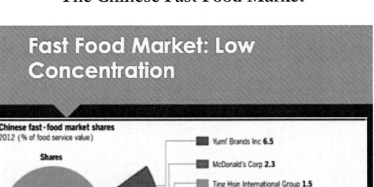

9.2 Monopolistic Competition

As we discussed in Chapter Four, monopolistic competition is a market structure that includes a mix of elements of monopoly and perfect competition. Monopoly elements come from market power, which comes with product differentiation. Perfect competition elements come from competition that comes with a large number of sellers.

Monopolistic Demand and Revenues

The demand for a monopolistic firm's product exhibits several similarities and differences compared to that of a true monopolist's. With regard to the similarities, the monopolistic firm's demand is also negatively sloped, meaning that the firm has considerable power to change the product price without losing a significant number of customers. With regard to the differences, the monopolistic firm's demand curve is relatively elastic, meaning that in deciding about price, the firm must take into consideration that consumers have many other firms to choose from (see Exhibit 9.5). For example, if one looks at the market for dental services, patients may like Doctor Smith's dental services, but if he raises the price of his services, some patients will turn away to other dentists. In other words, unlike a monopoly, monopolistic firms have limited market power, and if they abuse it they lose customers to other competitors.

Defining the demand curve, and applying the standard reasoning, total revenue is defined as the product of price and quantity sold in the market, with the relationship between total revenue and sales depending on the elasticity of demand, as in the case of monopoly (recall Exhibit 8.2). While average revenue is the same as with the demand curve, marginal revenue is below the demand curve (see Exhibit 9.6).

Short-Run Profit Maximization: Price Above Marginal Cost

As in a true monopoly, the monopolistic firm cannot choose price independently from output. The decision rule for either choice requires that marginal cost equal marginal revenue. Assuming that the cost curves have the usual shape, the rule is satisfied at point A in Exhibit 9.6. You may notice that, as with true monopoly, price is above the marginal cost, an indication that the monopolistic firm charges too high a price and produces too low an output compared to perfect competition. Nevertheless, such market distortion is not as bad as in the case of true monopoly.

Exhibit 9.5
Market Demand in Monopoly and Monopolistic Competition

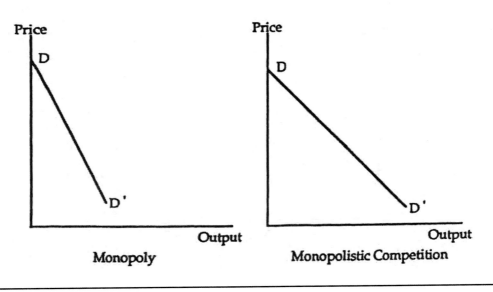

Monopoly   Monopolistic Competition

Exhibit 9.6
Price and Output Determination for a Monopolistic Firm:
The Short Run

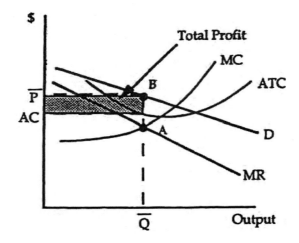

In choosing the output that maximizes profits, the monopolistic firm sets marginal cost equal to marginal revenue. As in the case of a true monopoly, price is set at P, above marginal cost.

Long-Run Profit Maximization: Excess Capacity

Unlike true monopoly, entry to a monopolistic competitive market, although restricted, is not completely blocked. If the industry makes a profit in the short run, new firms will enter the market. This will reduce the demand for the products of the existing firms and will drive profits down. Depending on how many firms enter the market, profits may even turn into losses and some firms will leave the industry. As in perfect competition, entry and exit to the market will continue until profits become equal to normal profits, i.e., the opportunity cost of capital and labor committed by the firm in this industry. This will be the point where the demand curve becomes tangent to the average total cost curve (see Exhibit 9.7). You should also notice that, unlike the perfect competitive firm which produces the profit maximizing output at the lowest long-run average cost, the monopolistic firm produces this output at a cost that is above the minimum. In other words, the monopolistic firm operates with an excess capacity that is reflected in the gap between Qm and Qo (see Exhibit 9.7). Moreover, you should notice that because each firm produces a different product than those of its competitors, we cannot determine an industry price and output level. What we can say is that price will differ across firms, and the more a firm differentiates its products from those of its competitors, the higher the price the firm can charge and the higher the market share to capture.

Non-Price Competition

Since product differentiation is a distinctive characteristic of this market, giving firms the power to influence price, it is in each firm's interest to attempt to magnify the differences of its products from those of other firms, an objective pursued with advertising and other marketing devices. Automobile companies, for instance, load cars with all kinds of extra equipment that are consumer catching devices rather than true improvements in car quality and performance. And so do the electronics companies that make VCRs, television sets, and home appliances. Do you use all the functions on your VCR? What about the functions on your microwave oven? Such practices mean that unlike perfect competition where firms compete with each other in terms of price, in monopolistic competition firms compete with each other by other means. This has given rise to what is often termed "non-price competition." It is important to notice that unlike price competition, non-price competition does not ensure the lowest price for consumers, neither does it provide for the efficient allocation of economic resources. However, monopolistic competition may benefit consumers in another sense: it gives them the choice to consume a variety of products. Therefore, whatever consumers pay above the competitive price could be considered as the premium that must be paid for such choice. At any rate, one should be careful in using the term competition and note the way it affects consumers and society.

Exhibit 9.7

Price and Output Determination for a Monopolistic Firm: The Long Run

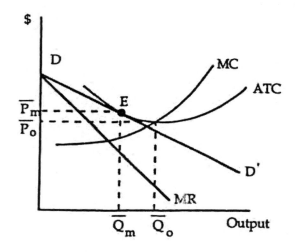

Entry and exit to the market dictate an output and a price level where profits are equal to normal profits. This holds true at point E, where the firm's demand curve becomes tangent to the average total cost curve.

9.3 Oligopoly

As we discussed in Chapter Four, oligopoly is a market of a few sellers who are interdependent, meaning that a seller's actions affect, and are affected by, the actions of other sellers. Entry to the market is restricted by physical, legal, financial, and marketing constraints, which allow sellers to acquire and perpetuate market control.

Oligopoly is loosely defined. Take the assumption of a few sellers, for instance. How "few" are "few"? Two, three, ten, twenty? What about size? The U.S. automobile industry, for instance, is an oligopoly of three sellers, with GM the largest seller. The home appliance industry is an oligopoly of five or six sellers. The soft drink industry is an oligopoly of two large sellers, Coke and Pepsi, and several small sellers. What about product differentiation? The steel industry is a homogeneous oligopoly. The home appliances, brewery, and tobacco industries are all differentiated oligopolies.

As oligopoly is a loosely defined market; no unique model exists that describes output and price determination for an individual firm and the industry as a whole. Instead, a number of models concerned with the strategic interactions among sellers that cover the special cases of oligopoly exist, the most important being the kinked demand model, the price leadership model, the rule-of-thumb model, and game models.

Product Differentiation as a Competitive Strategy

Product differentiation can be accomplished in two ways: by altering the physical characteristics of the product, or by altering the ways this product is delivered to customers, allowing international business to expand their market penetration in local established markets and to exploit market niches.

Intel, for instance, differentiates its products by speed, media, and customization, the development of "platforms" of multiple chips catered to four market segments: home computers, computers and servers, mobile gadgets and cellular phones, and network infrastructure devices. Estee Lauder's product divisions differentiate their products for different market segments. Estee Lauder targets the working woman. Clinique targets women in their 20s, while Jane targets teenagers. Applied Materials differentiates the technical characteristics of its products and services to address customers' productivity, cost, and return on investment needs. Texas Instruments customizes its analog signal products for different market segments, such as wireless, automotive, hard-disk drives, and printers. The company further customizes its digital signal processing products for several markets, including digital cameras, digital audio players, and multimedia storage disk drives. In the early 2000s, GE added more than a dozen new capabilities expected to contribute close to 90 percent of the company's 2005 earnings.

Product differentiation isn't a new competitive strategy. In the 1930s, automobile companies like GM differentiated their products by income, developing a broad line of automobile products catered to different market segments, for "every purpose and every purse": Cadillac for the upper class, the Oldsmobile and Buick for the middle class, and the Chevrolet for the lower class. In the 1960s and the 1970s, Japanese corporations expanded their presence in world markets by changing the attributes. Japanese automobile makers like Toyota and Honda, for instance, managed to gain substantial market share in the U.S. market by introducing smaller, more efficient, and better maneuverable cars with FWD. Japanese radio receiver makers like Sony managed to capture most of the U.S. market by miniaturizing radio receivers, while plain paper copy makers made their headway in the U.S. market by introducing simple, liquid toner copiers.

Product differentiation can be accomplished both internally and externally. In the consumer electronics sector, Sony relies on its own resources and expertise to differentiate its products. For the period 1950–2001, Sony Corporation developed successfully 27 innovative products, including: the first tape recorder, transistor radio, VCR, "Triniton" color TV, Digital Audio Tape (DAT), and Digital Video camcorder. Nokia has also relied on its own resources to develop new products. Korean conglomerates like Samsung Electronics produce internally almost every component going into their products. In the pharmaceuticals industry, Johnson and Johnson relies both on its own resources and on outside resources. The company's acquisition of McNeil Laboratories added a number of over the counter drugs popular in the U.S. market, including Tylenol. The acquisition of LifeScan Inc. added glucose monitors, the acquisition of Neutrogena added a number of beauty aids, while the acquisition of DePuy added a number of orthopedic products. In the soft drink industry, Coca Cola relies on its own resources for carbonated drinks, but on outside resources for non carbonated drinks. For this purpose, the company has formed alliances and joint ventures with consumer staples companies like Nestle to provide non carbonated drinks like iced coffee and iced tea. PepsiCo's acquisition of alternative drinks maker South Beach Beverage Co. and Quaker Oats, maker of leading sports drink Gatorade, expanded the company's drink portfolio to competing products.

In the electronic banking industry, companies rely on alliances to differentiate their products. The strategic alliance among Spain's Banco Popular, IBM, and German financial service company Allianz is a fourth case in point. The three companies agreed to create an Internet portal and to launch a business to business (B2B) partnership. Allianz and Banco Popular invested one billion pesetas ($5.66 million) as a seed capital for the portal. IBM provided the technology for the portal and the B2B project. In the food industry, J. M. Smuckers expanded its U.S. product portfolio by acquiring peanut butter product maker JIF. In the networking industry, Cisco Systems and Nortel Networks relied on a stream of mergers and acquisitions. In the 1990s, Cisco acquired about 70 companies, while Nortel Networks acquired ten companies, including IP Network maker Bay Networks, Internet protocol services Shasta, and enterprise network maker Peripheronics.

Price Rigidity: The Kinked Demand Model

The kinked demand model, first developed by Paul Sweezy in 1939, is an attempt to explain the observed price rigidity in a number of oligopolistic markets even in the face of considerable cost variations: recognizing mutual interdependence, firms arrive, through any appropriate or inappropriate business practice, at a commodity price they have no incentive to adjust upward or downward. Specifically, the kinked demand model rests on the following assumptions:

(a) the supply side of the market consists of a small number of large sellers of an approximately equal size,

(b) each seller has a good knowledge of how the other sellers would respond if it were to take the initiative to change the commodity price or output.

Taken together, these assumptions imply asymmetric price behavior among sellers. If a seller raised his price, others would not follow, and the seller's market share would diminish. If the seller lowered his price, others *would* follow, matching the lower price, and the seller's market share would remain unchanged. Such asymmetric price behavior implies a kinked demand and discontinuous marginal revenue (see Exhibit 9.8).

Exhibit 9.8
Asymmetric Price Responses:
Kinked Demand and Discontinuous Revenues

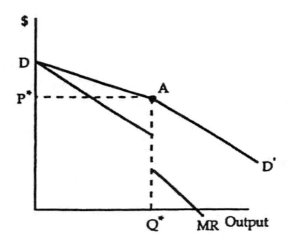

With an asymmetric price response, the firm's effective demand is DAD'. The firm expects that AD will apply for prices higher than the current price P, but AD' will apply for prices higher than the current price P. As a result of the kink, marginal revenue does not have the usual negative slope (as in the case of the monopoly), but it is discontinuous at the current price.

Profit Maximization and Price Rigidity

Following the conventional procedure, profit maximization requires a comparison between marginal revenue and marginal cost. Assuming that marginal cost has the usual shape and crosses the discontinuous range of the marginal revenue curve, the profit maximization price and output levels are P* and Q* respectively (see Exhibit 9.9). Although this point sounds like a trivial conclusion that follows the assumption of asymmetric behavior, what makes the model popular is the prediction that the profit maximizing price will remain unchanged even in the face of slight cost variations (see Exhibit 9.10). Notice, however, that this point is valid only as long as marginal cost stays within the discontinuous range of the marginal revenue. If the marginal cost gets outside, price changes will follow. Sharply lower marginal costs, for instance, could result in a price war.

Exhibit 9.9
The Kinked Demand Model:
Price and Output Determination

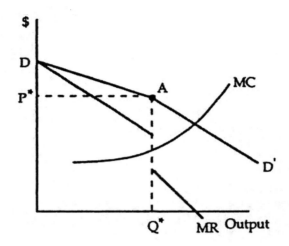

Following the conventional rule, profit is maximized at the output level where marginal cost equals marginal revenue. Because of marginal revenue discontinuity, price is determined at the current level, P*.

Exhibit 9.10
The Kinked Demand Model:
Price Rigidity in the Face of Cost Variations

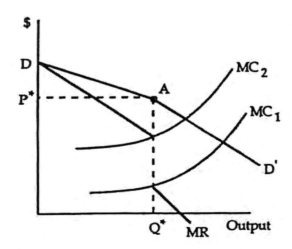

Because of the discontinuity of marginal revenue, the profit maximization price remains at the current, P*, level even in the face of slight cost variations.

Example

Gasoline stations located in remote areas are good examples of markets that comply with the requirements of the kinked demand model. Take, for instance, three gasoline stations located off Interstate 80. How do they set gasoline prices? Let us say that station A posts a price of $1, station B a price of $.98, and station C a price of $.95 (see Exhibit). Taking for granted that consumers are rational and well informed about these prices, they will end up buying gasoline at station C. Faced with this situation, stations A and B cut their prices below that of station C. This price war goes on until all three stations come up with an acceptable price.

	Round 1	Round 2	Round 3
A	$1.00	$.92	$.88
B	.98	.90	.88
C	.95	.88	.88

The kinked demand model is useful in explaining pricing in an oligopoly market of sellers of about equal size. What about pricing of oligopoly markets with a firm leader?

The Price Leadership Model

Not all oligopolistic markets comply with the kinked demand model. In some markets, firms of unequal size and unequal power influence price. An interesting case is that of one firm or a group of firms being the leader and the remainder being the followers. IBM, for instance, is the leader in the computer hardware market and all other producers are the followers. The leader does not always have to be the largest firm in the market. SONY Corporation, for instance, is a midget compared to NEC, and yet, it is the leader because of its product innovation. How are output and prices determined in this case? The firm leader plays a role similar to that of the market in perfect competition, in the sense that it sets the price that the followers take as given, choosing the output that maximizes its own profits. However, in order for the leader to leave room for followers, the price must be set above the average cost of the followers, allowing a portion of the market to their account; otherwise, the followers will be driven out of the market and the leader will become a monopoly (a not-so-happy prospect in a society of monopoly regulators!).

Rule-of-Thumb Models: Cost Markup Practice

As you may recall from Chapter One, the standard methodology of economics is based on formal modeling and hypothesis testing, a method we have adhered to in our discussion of output and price determination. Not all economists are happy with this procedure, however. As most of the models described thus far require precise knowledge of marginal cost and revenue curves, institutional economists have raised concerns about the practicality of conventional economic theory. As an alternative, they have launched several surveys in which they asked firms themselves about output and price determination. They found that firms follow routine rules (rules of thumb). A popular version of such models is the cost markup model.

The Cost Markup Model

According to this model, firms calculate prices as the sum of two components, average cost and a profit markup (see Exhibit 9.11).

$$P = AC + Markup$$

Both components are easy to calculate, and while average cost is determined by technological factors, the cost markup is set as a percent of the former and adjusted according to the absolute size and the elasticity of demand for a firm's product. A high demand/low elasticity product will allow a high markup. A low demand/high elasticity product will allow a low markup. In perfect competition, where all firms are faced with the same demand conditions, the markup will be equal to normal profit. In a monopoly and monopolistic competition the markup will exceed normal profit. These remarks connect the cost markup model to the traditional market models we have discussed in the previous chapters: cost markup will vary from industry to industry and from product to product. You should also notice that as a product may exhibit different demand conditions in different seasons, the profit markup could vary accordingly. For example, one would expect a low profit markup and a low price for ice cream during the winter months, when fewer people have a strong preference for ice cream (lower price is often reflected in coupon discounts). By contrast, one would expect a high profit markup and a high price for winter clothes at the beginning of the cold season, etc. Similarly, profit markup on roses is expected to be high on special occasions like Valentine's Day, and low on regular days.

Exhibit 9.11
Price Determination in the Cost Markup Model

Price

Markup
Average Cost

Commodity price is determined as the sum of average cost and a markup (a percent of the former).

Several studies support the cost markup pricing hypothesis. In a classical study of pricing policies of major U.S. corporations, economists Kaplan, Dirlam, and Lanzillotti confirm that profit margins depend on the size of product elasticity. Profit margins are high for demand-inelastic products and low for demand-elastic products. Within the steel industry, for instance, profit margins for a demand-elastic product like stainless steel were found to be low; and profit margins for demand-inelastic products like steel rails were found to be high.

Game Models[1]

In recent years, game theory has been gaining in popularity as an analytical tool in microeconomics. Game models describe strategic behavior among firms in an oligopolistic market due to the characteristics of oligopoly, such as the assumption of a few, mutually interdependent sellers. This section provides the basic concepts and applications of game theory and the Nash Equilibrium.

A game consists of three components: (i) number of players, (ii) number of strategies of each player, and (iii) payoffs. For example, in duopoly, firms have the choice to or not to invest a certain amount of money in advertisement. A payoff table can be derived from the model, which depends on their cost structure, demand schedule, and firms' strategies.

Basic Concepts

The concept of equilibrium for a game comes from John Nash, an American mathematician, who formulated the concept in 1951. A pair of strategies is defined as a Nash Equilibrium if player A's choice is optimal, given player B's choice, and player B's choice is optimal, given player A's choice. Remember that neither player knows what the other player will do when he or she has to make his or her own choice of strategy. The following table is an example of game theory in a Normal Form. There are two players—A and B, in the game. Each player has two strategies: player A can choose either TOP or BOTTOM; Player B can choose either RIGHT or LEFT. Player A receives $1, and B receives nothing, if A chooses TOP, and B chooses LEFT, and so on.

		Player B	
		LEFT	RIGHT
Player A	TOP	1,0	1,1
	BOTTOM	−10,0	2,1

Given that player B chooses RIGHT, player A would choose BOTTOM. Given player A's BOTTOM, B would chose RIGHT. Therefore, the pair of strategies (BOTTOM, RIGHT) is the Nash Equilibrium.

An Application: Duopoly

Let us consider the game of two firms, A and B. Each firm has two strategies—to advertise or not to advertise. Firm A receives $10 and firm B receives $5 if both firms choose to advertise. Firm A receives $15 and firm B receives nothing if A chooses to advertise and B chooses not to advertise.

		Firm B	
		ADVERTISE	DON'T
Firm A	ADVERTISE	10,5	15,0
	DON'T	6,8	10,2

Given firm B's ADVERTISEMENT, the best strategy for firm A is ADVERTISEMENT. Given A's ADVERTISEMENT, the best strategy for firm B is ADVERTISEMENT. Therefore, (ADVERTISE, ADVERTISE) is the Nash Equilibrium of this example. Furthermore, no matter what firm B does, firm A does best by advertising. So, advertising is a dominant strategy for firm A. The same is true for firm B. Assuming that both firms are rational, we know that the outcome for this game is that both firms will advertise.

To sum up, many real-world markets fall in between the two extreme market models in what economists call imperfect competition. Imperfect competition can be approached by two models, monopolistic competition and oligopoly.

In monopolistic competition, firms maximize profits in a fashion similar to that of a monopoly. They set marginal cost equal to marginal revenue, and sell at a price above marginal cost. Because of this pricing rule, monopolistic firms allocate resources inefficiently. As product differentiation is an important element of monopolistic competition, firms compete not only on price but also on advertising, new product development, and marketing gimmicks.

In oligopoly, profit maximization may take different forms. In one version of oligopoly, described by the kinked demand model, firms set a commonly acceptable price, which no firm has an incentive to change. In another version, the leadership model, the leading firm in the market sets the commodity price and the others follow that price. In the same way, each firm follows the market price in perfect competition. In a third version of oligopoly, firms set prices as the sum of average cost and a markup.

The discussion of monopolistic competition completes our investigation of commodity markets. It is now the time to turn to the resource markets, and in particular, the labor market.

9.4 Review

1. Imperfect Competition refers to market structures that exhibit a mix of the characteristics of monopoly and perfect competition. The two popular versions of imperfect competition are monopolistic competition and oligopoly.

2. Monopolistic Competition refers to a market structure that includes elements of monopoly and elements of perfect competition. A monopolistic firm maximizes profits at an output level that sets marginal cost equal to marginal revenue. As in the case of a monopoly, the commodity price is set above marginal cost.

3. Oligopoly refers to a market structure of a small number of large firms which sell either homogeneous or differentiated commodities. Entry into the market is restricted by economic, legal, and technical barriers. Because an oligopoly is not well defined, there is no unique model that describes output and price determination. Instead, there are many models that refer to particular cases: the kinked demand model, the price leadership model, the rule-of-thumb model, and game models.

4. The Kinked-Demand model is an attempt to explain price rigidity that appears in some oligopolistic markets even in the face of considerable cost changes. The model rests on the following assumptions: (a) each firm believes that a price increase would not be followed by other firms (b) each firm believes that a price decrease would be followed by other firms. As a result of these assumptions, each firm is faced with a kinked rather than a straight demand line and a discontinuous marginal revenue line. Given this setting and assuming that marginal cost and marginal revenue intersect with each other at the discontinuous part of the latter, price will be set at the current level, and stay there even in the presence of considerable cost changes.

5. The Price Leadership model refers to an oligopoly situation where one firm or a group of firms is recognized as the market leader while the remaining firms follow its behavior closely. Acknowledging the existence of followers, the leader behaves as a restricted monopolist: it sets price at a level that allows the other firms to capture a market share sufficient for their survival. In this sense, followers behave as perfect competitors with each other.

6. Rule-of-Thumb models refer to routine pricing policies, such as the cost markup model. According to this model, a commodity's price consists of two components—average cost and a profit markup. While average cost is determined by technological factors, cost markup is determined by the size of the product demand—how many customers there are—and the elasticity of demand (i.e., how sensitive customers are to changes in the price of the product).

7. Game models describe strategic behavior in oligopolistic markets, i.e., courses of action that are contingent on competitors' decisions.

Review Questions

1. What is market concentration? How is it measured?
2. What is monopolistic competition? How does a monopolistic firm maximize profits in the short run? In the long run?
3. Is the monopolistic profit-maximization rule consistent with efficient allocation of economic resources?
4. What is non-price competition? How does it affect consumers?
5. What is oligopoly? Is it well defined?
6. What are the assumptions and the implications of the kinked-demand model?
7. What is the reasoning behind the cost markup model? How does it compare to perfect competition and monopoly models? What is the relationship between cost markup and demand elasticity?

Note

1. The author is indebted to Dr. Laura Lu for her assistance in the preparation of this section.

Homework 9

1. Why is it difficult to draw the line between monopolistic competition and oligopoly?

2. What is market concentration? How is it measured?

3. What are the implications of the Kinked-Demand Model?

4. What determines the size of mark-up in the Cost mark-up model?

5. How does a monopolistic firm maximize profits in the short term?

6. How does a monopolistic firm maximize profits in the long term?

7. What is Nonprice competition?

Chapter 10

LABOR MARKET

Preview

In the previous chapters we took a closer look at the demand and the supply sides of the market for a product. In this chapter we are taking a closer look at the resource markets, especially the labor market. Among other things, we focus on the questions: What determines the wage rate and employment in an industry? Do unions play any role? What determines inter-industry and interpersonal earnings differences?

Introduction

Have you decided about the working career you would like to pursue? Have you checked the wages you could earn? Here are some interesting numbers for you. In 2007, college graduates in business earned an annual salary of $57,181. M.A. holders earned an annual salary of $70,186. Ph.D. holders earned an annual salary of $95,565.

While keeping an eye on wages is important, you must also look at job opportunities for each occupation. Between 1990–2005, occupations for mathematical and computer scientists, personal service, health care, and legal service have the greatest potential growth; and occupations for private household workers, machine operators, and financial records processing have the lowest growth potential. Between 2006–2008, professional service occupations had the highest potential, while production occupations had the least potential.

Why do earnings differ across occupations? Why do employment opportunities differ across occupations? To answer these questions, we must investigate the mechanics of the labor market, i.e., the demand for and supply of labor.

This chapter is in six sections. The first section is a discussion of the concept of a labor market. The second section discusses the demand side of the labor market. The third section discusses the supply side of the market. The fourth section puts together the two sides of the labor market. The fifth section discusses labor market issues, and the sixth section ends with a review of the labor market.

10.1 The Concept of Labor Market

The labor market can be analyzed from two perspectives, economy wide and industry specific. From the economy-wide perspective, the labor market refers to the process that facilitates the exchange of labor services among all firms and all households. From the industry perspective, the labor market refers to the process that facilitates the exchange of labor services between the firms of a particular industry and households. While both concepts are of interest to economists, for the purpose of answering the questions we have raised above, we focus our discussion on the labor market of a particular industry.

As with any other market, the labor market includes two sides: the demand side and the supply side. The demand side consists of firms (employers) which are ready to buy (hire) labor and employ it in the production of goods and services. The supply side consists of households (employees) which are ready to sell their labor services in return for wages. The interaction of the two sides of the market determines the equilibrium or market wage and the equilibrium employment. Formally:

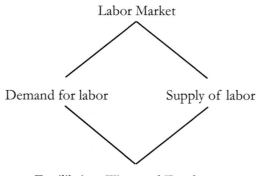

Labor Market

Demand for labor   Supply of labor

Equilibrium Wage and Employment

The interaction between firms and households is not without restrictions. It is subject to institutional constraints such as collective bargaining laws, contractual agreements, and employment practices. Through most of this chapter, in order to simplify matters, we assume there are no such restrictions. We make up a perfectly competitive labor market that exhibits the following characteristics: (a) a large number of small firms with identical job openings; households are indifferent about which firm they sell their labor services to, and therefore no firm (buyer) can influence wages, (b) labor mobility across jobs is costless, i.e., there are no contractual, relocation, or job search costs, (c) perfect information.

Given this setting, which factors determine the demand side of the market? Which factors determine the supply side of the market? How do the two sides determine the equilibrium wage and employment? Before we embark on these questions we must clarify the concept of labor input. It consists of two dimensions: hours of work and number of workers, the product of these two variables often being called man-hours. For example, the daily labor input of a company that employs 100 workers for eight hours a day is 800 man-hours. To simplify matters, we can assume that hours of work are fixed and labor input is measured in terms of numbers of workers.

10.2 The Demand Side: Firms

As stated in earlier chapters, labor is an input in the production of goods and services and therefore is useful to firms: they must hire labor, employ it along with other inputs in producing commodities that they expect to sell in the commodity market at a profit. In this sense the demand for labor is associated with the firm's output, and it is called derived demand. What is the appropriate quantity of labor input a firm must hire? To put it differently, which factors determine the quantity of labor input demanded? Several factors, the most important being

- The Wage Rate
- The Demand for the Firm's Product
- Technology
- The Price of Other Inputs

To discuss how each of these factors affects the firm's decision to hire labor, we discuss them one by one, starting with the wage rate. Other things being equal, would the firm hire more or less labor at a higher wage rate? To answer this question we must discuss the firm's hiring decisions.

The Firm's Hiring Decision

The firm's decision to hire additional labor involves the deployment of concepts we learned in Chapter Six, especially the concept of marginal physical product of labor. As you will recall from that chapter, marginal product refers to the contribution of additional labor to the firm's total output. To put it differently, marginal product shows how much each additional labor unit is worth to the firm. However, employing additional labor is not without cost. The firm must pay wages. This means that for each additional unit of labor the firm must weigh the marginal product against the wage rate.

To understand this process, we can recall from Chapter Six the marginal product of a bakery firm (see first two columns of Exhibit 10.1). Before we pursue the comparison between marginal product and the wage rate, and in order for the two variables to be comparable, marginal product must be converted to dollars. Assuming that the firm sells output in a competitive market, this exercise can be carried out by multiplying the marginal product with the commodity price (see columns two, three, and four of Exhibit 10.1). The outcome of this exercise is called Value of Marginal Product. Formally:

$$\text{Value of Marginal Product (VMP)} = (\text{Marginal Product}) \times (\text{Price})$$

Now, we can proceed with the comparison between the value of marginal product and the wage rate, deriving the firm's hiring rule: the firm must hire workers until the last worker's dollar contribution to the total output is equal to the wage rate. Formally,

$$\text{VMP} = \text{W}$$

Another way of looking at this rule is to think of it as a cutting point between hiring and not hiring additional labor. As long as VMP exceeds the wage rate, the firm is better with that additional unit of labor than without it.

Exhibit 10.1
The Bakery Firm's Hiring Decision:
The Value of Marginal Product versus the Wage Rate

Labor Input	Marginal Product	Price	Value of Marginal Product	Wage Rate
1	—	$10	—	$70
2	$8	10	$80	70
3	10	10	100	70
4	9	10	90	70
5	7	10	70	70
6	5	10	50	70
7	3	10	30	70
9	–3	10	–30	70

The first two columns of the table are taken from Exhibit 6.1 of Chapter Six. The third column is constructed under the assumption that the firm sells bread in a competitive market at ten dollars per unit. The fourth column gives the Value of the Marginal Product (the product of the second and third columns), and the fifth column gives the wage rate, which we have assumed to be seventy dollars. Applying the hiring rule, the firm must hire workers until the value of the marginal product is equal to the wage rate, i.e., they must hire five workers.

The Value of the Marginal Product Is the Firm's Demand Curve

Deriving the firm's hiring decision rule, we have assumed a fixed wage rate. How would the firm adjust hiring if the wage rate were to change? The firm would adjust the quantity of labor accordingly, moving along the curve of the value of marginal product. This means that the value of the marginal product curve constitutes the firm's demand for labor. You should notice that the firm has no problem in hiring additional units of labor as long as the value of marginal product is increasing. Conversely, the firm is not interested in hiring labor with a negative marginal product. Therefore, it is only the *diminishing part* of the value of marginal product, but not the negative one, that is relevant for a firm's decisions and constitutes the firm's demand curve. It shows the amount of labor input an employer is willing to hire at different wage rates: the firm plans to hire additional labor at a lower wage (see Exhibit 10.2). Reflecting the law of diminishing returns, the firm's demand curve is negatively sloped.

Exhibit 10.2
The Demand for Labor

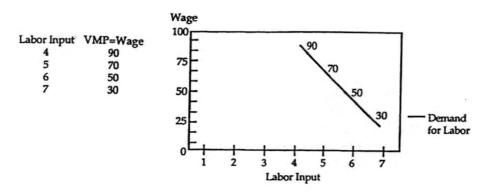

Labor Input	VMP=Wage
4	90
5	70
6	50
7	30

The table on the left is a numerical exhibition of the competitive firm's demand for labor. The figure on the right is a graphical exhibition of the firm's demand curve. Both exhibits give the quantity of labor input a firm is willing to hire at different wages. Reflecting the law of diminishing returns, the firm's demand for labor is negatively sloped.

From the Individual to the Market Demand Curve: Summing up the Individual Demand Curves

Now, after we have rationalized the shape of the individual demand curve, we can derive the market demand curve. This exercise can be carried out through a horizontal summation of all individual demand curves (see Exhibit 10.3). In this exhibit we have assumed that there are one hundred firms in the market with identical demand curves. So the first column of the table was derived by multiplying the first column of the exhibit 10.4 by 100. Consequently the market demand in a particular industry such as the bakery industry, the computer industry, or the coal mining industry is the sum of all employers' demands for labor: it shows the firms' hiring plans at different wage rates.

Exhibit 10.3
From the Individual to the Market Demand Curve:
The Bakery Industry

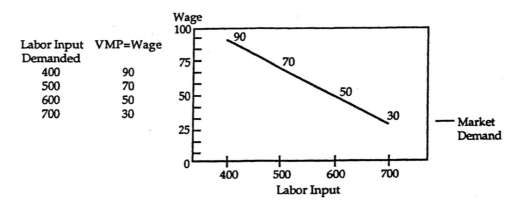

Labor Input Demanded	VMP=Wage
400	90
500	70
600	50
700	30

The market demand for labor is the sum of all individual demands. The exhibit shows the amount of labor input all employers are willing to hire at a different wages. Reflecting the law of diminishing returns that characterizes the production process of each firm, the market demand is negatively sloped: firms plan to hire less labor at higher wages.

After we have established the relationship between wage and the quantity of labor input demanded, we return to the other factors that we have assumed constant, namely the demand for the firm's product, the state of technology, and the price of other inputs. What would happen to the demand for labor if any of these factors were to change? The whole demand labor curve would shift to the left or to the right (see Exhibit 10.4). But let us say a few words about how each factor affects the demand for labor.

• *The Demand for the Firm's Product.* As you may recall from our earlier discussion, the demand for labor is a derived demand; i.e., it is associated with the firm's production. Changes in the demand for the product will be reflected in changes in the demand for labor. For example, an increase in the demand for bread will result in a higher demand for labor in the bread industry (the whole demand curve shifts to the right).

• *The State of Technology.* As another factor of production, technology determines productivity, i.e., the number of units each additional labor unit can produce. Improvements in technology make labor more productive and therefore result in an increase in the demand for labor (the whole demand curve shifts to the right)—see end of the chapter for a case study.

• *The Price of Other Inputs.* Although labor is needed to produce commodities, it is not the only factor of production. The firm must employ labor along with other human and nonhuman inputs in a way that minimizes production costs. In doing so, the firm must take into consideration not just the price of labor (wage) but also the price of other inputs. The choice of the lowest cost combination depends on the price of other factors of production. For example, an increase in the price of capital may reduce the demand for capital and increase the demand for labor (the whole curve will shift to the right).

The demand for labor is only one part of the labor market story, the other being the supply of labor.

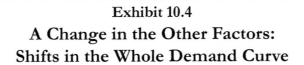

Exhibit 10.4
A Change in the Other Factors:
Shifts in the Whole Demand Curve

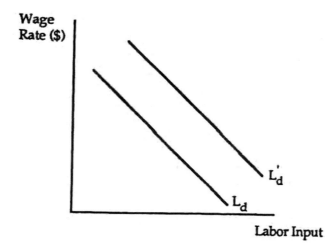

While changes in the wage reflect an adjustment in labor input along the demand curve for labor, changes in any other factors reflect a shift in the whole demand curve.

10.3 The Supply Side: Households

As stated in Chapter Two, labor is a source of income for almost all households. Specifically, about 75 percent of income of American households is derived from selling labor services to firms. How do households decide to allocate time between market and non-market activities? What about decisions to choose to work for a particular industry?

Household decisions to allocate time between market and non-market activities depend on the wage rate. Changes in the wage rate affect labor supply decisions in two ways. First, as the wage rate is the opportunity cost of any non-market activity, a higher wage induces households to substitute nonmarket activities with market activities. This effect known as the *substitution effect* suggests a direct relationship between wages and time supplied to labor markets. Second, as the wage rate increases, households can earn the same income by working less. This effect, known as the *income effect,* suggests an inverse relationship between wages and time allocated to market activities. The net impact of the wage rate on work depends on the relative strength of the substitution and income effects.

Household decisions to choose to work in a particular industry depend on the wage rate and benefits paid in that industry, working conditions, and wage rates and working conditions in other industries. In sum:

- Wage Rate Paid in the Occupation
- Other Pecuniary and Nonpecuniary Benefits
- Working Conditions
- Wage Rates Offered in Related Industries

To understand how these factors determine the amount of labor services that households are willing to supply to the market, we discuss them one by one. First we establish the relationship between the wage rate and the quantity of labor input supplied, assuming all the other factors away. Then we discuss how each of the other factors affects that relationship.

In general, as the wage rate increases in a particular industry, the industry becomes more appealing to workers in other industries, some of whom may quit their jobs and opt to work for this industry. To understand this relationship, we appeal to a numerical and a graphic presentation (see Exhibit 10.5). As you can see from the table on the left, as the wage rate increases from 30 to 50 and then to 70, the quantity of labor supplied increases from 400 to 600 and then to 800. This direct relationship between the wage rate and the quantity of labor supplied is reflected in the positive slope of the curve on the right of the exhibit.

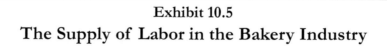

Exhibit 10.5
The Supply of Labor in the Bakery Industry

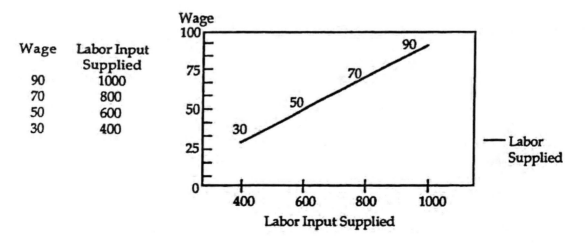

Wage	Labor Input Supplied
90	1000
70	800
50	600
30	400

The table on the left gives a numerical example of the labor supply to the bakery industry. As the wage increases from $30 to $50, the labor input supplied increases from 400 to 600 workers. On the right of the exhibit, reflecting the direct relationship between the wage rate and the quantity of labor supplied, the supply curve is positively sloped.

Now that we have established the relationship between the wage rate and the quantity of labor supplied, we can turn to the other factors that we have assumed away and see how they affect the supply curve. As in the case of the demand curve, a change in the "other factors" results in a shift in the whole supply curve to the left or to the right from its initial position. For example, an increase in the wages offered in other industries will draw laborers away from this industry: the supply curve shifts to the left (see Exhibit 10.6). Similarly, an improvement in the nonpecuniary characteristics of the industry will result in a shift of the supply curve to the right.

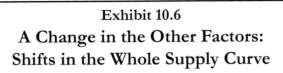

Exhibit 10.6
A Change in the Other Factors:
Shifts in the Whole Supply Curve

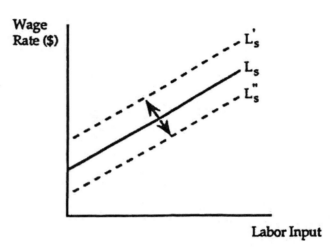

While a change in the wage rate is reflected by an adjustment in labor input along the supply curve, a change in any of the other factors is reflected in a shift in the whole supply curve.

10.4 Putting the Two Sides Together: Equilibrium Wage and Equilibrium Employment

Now that we have become familiar with the two sides of the labor market, we can proceed to pull the two sides together and determine the equilibrium employment and equilibrium wage. This exercise is carried out in Exhibit 10.7 As we can see, the equilibrium wage rate is determined at the intersection of the demand and the supply curve, that is, at a wage rate of $50 and the equilibrium employment that corresponds to this wage is 600 workers.

Exhibit 10.7
A. Putting the Two Sides Together:
The Equilibrium Wage and Equilibrium Employment

Labor Input Demanded	Wage Rate	Labor Input Supplied
400	90	1000
500	70	800
600	50	600
700	30	400

This table puts together the two sides of the labor market in the bakery industry. The market is at equilibrium at a wage rate of $50 and an employment of 600 workers.

B. The Equilibrium Wage and Employment

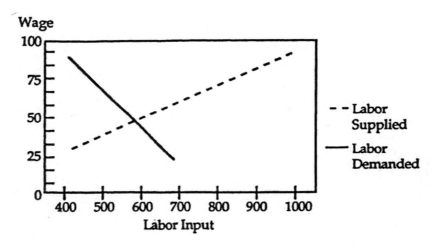

The equilibrium wage and equilibrium employment and determined at point A, the intersection of the demand and the supply of labor. At this point the wage rate is $50 and the employment level is 600 workers.

10.5 Labor Market Issues

Minimum Wage

In an attempt to alleviate poverty, labor unions and other social organizations have campaigned for a minimum wage, i.e., a legal benchmark for the hiring of workers. Although the state of Massachusetts introduced a minimum wage act as early as 1812, the Fair Labor Standards Act that established minimum wage nationwide was not introduced until 1938, when minimum wage was set at 25 cents. Responding to changes in the cost of living, Congress has occasionally raised the minimum wage (see Exhibit 10.8). But despite these adjustments, minimum wage is far below the average wage with the gap ever widening. In 1988, with an average wage of close to $10, minimum wage was $3.10 (see Exhibit 10.9).

According to the U.S. Department of Labor, about 3.3 million workers earned the minimum wage or less in 1999. Of these workers, 80 percent were eighteen years or older, 78 percent non-Hispanic whites, 57 percent women, 88 percent in service occupations, 36 percent come from poor families. These percentages may be misleading, however. Not every worker is covered by the minimum wage legislation, and many workers still receive a wage below the minimum.

Exhibit 10.8
Federal Minimum Wage 1938–2021

Year	Minimum Wage
1938	$0.25
1945	0.40
1956	1.00
1963	1.25
1968	1.60
1975	2.10
1980	3.10
1990	3.80
1994	4.75
1998	5.15
2007	5.85
2009	7.25
2021	$11

Source: U.S. Department of Labor
Reflecting changes in economic conditions, minimum wage has increased from $0.25 in 1938 to $11 in 2021.

Ever since introduced, the minimum wage has been the focus of controversy in economic literature. The question often asked is whether the minimum wage serves its purpose, i.e., provides for a minimum income for workers at the lower end of the labor force.

Depending upon the assumptions one makes about the labor market, there are three different answers to this question. First, the minimum wage may hurt those it was designed to help. As with any other market restriction, a minimum wage constitutes a wedge between the two sides of the market. Being forced to pay higher wages, firms reduce hiring. This results in a labor surplus or unemployment (see Exhibit 10.10). Thus, there is a trade-off between higher wages and employment opportunities. While jobs pay more, the chance of getting a job is lower. A study finds that a 10 percent increase in the minimum wage decreases employment by 1 percent. Second, the minimum wage legislation may benefit skilled labor at the expense of unskilled labor. As the minimum wage is most likely to raise wages of unskilled labor, employers may decide to substitute skilled labor for unskilled labor. Third, in an attempt to cope with higher wages, firms may trade higher wages for lower fringe benefits; thus a minimum wage may hurt both skilled and unskilled labor by lowering fringe benefits.

Exhibit 10.9

The Effect of Minimum Wage on the Labor Market

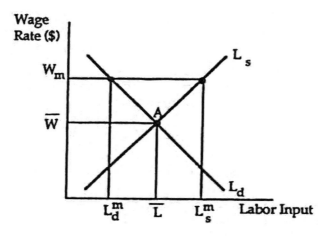

A minimum wage imposes a wedge between the two sides of the market, preventing the market from reaching equilibrium, something that results in a labor surplus or unemployment.

Amnesty Brings Lower Wages in California Farms

The year 1986 was a relief year for illegal aliens. The Federal Immigration Reform and Control Act allowed hundreds of thousands of illegal immigrants to live and work legally in the U.S. How has this legislation affected the labor market in states with a large number of illegal immigrants like California? Legality increased the supply of labor and wages dropped. According to a *New York Times* report, 1.3 million people applied, 55 percent or 700,000 workers were in California. In Salinas, wages dropped from an average of $7 an hour to $5.50 an hour (see Exhibit 10.10).

Exhibit 10.10

The Effect of 1986 Amnesty on the California Labor Market

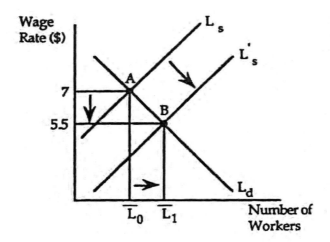

As labor supply increased with amnesty, wages in California farms dropped.

Wage Differentials

As labor is the main source of income for the majority of households, wage differentials are the clue to investigating the income inequalities characterizing market economies. As a result, exploring wage differentials has always been a challenge to economic theory. Many economists, including the classical economists Adam Smith and David Ricardo, have attempted to identify the causes of inter-industry and interpersonal wage differentials.

Inter-industry Wage Differentials

To get an idea about wage differentials across industries just take a look at Exhibit 10.11. Wholesale trading and mining paid the highest hourly wages in 2021, in the low 30s, while retail trade and construction paid the lowest wage per hour, in the low $20s. What accounts for such wage differentials? Since wages in any industry are determined by demand and supply, differences in wages across industries must be found in differences in demand and supply conditions (see Exhibit 10.12).

Exhibit 10.11
Average Hourly Earnings by Industry in 1999 and 2021

Industry	1999 Average Hourly Earnings	2021 Average Hourly Earnings
Mining	$17.04	$31.13
Construction	17.13	20.67
Manufacturing	13.91	17.13
Transportation and Public Utilities	15.67	26.07
Wholesale Trade	14.59	33.34
Retail Trade	14.61	21.40
Services	13.28	26.17

Source: U.S. Department of Labor

Wage Differentials Due to Demand Factors

The demand for labor is not evenly distributed across industries. At any moment, there are industries that grow fast and therefore demand a large number of new workers, and industries that grow slowly, and therefore demand a small number of new workers. Assuming an even supply of labor across industries, fast-growing industries are expected to pay higher wages and provide more jobs than the slow-growing ones (see Exhibit 10.12).

Wage Differentials Due to Supply Factors

Not all industries are equally popular among prospective workers. As a result the supply of labor is unevenly distributed across industries. Working several hundred feet under the ground is neither safe nor pleasant, and not very many people are qualified to take or thrilled to get such a job. By contrast, working in retail trade is fairly safe, and the working conditions are in no way similar to mining, and many people are qualified for and happy to get such a job. Assuming the same demand for labor in both industries, wages will be higher in the mining industry, and the wage differential could be considered a premium to those who choose to put up with the hardships of mining (see Exhibit 10.13).

Exhibit 10.12
Wage Differentials Attributed to Demand Factors

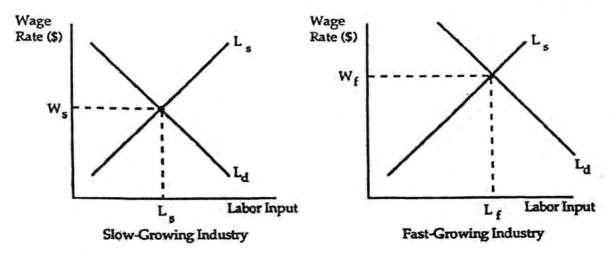

Assuming an even supply of labor to the two industries, the fast-growing industry pays higher wages.

Exhibit 10.13
Wage Differentials Due to Supply Factors

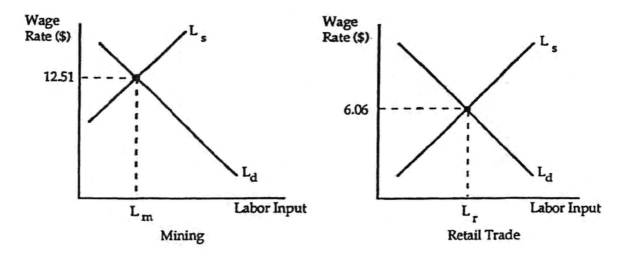

Assuming an even demand for labor in the two industries, the mining industry pays higher wages that the retail trade industry.

Interpersonal Wage Differentials

Wage differentials are not confined just to the industry level. They extend to persons. In other words, even persons working in the same industry earn different wages. What is the reason for such differences? Personal characteristics such as age, quantity and quality of education, gender, and social status.

Age

Age has a positive effect on earnings: other things being equal, workers with a longer service record are expected to earn more than workers with a shorter record of service (see Exhibit 10.14A). Chemists, for instance, with a B.A. and fifteen to nineteen years of experience earned $41,400, almost twice the earnings of chemists with a B.A. and zero to one years of experience (see Exhibit 10.15). In other words, age is a proxy for experience. And as experienced workers are normally more productive than inexperienced workers, they hold better paying positions.

While age is an important determinant of interpersonal wage differentials, so is the quantity and quality of education.

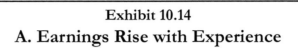

Exhibit 10.14

A. Earnings Rise with Experience

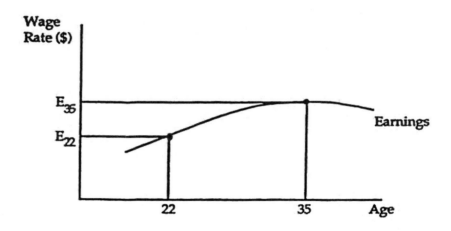

Being a proxy for experience, age has a positive effect on earnings. Other things being equal, a thirty-five year old worker is expected to earn more than a twenty-two year old worker.

Seniority Wages in Japan

In the conventional economic wisdom, the term *seniority wages* is used to describe the direct relationship between on-the-job experience and wage growth. The longer the service in a job the higher the wage.

When applied to the Japanese economy, the term has a slightly different meaning: First, company-specific experience exerts a higher impact on wage increments than general experience. Professor Higuchi of Keio University estimates that a year of general experience of male workers in Japan contributes 0.6 percent to wage increases as compared to a corresponding 0.9 percent in the U.S., while a year of experience within the company contributes 4.1 percent to wage increases as compared to a corresponding 1.2 percent in the U.S. Second, wages are primarily assigned to workers, not to jobs. This factor facilitates labor deployment, i.e., worker rotation and re-assignment to different jobs as market conditions may dictate.

Why does the Japanese employment system emphasize experience within the same company rather than general experience? Many observers trace the origins of the Japanese-style seniority wage system back to the vestiges of feudalism and the egalitarian spirit of the Occupation. This system is another vehicle that rewards and reinforces worker loyalty to the company; it also promotes wage equity across occupations. Workers identify themselves with the company and promote the interests of the company as family members promote the interests of the family.

Other observers argue that seniority wages are consistent with the rational behavior of employers and employees, in the presence of labor supervision and turnover costs. Seniority wages are a vehicle that discourages quitting and labor shirking and so minimizes such costs. Seniority wages also represent the labor share in the rents generated through joint labor-management investments in human capital.

Quantity and Quality of Education

Economists have placed special attention on the impact of education on wage differentials. They view time and money people spend on education as an investment in themselves, an investment that can be rewarding in terms of higher earnings (see Exhibit 10.14). Why do earnings rise with education? First, education prepares workers for prospective jobs and, therefore, they can adapt faster to the job requirements than can those without it. Second, educational success is a sign of commitment and discipline, both of immense importance for businesses. In other words, businesses are willing to pay higher wages to those with a degree than those without a degree because they take fewer chances of hiring the wrong person in the former group than in the latter.

For any given education level, workers with more education earn more. Workers with five to nine years of experience and a Ph.D. earned $1269 per week in 2019 while workers with the same experience and a B.A. earned $592.

Exhibit 10.14
B. Earnings Rise with Education

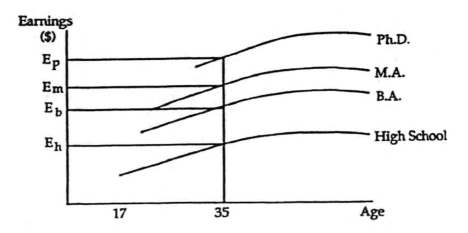

At any age workers with more education are expected to earn more. At the age of 35, workers with an M.A. are expected to earn more than workers with a B.A. And so do workers with a Ph.D.

C. Median Weekly Earnings by Educational Attainment, 2019

Education Level	Median Annual Earnings	Premium over High School Graduates
Professional	$1,861	$1,269
Ph.D.	1,883,	1,291
Master's	1,497	905
Bachelor's	1,249	657
High School	592	—

Source: U.S. Department of Labor.

Gender

Gender is a source of earnings differentials in any society. According to the U.S. Census Bureau, in 2016 women earned about 22 percent less than men. Do not women in the computer industry perform as well as men? There are two prevailing views here. The first view is that women are victims of discrimination. Some employers may want to believe that women are not as productive as men, and, therefore, they can get way paying lower salaries. As affirmative action takes full effect, gender discrimination, although not ruled out, is limited. The second view claims that as women become mothers, the chances of dropping out of the labor market for a period of time are higher than those of men. Withdrawing from the labor market makes investment in human capital obsolete and has a negative impact on job promotion and earnings.

Social Status

In spite of progress with affirmative action, social status is still an important determinant of earnings differential. Ability aside, rich and poor do not have equal chances to acquire the same education. And even if they do so, the chances for success may not be the same. A Harvard University M.B.A. may have more chances to become the president of a big company if his father is already the president of one.

To summarize, wages and employment in an industry are determined by the demand for and the supply of labor. Any interference with the market can generate labor shortages or labor surpluses. For instance, minimum wage legislation results in labor surpluses. Wages are higher for those who manage to get a job, but the chances of getting a job are smaller.

Differences in demand and supply conditions impact on wages and employment across industries. Given the supply of labor, a high demand for labor results in high wages. Given the demand for labor, a low supply of labor results in high wages, too.

Personal differences such as experience, education, gender, and social status impact on wage differences across people within the same industry. Experience, education, and good social status exert a positive impact on earnings. Discrimination and frequent labor market withdrawals exert a negative impact on female earnings.

What Students Should Know Before Pursuing a College Degree

Pursuing a successful career is a dream for every young individual. For some individuals the dream comes true, as they quickly find a fulfilling and highly paying job. For other individuals, it remains just a dream. The difference between the dream and reality is in the education choices they make while in college, the undergraduate and the graduate degree they pursue; that's where the secret is:

Try something different, march against the crowd.

Pursuing a career is similar to pursuing a business. You must begin with a vision; a place you want to be four, ten, twenty years down the road, and a service you want to provide to the business community and society, but make sure that there will be a sustained demand for these services. Then, you must think of the educational degree that will provide you the skills for this career; and the competition, the other people that pursue the same degree at the same time as you. Basic economics dictates that if too many individuals pursue the same career, it will become increasingly difficult for each individual to find a job. That's why you should study something different than the rest of the crowd, prepare for careers with little competition.

The story of James is a good case in point. Back in the early 1980s, when his university classmates were studying Spanish and French, he was studying Japanese. And when his classmates were heading for American MBA programs, he headed for Japan on a *mombusho* (Japanese Ministry of Education) scholarship that paid for his master's degree in economics. It sounded crazy at the time, but it paid off handsomely in the end. As soon as he graduated, and while his classmates were busy looking for a job to pay for student loans, he landed a job at Toyota Europe, debt free.

The story of Jeffrey is another case in point. After receiving his applied physics degree, he chose to enter the law school and study intellectual property law over the popular choice of an MBA program, as most of his classmates pursued. Three years later, Jeffrey's unique combination of technology and legal skills landed him a job in a large law firm, riding the rising trend of technological innovation and the needs of companies for intellectual property protection.

The bottom line: Don't be a follower; be a leader, have a vision for a career few people pursue, and get the right education for it.

Real World Link 13: The Career-Development Gap:
Why Employers Fail to Retain Top Talent

Top talent is the most important source of competitive advantage for every corporation, especially in high tech industries that compete on creativity and innovation. That's why these companies have the proper management techniques and the right career-development programs to retain top talent, or do they?

In a recent piece, *Forbes* editor Frederick E. Allen points to "stack ranking," a management technique applied by Microsoft that undermines talent retention and company creativity rather than fostering them. In a study of 1,200 top young managers published in the July–August 2012 *Harvard Business Review*, Monika Hamori and Burak Koyuncu identify a career-development gap between the support top young managers expect to get from their employers and the actual services they receive in the areas of mentoring, coaching, training, support from direct manager, support from the senior management, working as part of global virtual team, and a job in a new function product division, or market.

On a scale of 1–5 (5 being the most important), for instance, young managers assigned a value of 4 to mentoring and coaching, but they valued the service they received from their employers slightly below 3. The expectation gap was even greater in training, where the assigned value was close to 4.5, while the actual value was slightly above 3. That could certainly explain why these young managers were looking for jobs elsewhere. Seventy-five percent sent out resumes or contracted recruiters to move to other companies; and 95 percent engaged in networking activities, and eventually left their companies 28 months after they were hired. But why do companies fail to accommodate the expectations of their talented employees?

Because of time and money that may end up subsidizing the competition. Mentoring and coaching require a great deal of time, for both the mentor and the apprentice. Formal training is costly and requires paid time off work for the employees involved; and there's a dilemma over its effectiveness. "Employers are understandably reluctant to make big investments in workers who might not stay long. But this creates a vicious circle: companies won't train workers because they might leave, and workers leave because they don't get training."

The Bottom Line: top talent retention is an expensive proposition. Companies must either come up with the resources to meet up the expectations of their talented employees or be constantly in the market to replenish them.

Source: *Forbes Magazine*

Real World Link 14: Three Things That Determine the Market Value of a College Degree

What is the value of a college degree? Why do some college graduates get multiple job offers, while others end up with jobs that do not require a college degree?

These questions aren't new, but they're raised anew this time of the year, as colleges around the country award degrees and graduates head for the job market.

A college degree is official recognition of the formal education accumulated in college, which has a dual value: an intrinsic value, enhancing the student's personality; and a market value, increasing the student's chances of getting a "rewarding" job.

How rewarding? It depends on three things, according to a recent report titled "Degrees of Value: Evaluating the Return on the College Investment," published by the Education Sector.

First is academic performance. While college degrees do not say much about student performance, transcripts and records do, providing prospective employees an indication about student intelligence and commitment to coursework. According to the report, "students at the top of their classes have more job opportunities than their less academically stellar peers, and the quality of those jobs in terms of financial compensation also is generally better."

Second come majors, as demand and supply conditions differ across majors. Median earnings, for instance, can differ from $29,000 for psychology majors—where supply of graduates exceeds demand—to $120,000 for petroleum engineers, where demand outstrips supply.

Finally there is the reputation of the college attended. Students enrolled in top colleges earn, in some cases, 20% more than students who enrolled in lower ranking schools, according to a study cited in the report.

The Bottom Line: not all college degrees are valued equally in the marketplace. Academic performance, major, and college selectivity do matter. Students should consider all these factors before applying to college rather than finding out after graduation.

Source: *Forbes Magazine*

Real World Link 15: Seattle Reveals The Ugly Truth About The $15 Minimum Wage Movement

A minimum wage hike back in 2016 in Seattle resulted in lower, not higher, pay for low-wage earners, revealing the ugly truth of the $15 minimum wage movement—a "living wage" isn't an entitlement, it must be earned by delivering value to the consumer.

That's the key finding of a recently released study by a team of economists at the University of Washington. "Using a variety of methods to analyze employment in all sectors paying below a specified real hourly rate, we conclude that the second wage increase to $13 reduced hours worked in low-wage jobs by around 9 percent, while hourly wages in such jobs increased by around 3 percent," write the authors of the study. "Consequently, total payroll fell for such jobs, implying that the minimum wage ordinance lowered low-wage employees' earnings by an average of $125 per month in 2016. Evidence attributes more modest effects to the first wage increase."

The minimum wage movement has a pretty side and an ugly side. The pretty side is about the promise it makes to low wage earners—a "living wage." The ugly side is the way it wants to deliver on this promise—by disconnecting pay from performance, turning business enterprises into welfare agencies.

That's a radical idea that can be traced back to Maoist China and the Soviet Union, where corporations were "units" within a centrally planned economy; and in countries that fell in love with these systems—like pre-crisis Greece, where government bureaucrats and union bosses rather than markets set wages.

We all know what happened to those economies.

Fortunately, these systems never gained popularity in America. That's why corporations of all sizes remained for-profit businesses in a free enterprise system, where markets—not government bureaucrats or union bosses—set wages.

But there are a few exceptions to this rule. Like the minimum wage mandate, too, which sets a floor on what companies can pay for labor, irrespective of what workers who receive it deliver to the other side, the customer.

While the government can set the minimum wage, however, it cannot tell corporations how to organize their operations, or how much labor to use vis-a-vis other resources, capital and technology.

So, when the government hikes the minimum wage, corporations change the way they produce things, replacing workers—who are now more expensive—with machines, which usually become more efficient and less costly overtime.

In response to minimum wage hikes, for instance, major retailers like Wal-Mart and Target are already replacing cashiers with self-checkout counters. Restaurant chains like McDonald's and Panera Bread and the like are also replacing cashiers with apps and ordering kiosks.

That's a trend that is expected to accelerate, as America is advancing towards a $15 minimum wage, completely eliminating the need for cashiers and other low skilled labor.

That's bad news for people earning a living from these occupations.

While mandates like the minimum wage help low paid workers bring home a higher pay in the short term, they send these workers to the unemployment lines in the long term, as companies replace labor with machines.

Worse, minimum wage hikes, together with other regulations that restrict economic freedoms, undermine business creation, which makes it even harder for younger people to find jobs.

It should come to no one's surprise, therefore, that countries like Greece and France have been suffering from astronomically high youth unemployment rates; and the same is true for American states with high minimum wages.

That's how a good cause turns into a bad cause. And that's the ugly truth for the $15 minimum wage movement.

Source: *Forbes Magazine*

10.6 Review

1. The market for labor services in a particular industry has two sides, the demand side with firms that are ready to hire labor in order to produce goods and services and the supply side with households that are ready to supply labor in order to earn income.

2. In hiring labor, a firm weighs marginal costs and marginal benefits. The marginal cost of hiring an additional worker is the wage the firm must pay. The marginal benefit from hiring an additional worker is the value of marginal product, i.e., the dollar value of the marginal product of labor. To the extent that the latter exceeds the former, the firm is better off hiring the additional worker than not doing so. Therefore, the firm hires workers up to the point where the value of marginal product is equal to the wage rate. Applying this decision rule at different wage rates, we derive the firm's demand for labor, which is the same as the diminishing part of the value of marginal product.

3. Knowing each firm's demand for labor, we can add them horizontally and get the market or industry demand for labor, showing the number of workers all firms are willing to hire at different wages.

4. The supply of labor to an industry refers to the number of workers that are willing to supply their labor in that industry at different wage rates. In general, the industry supply is positively sloped: as the wage rate increases, more workers are willing to join that industry.

5. The two sides of the market determine the equilibrium (market) wage and equilibrium employment.

6. A minimum wage may end up hurting rather than helping those it was designed to help. As a minimum wage makes labor more expensive, firms are induced to hire fewer workers.

7. Wage differences can be classified into two categories: inter-industry and interpersonal. Inter-industry wage differentials can be attributed to differences in demand and supply conditions across industries. Interpersonal wage differences can be attributed to personal characteristics, such as sex, age, education, and social status.

Review Questions

1. How do firms make hiring decisions?

2. Which factors may cause a shift in the demand for labor?

3. Which factors may cause a shift in the supply of labor?

4. What are the major issues concerning a minimum wage?

5. How does an immigration amnesty affect wages?

6. What are the sources of inter-industry wage differentials?

7. What are the sources of interpersonal wage differentials?

8. How does automation affect employment?

REVIEW QUESTIONS

Chapters 1–3

A. Multiple Choice Questions

1. We study economics in order
    - (a)   to become better citizens
    - (b)   to become better managers
    - (c)   to understand our business world
    - (d)   (a) and (c)
    - (e)   (a), (b), and (c)

2. Which one is *not* a part of a model
    - (a)   assumption
    - (b)   refutable hypotheses
    - (c)   postulates
    - (d)   experiments
    - (e)   all of the above

3. The cost of going to school is lower for an eighteen-year-old student as compared to a thirty-year-old because of
    - (a)   a higher tuition
    - (b)   more expensive books
    - (c)   a higher room and board charge
    - (d)   lower forgone earnings
    - (e)   none of the above

4. The existence of unemployment in an economy implies that
    - (a)   economic resources are allocated inefficiently
    - (b)   economic resources are allocated efficiently
    - (c)   the economy produces at its full potential
    - (d)   the economy runs deficits
    - (e)   none of the above

5. Over time the production possibilities frontier of our economy expands because of
    - (a)   technological advances
    - (b)   population growth
    - (c)   capital accumulation (savings)
    - (d)   more efficient organization techniques
    - (e)   all of the above

6. If two goods are complementary (say record players and records), then
   (a)   an increase in the price of record players will increase the demand for records
   (b)   a decrease in the price of record players will increase the demand for records
   (c)   a decrease in the price of record players will not affect the demand for records
   (d)   a decrease in the price of record players will decrease the quantity demand for record players
   (e)   (b) and (d)

7. Other things being equal, a decrease in the demand for a product will tend
   (a)   to increase the equilibrium price and decrease the equilibrium quantity
   (b)   to decrease both the equilibrium price and quantity
   (c)   to decrease the equilibrium price and increase the equilibrium quantity
   (d)   to have no effect on either its price or quantity
   (e)   none of the above

8. Other things being equal, a decrease in the supply for a product will tend
   (a)   to increase the equilibrium price and decrease the equilibrium quantity
   (b)   to decrease both the equilibrium price and quantity
   (c)   to decrease the equilibrium price and increase the equilibrium quantity
   (d)   to have no effect on either its price or quantity
   (e)   none of the above

9. The demand curve shows
   (a)   the maximum prices that consumers are willing to pay for different quantities of a given product
   (b)   the minimum prices that sellers are willing to accept for different quantities of a product
   (c)   the prices that different amounts of a product have actually fetched in the market
   (d)   the most profitable prices of the product at the time
   (e)   (a) and (b)

10. The law of supply states that:
    (a)   at lower prices firms will offer for sale greater amounts of a given product than at higher
    (b)   at higher prices firms will sell greater amounts of a given product than at lower
    (c)   prices and quantities sold are inversely related
    (d   prices and quantities supplied are directly related
    (e)   (b) and (d)

11. A change in any one of the following factors will shift the supply curve, except
    (a)   a change in the price of a related product
    (b)   a change in resource prices
    (c)   an increase in the number of firms producing the product
    (d)   a change in consumers' income
    (e)   (b) and (c)

12. Other things being equal, a joint decrease in the demand for and the supply of a product will tend
    (a)   to increase the equilibrium price
    (b)   to decrease both the equilibrium price and quantity
    (c)   to decrease the equilibrium price and increase the equilibrium quantity
    (d)   to have no effect on either equilibrium price or quantity
    (e)   cannot tell

13. Which of the following statements is correct?

    (a)   supply refers to the different amounts of a given product that firms are willing to offer for sale at alternative prices

    (b)   supply refers to the amounts of a given product that firms have withheld from the market

    (c)   supply refers to the amount of a product which firms will offer for sale at a given price

    (d)   supply refers to the amounts of a product coming out of a plant during a given period of time

    (e)   (a) and (b)

14. Other things being equal, an increase in demand for a product will tend

    (a)   to increase the equilibrium price and decrease the equilibrium quantity

    (b)   to decrease both its price and quantity

    (c)   to increase its price and quantity

    (d)   to have no effect on either its price or quantity

    (e)   none of the above

15. Scarcity refers to the fact that

    (a)   commodities are limited in supply

    (b)   human needs are unlimited

    (c)   commodities are limited compared to the desire for them

    (d)   commodities cost money

    (e)   commodities are purchased in the market

16. Entrepreneurship is the risk-taking skill in the

    (a)   initiation of business

    (b)   organization of business

    (c)   expansion of business

    (d)   survival of business

    (e)   all of the above

17. A market is the mechanism that

    (a)   brings buyers and sellers together

    (b)   facilitates transaction of goods, services, and resources

    (c)   facilitates the transfer of property rights from buyers to sellers

    (d)   all of the above

18. Consumer sovereignty means that

    (a)   consumers' preferences guide production

    (b)   advertising guides production

    (c)   large corporations influence consumers' decisions

    (d)   (b) and (c)

    (e)   none of the above

19. In a mixed market economy

    (a)   all important decisions are made by individuals

    (b)   all important decisions are made by big firms, unions, and the government

    (c)   a large percent of the GDP is produced and/or distributed by the government

    (d)   (b) and (c)

    (e)   none of the above

20. Which one is *not* a function of government in a mixed economy?

    (a)   allocation of public goods

    (b)   redistribution of income

    (c)   planning of economic activity

    (d   protection of property rights

    (e)   stabilization of the economy

21. A government policy that sets a commodity's price below the equilibrium level will result in

    (a)   a surplus

    (b)   a shortage

    (c)   lower prices for all consumers

    (d   higher prices for all consumers

    (e)   none of the above

22. The 1988 midwest summer drought resulted in

    (a)   lowering the price of soybeans

    (b)   increasing the price for soybeans

    (c)   increasing the price for salad dressings

    (d)   (a) and (c)

    (e)   (b) and (c)

B. Essays

1. Define and distinguish between "an increase in demand" and "an increase in the quantity demanded."

2. Define and distinguish between models and theories.

3. Define and distinguish between human and nonhuman resources.

4. Define and explain the concept of opportunity cost.

C. True and False Questions

1. T   F   "Quantity Demanded" refers to the amount firms sell to consumers.

2. T   F   A decrease in the quantity demanded is caused by an increase in price.

3. T   F   Given the supply for a commodity, an increase in consumers' income will result in a lower equilibrium price for the commodity.

4. T   F   Consumers like ice cream more in summer than in winter, therefore, the equilibrium price of ice cream is higher in summer.

5. T   F   Any time the quantity supplied exceeds the quantity demanded, there is a surplus in the market.

Chapters 4–5

A. Multiple Choice Questions

1. Which of the following is *not* a characteristic of monopolistic competition?

    (a)   a relatively large number of sellers

    (b)   homogeneous commodities

    (c)   restricted entry

    (d)   imperfect information

2. The steel industry is
   (a)   a monopoly
   (b)   a homogeneous oligopoly
   (c)   a differentiated oligopoly
   (d)   a perfectly competitive industry

3. The brewery industry is
   (a)   a monopoly
   (b)   a homogeneous oligopoly
   (c)   a differentiated oligopoly
   (d)   a perfectly competitive industry

4. Coupons are price discounts designed to attract consumers with
   (a)   an inelastic demand
   (b)   an elastic demand
   (c)   a unitary demand
   (d)   any kind of demand elasticity
   (e)   cannot tell

5. Given an inelastic demand for a product, the pricing policy that maximizes total revenues is to
   (a)   lower the price
   (b)   increase the price
   (c)   leave the price the same
   (d)   spend more money on advertising
   (e)   spend less money on advertising

6. Substitute commodities are those with
   (a)   a negative cross elasticity
   (b)   a positive cross elasticity
   (c)   a negative income elasticity
   (d)   a positive income elasticity

7. Normal commodities are those with
   (a)   a positive cross elasticity
   (b)   a negative cross elasticity
   (c)   a negative income elasticity
   (d)   a positive income elasticity
   (e)   an income elasticity greater than one

8. Rationing of a commodity results in
   (a)   higher satisfaction for some consumers
   (b)   a lower satisfaction for all consumers
   (c)   a lower satisfaction for some consumers
   (d)   higher satisfaction for businesses
   (e)   none of the above

9. In cases of commodity rationing, economists favor black markets because they
   (a)   decrease the satisfaction of some consumers
   (b)   increase the satisfaction of some consumers
   (c)   are immoral
   (d   (b) and (c)
   (e)   none of the above

10. For products with an elastic demand, a lower price means
    (a)   higher total revenues
    (b)   lower total revenues
    (c)   the same total revenues
    (d   cannot tell

11. Assume you are in charge of the marketing department of a company which sells automobiles and automobile parts. Which of the two products will you place on sale?
    (a)   the automobile parts
    (b)   the automobiles
    (c)   neither
    (d)   both

12. In the U.S., traditional tube TVs are
    (a)   normal goods
    (b)   inferior goods
    (c)   neutral goods
    (d)   inelastic goods
    (e)   complements

B. Essays

1. For the following Demand Schedule calculate the price elasticity of demand and comment on the size of it.

P	Q
10	50
12	45
14	30

2. Briefly explain the concept of consumer equilibrium
3. Briefly explain the factors that determine the size of the price elasticity of demand.

Chapters 6–7

A. Multiple Choice Questions

1. Normal profit is
   (a)   the opportunity cost of capital
   (b)   the profit any firm makes in the market
   (c)   the minimum capital return required in order to stay in a certain type of business
   (d)   (a) and (c)
   (e)   all of the above

2. Economic costs differ from accounting costs because
    (a)   accounting costs do not include implicit costs
    (b)   economic costs include both implicit and explicit costs
    (c)   of accounting mistakes
    (d)   either (a) or (b)
    (e)   none of the above

3. Which one is *not* a part of the short-run fixed cost?
    (a)   payments for raw materials
    (b)   rental payments
    (c)   insurance premiums
    (d)   salaries of top managers
    (e)   none of the above

4. Marginal cost is
    (a)   the sum of fixed and variable cost at each level of output
    (b)   the same as the per unit cost
    (c)   the change in total cost over the change in output
    (d)   the same as fixed cost
    (e)   all of the above

5. Marginal revenue is
    (a)   the revenue from an additional unit sold in the market
    (b)   the profit from an additional unit sold in the market
    (c)   what a firm makes in the market
    (d)   the dollar value of all units the firm sells in the market
    (e)   all of the above

6. A competitive firm maximizes profit at the level of output where
    (a)   average cost equals total cost
    (b)   marginal cost equals marginal revenue
    (c)   average cost is minimized
    (d)   marginal cost equals marginal revenue and marginal cost is not increasing
    (e)   cannot tell

7. In economics, zero profits means that
    (a)   the firm breaks down
    (b)   the firm makes just normal profits
    (c)   the firm must close down
    (d)   the firm must raise the price of the commodity
    (e)   all of the above

8. In perfect competition the firm
    (a)   has no control over the market
    (b)   is a price taker
    (c)   is very small as compared to the market
    (d)   makes just normal profits
    (e)   (a), (b), and (c)

9. In the long run a competitive firm
   (a)   makes just normal profits
   (b)   produces at the minimum cost
   (c)   operates with the best available plant size
   (d)   (a), (b), and (c)
   (e)   closes down

10. Marginal product is
   (a)   the increase in total output
   (b)   the increase in the total cost
   (c)   the change in the total output over the change in employment
   (d)   the per unit output
   (e)   all of the above

B. Essays

1. Compare and contrast the short-term and the long-term equilibrium of a competitive firm.
2. Formally, derive and discuss the supply curve of a perfectly competitive firm.
3. State and explain the law of diminishing returns.

Chapters 8–10

A. Multiple Choice Questions

1. A monopolist controls
   (a)   the price of the commodity
   (b)   the quantity of the commodity
   (c)   both the price and the quantity
   (d)   either the price or the quantity
   (e)   the market shares

2. The kinked demand model predicts that
   (a)   oligopolists will soon enter a price war
   (b)   oligopolists will "stick" with the same price
   (c)   a small change in marginal costs will have no effect on price
   (d)   (b) and (c)
   (e)   (a), (b), and (c)

3. Which one is *not* a characteristic of monopolistic competition?
   (a)   relatively large number of sellers
   (b)   restricted entry
   (c)   homogeneous products
   (d)   imperfect information
   (e)   all of the above

4. Monopolies arise because of
   (a)   patents
   (b)   economies of scale
   (c)   possession of a license

(d)   (a) and (c)

(e)   (a), (b), and (c)

5. A monopolist maximizes profit at the point where

   (a)   MC = AC

   (b)   MC = MR

   (c)   MC < P

   (d)   MR = P

   (e)   (b) and (c)

6. Economists argue that monopolies should be regulated because

   (a)   they allocate resources efficiently

   (b)   they allocate resources inefficiently

   (c)   they have too much power

   (d)   they charge consumers a too-high price

7. The most appropriate model to explain pricing in the hardware computer market would be

   (a)   perfect competition

   (b)   monopolistic competition

   (c)   the price leadership model

   (d)   the kinked demand model

   (e)   monopoly

8. In the cost-markup model

   (a)   the higher the elasticity of demand the higher the markup

   (b)   the lower the elasticity of demand the higher the markup

   (c)   the higher the elasticity the lower the markup

   (d)   (b) and (c)

   (e)   cannot tell

9. In the long term, a monopolistic firm produces

   (a)   at the minimum AC

   (b)   at AC is equal to price

   (c)   at AC is equal to MR

   (d)   (a) and (b)

   (e)   none of the above

10. Economists argue that advertising does not necessarily

   (a)   improve economic efficiency

   (b)   result in lower prices for consumers

   (c)   result in a better product quality

   (d)   (a) and (b)

   (e)   all of the above

11. A monopolist produces an output level consistent with

   (a) $e < 1$

   (b) $e > 1$

   (c) $e = 1$

   (d)   none of the above

12. At the inelastic part of the monopolist's demand curve
    (a)   total revenue is increasing
    (b)   total revenue is decreasing
    (c)   marginal revenue is negative
    (d)   marginal revenue is positive
    (e)   (b) and (c)

13. A competitive firm maximizes profit at the level of output where
    (a)   average cost equals total cost
    (b)   marginal cost equals marginal revenue
    (c)   average cost is minimized
    (d)   marginal cost equals marginal revenue and marginal cost is increasing
    (e)   cannot tell

14. In economics, zero profit means that
    (a)   the firm breaks down
    (b)   the firm makes just normal profits
    (c)   the firm must close down
    (d)   the firm must raise the price of the commodity
    (e)   all of the above

15. In perfect competition the firm
    (a)   has no control over the market
    (b)   is a price maker
    (c)   is very small as compared to the market
    (d)   (a) and (c)

16. The law of diminishing returns states that as more and more workers are added to a given number of machines, there is an employment level beyond which
    (a)   production increases
    (b)   production decreases
    (c)   the marginal product decreases
    (d)   the marginal product increases
    (e)   the marginal revenue increases

17. The law of diminishing returns can be attributed to
    (a)   lazy workers
    (b)   overcrowding of resources
    (c)   machines breaking down
    (d)   machines wearing out
    (e)   none of the above

18. Marginal product is
    (a)   the increase in total output
    (b)   the increase in total cost
    (c)   the change in total output over the change in employment
    (d)   the change in average product
    (e)   all of the above

B. *Essays*

1. Define and explain the "kinked" demand curve.

2. Define and explain the method of cost markup pricing.

3. Compare and contrast "price competition" with "non-price competition."

4. It is sometimes stated that a pure monopoly never exists because there are always substitutes for whatever is produced. Do you agree? Why or why not? Does a monopolist always make a positive profit? Explain.

5. What would be the effect of a crude oil shortage on (a) the price of crude oil?, (b) the price of gasoline?, (c) the price of furniture?, (d) employment in the oil refining industry?, and (d) wages in the oil refining industry?

6. The Tokogawa regime, established in early 17th century Japan, prohibited the use of land for tobacco plantations. What would have happened to the price of rice in the absence of such a prohibition?

7. In 2021, anesthesiologists earned $300,000 annually while pediatricians earned $200,000. Draw two diagrams which reflect the earnings differentials between the two professions.